THE TRUTH ABOUT UFO'S AND THE NEW WORLD ORDER CONNECTION

COMPILED AND WRITTEN BY:
WILLIAM JOSIAH SUTTON

2005 EDITION
© COPYRIGHT 1997
THE INSTITUTE OF RELIGIOUS KNOWLEDGE
WITH SPECIAL ARRANGEMENTS WITH
SIM & SONS' PUBLISHING HOUSE
HENDERSON, NV

ALL RIGHTS RESERVED

PRINTED IN THE UNITED STATES OF AMERICA

BOOKS WRITTEN BY WILLIAM JOSIAH SUTTON:

Vol. I: *Beware It's Coming - The Antichrist 666*
Vol. II: *The New Age Movement and The Illuminati 666*
Vol. III: *The Real Truth About UFOs and The New World Order Connection*
Vol. IV: *Ancient Prophecies About Mysticism, Hollywood, and The Music Industry*
Vol. V: *Ancient Prophecies About The Dragon, The Beast, and The False Prophet*
Vol. VI: *The Great Apostasy of European and American Leaders: In Gog They Trust?*, Book I
Vol. VII: *In Gog They Trust?*, Book II

TABLE OF CONTENTS

CHAPTER I: UFOLOGY AND THE NEW AGE CONNECTION..page 15
1. UFO's and the Ancient Mayan, Toltec, and Aztec Connection.
2. The Mysterious Dog Star Sirius and the UFO Connection.
3. The Revival of the Ancient Mayan and Toltec gods and their 520-Year Prophecy from 1475 A.D. to 1995 A.D. by Modern-Day New Agers.
4. The Strange Play of Sunlight and Shadows on March 21st During the Spring Vernal Equinox at Chichén Itzá, Yucatán Mexico.
5. New Agers Believe that the Aztecs, Toltecs, and Mayan Indians are Descendants of Atlanteans.
6. Plato's Atlantis and its Division of Ten Kingdoms.
7. The Warning about the Seven-headed Dragon of Revelation, Chapters 12 and 13.
8. UFO's: Are They Ancient Astronauts? Marshall Applewhite and the Heaven's Gate Tragedy.
9. The Double Star Sirius Rediscovered and the Mystery Involved around it Today and the Illuminati Connection.
10. The Promotion of the Galactic Age and a Socialist Federation by New Agers and Heathen Deities' Manifestations.
11. Are UFO's Coming to Take Over this Planet?
12. Chariots of the Gods?
13. The Age of Aquarius and Just Who Are These UFO's?
14. Jesus' Prophecy about UFO's.
15. Why Satan was Symbolized as a Great Red Dragon, and What the Symbols of the Beast and the False Prophet Signify.
16. Hermes, Not Only the Messenger of the gods, but Also the god of Merchants and Bankers and the Mural Painting Exalting Him.
17. Jesus' Prophecy about Businessmen in the Last Days.
18. Origin of Transmigration of the Soul among New Agers.
19. Modern Spiritualism's Doctrines are All Centered around the Belief in UFO's and Star People.
20. New Age Writers who made Popular that People Originally came from the Stars.

21. The Great White Brotherhood and the Most Powerful Interfaith Trap in the World Promoting It.
22. How Many Hollywood Citizens Were in the Past and Are at Present Involved in Spiritualism.

CHAPTER II: HOW THE NEW AGE AND THE NEW WORLD ORDER BEGAN..page 58
1. Jesus' Warning to Not Follow the Majority.
2. These Have One Mind.
3. The Prevailing Ignorance of Pastors of Bible Prophecy.
4. Revelation, Chapter 14:6–12: The Most Solemn Warning from God.
5. Just what Is the Illuminati?
6. Germany and New England, Birthplaces of the New World Order.
7. The Seven Ages of Astrology and Its Novus Ordo Seclorum.
8. What was Behind the New Age Harmonic Convergence?
9. Thomas Paine was Not a Christian, but a Deist, and an Apostle of the New World Order.
10. Thomas Jefferson was Not a Christian, but a Deist, and an Apostle of the New World Order.
11. Benjamin Franklin was Not a Christian, but a Deist, and an Apostle of the New World Order.
12. Simón Bolívar was Not a Christian, but a Deist, and an Apostle of the New World Order.
13. The Age of Reason, the Age of Enlightenment Deception.
14. James Shaw, a Confession of a Former 33° Freemason and Past Master to All Scottish Rite Bodies.
15. More on Freemasonry and Its Involvement with the New World Order Conspiracy.
16. How Learned People are Claiming to have Communicated with Extraterrestrial Visitors.

CHAPTER III: THE NEW WORLD ORDER AND THE PROMOTION OF METAPHYSICS................................page 99
1. The Three Unclean Spirits.
2. The Two Mainstreams of Modern Spiritualism.

3. Witches Fighting Christianity in Court.
   4. The Huge Order of Wicca Witchcraft in the United States.
   5. The Evil Origin of Halloween and How Christians Are Ignorantly Promoting It.
   6. How Christians Are Being Drawn into Modern-Day Witchcraft by Interfaith Organizations.
   7. The Worship of Fairies, Satyrs, Pan, and Devas by New Agers.
   8. Satan and His Angels appear in Human Form as Mahatmas.
   9. Baal Worship, Alive and Well Today.
   10. Human Sacrificing, Alive and Well Today.
   11. The Elijah Message.
   12. Do Not Get Involved in the Cares of This World or with Political Candidates.
   13. Law Enforcement Agencies are Warning about Satanism and Human Sacrificing.
   14. More Reasons Why Christians Fall for Spiritualism.
   15. Jesus is Calling the People of the World to Turn from the Dragon and Worship Him.

CHAPTER IV: SOCIALISM, COMMUNISM, AND THE AQUARIAN CONSPIRACY ARE BROTHERS AND SISTERS……………………………………………page 147
   1. The Reign of Terror of France Will Be Repeated in Our Day.
   2. Jesus' Kingdom is Not of This Present World.
   3. Jesus and the New Heaven and the New Earth.
   4. The Popular Belief in Christianity that Christ will Reign Here on Earth for 1,000 Years is a Hoax.
   5. The Prophecies of Christ's Reign of 1,000 Years are Pointing to Heaven.
   6. Eastern Religions, Jews, and Christians are being Ushered In Together into the Age of Aquarius Deception.
   7. Hitler and the Age of Aquarius.
   8. The Millennium or Golden Age of Peace made Popular by Plato, Adam Weishaupt, and Karl Marx.
   9. The Age of Aquarius – Called Utopia by Communists.
   10. The Age of Aquarius – Called the Millennium by Christians.

11. Forced International Socialism Is the Harbinger for the New Age Conspiracy.
12. Communism and Socialism Are Brothers and Sisters.
13. The Illuminati Gave Birth to Communism and Socialism.
14. Socialism Made War on Christianity During the French Revolution.
15. The Year 1848 Gave Birth Not Only to *The Communist Manifesto*, but Also to Modern Witchcraft in America.
16. The Fox Sisters.
17. Karl Marx, George Bernard Shaw, Antonio Gramsci, H.P. Blavatsky, Annie Besant, Alice Bailey, Aleister Crowley: The Most Read Authors for World Revolution.
18. The Theosophical Society.
19. The Great White Brotherhood.
20. Elizabeth Clare Prophet.
21. Carlos Castaneda and Don Juan.

CHAPTER V: HOW THEOSOPHY DECEIVED THE WORLD IN ANCIENT DAYS AND HOW IT WILL BRING ITS HEADQUARTERS TO ISRAEL..................................page 195
1. The Two Ecumenical Movements.
2. Plato and Atlantis.
3. Cush, Nimrod, and Semiramis.
4. Nimrod, the Great Rebel and First Sun-God.
5. The Seven-headed Dragon Symbolizes Astrology.
6. The Antediluvian Giants and the Descendants of Noah.
7. Eber Was the First Hebrew; The First Christians Were Jews.
8. Abraham's and the Hebrew Jew's Promises from God.
9. The Ashkenazi Jews, Zionism, and the Rothschilds.
10. The Sephardim Jew.
11. The Merger of Judaism and Babylonian Witchcraft.
12. The Kabbalah, the Jewish Book of Magic.
13. The Sephardim Jew and the Spanish Inquisition.
14. The Origin of the Ashkenazi Jew.
15. Ashkenazi Jews, not Hebrew or Semitic, but Mainly Aryan (European).

16. Ashkenazim, a Mixture of Judaic and Pantheistic Doctrines. How Modern Jews Are Deceived Today by Spiritualism.
17. The Hexagram Is Not the Star of David, but the Most Evilest Sign in Astrology.
18. All Secret Societies Draw Their Beliefs from the Kabbalah, the Jewish Book of Magic.
19. The Lie of Immortality of the Soul.
20. David Berkowitz.
21. How Jews, Muslims, Christians, and Eastern Religions Have Been Deceived Today by Satan's First Lie.
22. Jesus Will Bring All His People Who Choose Him as Saviour Out from All the Religions of the World into One Fold.
23. The New World Order Conspiracy – Not a Jewish Conspiracy, but Actually Luciferian.
24. Jesus Was a Jew.
25. Real Jews Are of the Heart, Not of the Flesh.
26. How Satan Today is Using Modern Israel.
27. Satan Will Move His Headquarters to Israel.
28. Gog and Magog: Who Really Are They?
29. Armageddon, Literal or Spiritual?

SOURCES

1. *The Holy Bible*, King James Version, Cambridge University Press, NY.
2. *Chariots of the Gods?*, Erich Von Däniken, G.P. Putnam's Sons, NY, 1968.
3. *Morals and Dogma of the Ancient and Accepted Scottish Rite of Freemasonry*, Prepared for the Supreme Council of Thirty-third Degree, Albert Pike, 1871.
4. *Mysteries of the Unknown -- The UFO Phenomenon*, Time-Life Books, Inc., 1987.
5. *The Two Babylons*, Hislop, Loiseaux Brothers, Inc., Neptune, NJ, 1916.
6. *Greek Gods and Heroes*, Graves, Doubleday and Company, NY, 1960.
7. *The New Book of Knowledge*, Grolier Inc., 1982.
8. *Bulfinch's Mythology*, Bulfinch, The Modern Library Random House, NY, 1970.
9. *Beware It's Coming – The Antichrist 666*, Sutton, WFG, Inc., TX, 1980.
10. *The New Age Movement and The Illuminati 666*, Sutton, The Institute of Religious Knowledge, TN, 1983.
11. *The Occult Illustrated Dictionary*, Day, Oxford University Press, NY, 1976.
12. *The New Age Encyclopedia*, Melton/Gordon, Gale, 1990.
13. *Encyclopaedia Judaica*, Keter Publishing House, Jerusalem Ltd., 1972.
14. *Finding Your Place in the Golden Age*, Chaney, Astara Inc., 1993.
15. *Rosicrucian Questions and Answers with Complete History*, Lewis, Rosicrucian Press.
16. *Hollywood and The Supernatural*, Steiger, St. Martin Press.
17. *The Hidden Dangers of the Rainbow*, Cumbey, Huntington House Inc., 1983.
18. *The Compleat Astrologer*, Parker, McGraw-Hill Book Company, 1971.
19. *The Los Angeles Times*, January 21, 1993.

20. *Newsweek*, August 17, 1987.
21. *Discover*, January 1988.
22. *People Weekly*, August 31, 1987.
23. *Time*, August 31, 1987.
24. *People Weekly*, January 1988.
25. *American Health*, January/February 1987.
26. *The Encyclopedia of Religion*, MacMillian Pub., NY, 1987.
27. *An Encyclopedia of Freemasonry and Its Kindred Sciences*, Mackey, 33rd Degree, The Masonic History Company, Chicago, NY, London, 1921.
28. *Coil's Masonic Encyclopedia*, Coil, 33rd Degree, Macoy Publishing and Masonic Supply Company, 1961.
29. *The Great Controversy*, White, Pacific Press Pub. Assoc., 1939.
30. *Daniel and The Revelation*, Smith, Southern Publishing Company, 1972.
31. *The San Juan Star*, June 30, 1991.
32. *The American Heritage Dictionary of the English Language*, American Heritage Publishers, 1969.
33. *The Encyclopaedia Britannica*, Macropaedia, Encyclopaedia Britannica, William Benton, Pub., 1983.
34. *The Cincinnati Enquirer*, Saturday, October 18, 1986.
35. *The New Age Magazine*, The Supreme Council, 33rd Degree, Ancient and Accepted Scottish Rite of Freemasonry, April, 1986.
36. *The Masonic Report*, McQuaig/Shaw, Published by authors.
37. *The World Book Encyclopedia*, Grolier Inc., 1993.
38. *Encyclopedia of World Biography*, McGraw-Hill Inc., 1973.
39. *The St. Petersburg Times*, October 30, 1990.
40. *The Boston Herald*, Massachusetts, October 27, 1991.
41. *The Buffalo News*, New York, May 18, 1991.
42. *Mythology of All Races*, Louis H. Gray, Ed., Cooper Square Publishers, 1964.
43. *The Houston Chronicle*, July 28, 1996.
44. *People Weekly*, May 23, 1988.
45. *Encyclopedia of World Mythology*, Galahad Books, NY, 1975.
46. *Larousse World Mythology*, Hamlyn Publishing Group Limited, 1965.
47. *Adonis Attis Osiris*, Frazier, University Books, Inc., 1961.

48. *The New Columbia Encyclopedia*, Harris/Levey, Columbia University Press, NY, 1975.
49. *La Popessa*, Murphy/Arlington, Warner Books, Inc., NY, 1983.
50. *Time*, December 30, 1991.
51. *The Evansville Courier and Press*, April 8, 1990.
52. *The Tampa Tribune*, October 31, 1988.
53. *Cape Cod Times*, November 16, 1991.
54. *The Buffalo News*, April 19, 1989.
55. *Funk and Wagnall's New Standard Dictionary of the English Language*, Funk and Wagnall's Company, 1945.
56. *The Rockefeller's, An American Dynasty*, Collier/Horowitz, New American Library, 1976.
57. *Dateline*, NBC News Transcript, February, 9. 1993.
58. *48 Hours*, CBS News Transcript, February 9, 1994.
59. *The Wall Street Journal*, May 31, 1991.
60. *Time*, May 13, 1991.
61. *The Environmental Magazine*, January/February 1993.
62. *Encyclopedic Psychic Dictionary*, Bletzer, The Donning Co. Pub., 1986.
63. *Feet First/A Guide to Foot Reflexology*, Norman/Cowan, Simon and Schuster, Inc., NY, 1988.
64. *Testimonies to the Church*, Volume 4, White, E.G. White Publications, 1948.
65. *Make Your Juicer Your Drug Store*, Newman, Benedict Lust Pub., 1970.
66. *Back to Eden*, Kloss, Review and Herald Pub. Assoc., 1949.
67. *Origins of Astrology*, Lindsay, Barnes and Noble, Inc., 1971.
68. *Young's Analytical Concordance to the Bible*, Young, William B. Eerdman's Pub. Co., 1970.
69. *The Encyclopedia Americana*, Grolier Inc., 1978.
70. *The Academic American Encyclopedia*, Grolier Inc., 1989.
71. *The Encyclopedia of Philosophy*, Edwards, MacMillian Pub. Co., Inc., Great Britain, 1967.
72. *The Fringes of Reason, A Whole Earth Catalog*, Schultz, Harmony Books, NY, 1989.
73. *The New Encyclopaedia Britannica*, Micropaedia, Encyclopaedia Britannica, 1990.
74. *The Jewish Encyclopedia*, Funk and Wagnall's Co., NY, 1925.

75. *The Story of Prophets and Kings,* White, Pacific Press Pub. Assoc., 1915.
76. *The World Book Encyclopedia*, World Book Inc., 1989.
77. *Wainwright House Fall/Winter 1990 Guide*, Rye, NY.
78. *Collier's Encyclopedia*, MacMillian Educational Co.,NY, 1991.
79. *The New International Dictionary of Quotations*, Rawson/Miner, Pub. E.P. Dutton, NY, 1986.
80. *The Fabians*, MacKenzie, Simon and Schuster Pub., 1977.
81. *Encyclopedia of Occultism and Parapsychology*, 3rd ed., Sheppard, Gale Research Inc., NY, 1991.
82. *People Weekly*, May 23, 1988.
83. *Man, Myth, and Magic*, Cavendish, Marshall Cavendish Limited, 1983.
84. *Macleans*, May 7, 1990.
85. *The Teachings of Don Juan: A Yaqui Way of Knowledge*, Castaneda, Univeristy of Cal. Press, 1968.
86. *The Interpreter's Bible*, Abingdon Press, NY, 1956.
87. *Testimonies to Ministers*, White, Pacific Press Pub. Assoc.,1944.
88. *Childcraft, The How and Why Library*, World Book Inc., Chicago.
89. *The Maryknoll Catholic Dictionary*, Nevins, Dimension Books, NY, 1965.
90. *Standard Dictionary of Folklore, Mythology, and Legend*, Edited by Maria Leach, Funk & Wagnalls Co., NY, 1950.
91. *The Buffalo News*, May 19, 1982.
92. *The Encyclopedia of Religions*, Ferm, The Philosophical Library, NY.
93. *Look Magazine*, January 16, 1962.
94. *Cyclopedia of World Authors*, Magill, Harper and Brothers, 1958.
95. *People Weekly*, June 4, 1990.
96. *Contemporary Authors,* Volume 116, Gale Research Co., 1986.
97. *Strong's Exhaustive Concordance to the Bible*, Thomas Nelson Publishers, TN, 1990.
98. *Time*, April 7, 1997.
99. *Atlantis: The Eighth Continent*, Berlitz, Ballantine Books, NY, 1984.
100. *Encyclopedia of Mythology*, Cotterell, Anness Publishing Limited, NY, 1996.

101. *World Mythology*, Willis, Henry Holt & Co., NY, 1993.
102. *The Encyclopedia of Parapsychology and Psychical Research*, Berger, Paragon House, NY, 1991.
103. *The Arizona Republic*, March 27, 1997.
104. *World Religions from Ancient History to the Present*, Parrinder, The Hamlyn Publishing Group Ltd., 1971.
105. *The Encyclopedia Americana*, Grolier Inc., Danbury, Conn., 1996.
106. *Mayan Initiation Centers* flyer, Merida 7, Yucatán, Mexico.
107. *The Unknown Hitler*, Schwarzwaller, National Press, Inc., 1989.
108. *Atlantis*, Stein, Greenhaven Press, Inc., San Diego, CA, 1989.
109. *Ruth Montgomery: Herald of the New Age*, Montgomery/Garland, Doubleday/Dolphin, Doubleday & Co., Inc., Garden City, NY, 1986.
110. *The Keys of This Blood*, Martin, Simon & Schuster, NY, 1990.
111. *Nineteen Eighty-four*, Orwell, Penguin Group, NY, 1984.
112. *Funk & Wagnall's New Encyclopedia*, Vol. 12, Funk & Wagnall's Inc., 1988.
113. *Gandhi: Voice of a New Age Revolution*, Green, The Continuum Publishing Company, NY, 1993.
114. *Harper's Encyclopaedia of the United States*, Vol. 5, Harper & Brothers Publishers, NY, 1905.
115. *Dictionary of Symbolism*, Biedermann, Facts on File, NY, 1992.
116. *The Mystical Year,* Time-Life Books, Alexander, VA.
117. *A Guide To The Gods*, Carlyon, William Morrow and Company, NY, 1982.
118. *The Jews: Their History, Culture, and Religion*, Finkelstein, Harper & Brothers Publishers, NY, 1960.
119. *Who's Who in Jewish History*, Comay, David McKay Company, Inc., NY, 1974.
120. *The Universal Jewish Encyclopedia*, The Universal Jewish Encyclopedia Inc., NY, 1943.
121. *A New Encyclopaedia of Freemasonry*, Vol. 1, Waite, University Books, New Hyde Park, NY, 1970.
122. *Mackey's Revised Encyclopedia of Freemasonry*, Vol. 1, Macoy Publishing and Masonic Supply Co., Inc., 1946.
123. *Council on Foreign Relations, Inc., Annual Report*, 1979-80.

124. *Council on Foreign Relations, Inc., Annual Report*, 1995.
125. *The Cult of the All-Seeing Eye*, Spenser, Monte Cristo Press, 1964.
126. *The Interfaith Community flyer*, May 1990.
127. *Parade* magazine, April 3, 1994.
128. *Externalization of the Hierarchy*, Bailey, Lucis Trust, 1971.
129. *Ben Gurion: The Burning Ground 1886-1948*, Shabtai Teveth, Houghton Mifflin Co., 1987.
130. *Chronicle of the 20th Century*, December 1973, Chronicle Publications.
131. *Pathway To Light*, The Unarius Academy of Sciences, El Cajon, CA.
132. *A Dictionary of World Mythology*, Cotterell, G.P. Putnam's Sons, NY, 1979.
133. *The International Encyclopedia of Secret Societies & Fraternal Orders*, Axelrod, Facts on File, Inc., NY, 1997.
134. *Sedona: Journal of Emergence!*, April 1999.

ILLUSTRATIONS

1. Illustration of Hebrews Worshipping the Sun...............p. 16
2. Photograph of Sedona New Age Center.....................p. 33
3. Photograph of Von Däniken's Theories....................p. 35
4. Chart of the Seven Ages of Astrology........................p. 39
5. Illustration of UFO Flyer...p. 44
6. Illustration of the Ten Divisions of the World...............p. 47
7. Illustration of the Wand of Hermes (Caduceus)............p. 49
8. Photograph of Unarius Academy of Sciences...............p. 51
9. Photograph of Thomas Paine's Cottage....................p. 76
10. Illustration of Thomas Jefferson.............................p. 77
11. Illustration of Benjamin Franklin............................p. 83
12. Photograph of Prophet's Ranch Restaurant.................p. 187
13. Map of Descendants of Noah................................p. 200
14. Illustration of Jesus...p. 226
15. Photograph of *Wainwright House 1990 Guide*............p. 255
16. Photograph of Wainwright House...........................p. 257
17. Photograph of U.N. Meditation Room.....................p. 263
18. Photograph of Original Pagan Altar of U.N................p. 265
19. Photograph of U.N. Meditation Room Mural...............p. 267
20. Photograph of Wainwright House...........................p. 269

CHAPTER I

UFOLOGY AND THE NEW AGE CONNECTION

It was back in 1975 on the island of Oahu, Hawaii, that I was astonished with amazement along with three other companions as we silently gazed into the night skies and watched a formation of UFO's, about five in number, pass before our eyes! These UFO's were not in the form of saucers for they were too distant into the earth's atmosphere to recognize their shapes. We saw them as bright lights like stars moving together in formation. When they suddenly wisked away and disappeared, then we all shouted in unison, "Did you see **THAT**!"

Again, while holding lectures in Phoenix, Arizona, in the month of March of 1997, over 10,000 people saw saucer-like disks hovering over Phoenix. Even the news media captured them on their cameras, however, the Air Force, who refused at first to comment, announced later they were only flares. Nevertheless, there are UFO's flying through the skies of this planet. But, just *who* are they? Some New Agers believe that there are extraterrestrials from the Dog Star Sirius, which modern shamans say they have contacted. Sirius is a double star and, in Egyptian mythology, Sirius a.k.a. Sothis was the abode of their gods named Isis and Osiris.[1] The reader shall discover that both New Age beliefs and UFOlogy are centered around this mysterious double star. This eight-pointed star was widely venerated by ancient pagan civilizations.

In Egypt, at one time, Sirius first appeared at dawn during the hottest time of the year and the pagan Romans coined the phrase "dog days,"[2] meaning the time of Sirius, the Dog Star.

In early Babylonian mythology, which is the mother of all pagan religions, Sirius was the symbol of Ishtar, the pagan war goddess who was the equivalent of the Greek goddess Aphrodite. Today, this

---

[1]*World Religions from Ancient History to the Present*, Parrinder, The Hamlyn Publishing Group, Ltd., 1971, p. 140.
[2]*The Encyclopedia Americana*, Grolier Inc., Danbury, Conn., 1996, p. 848.

The Real Truth About UFO's and the New World Order

Israel, Worshiping the Sun, With Their Backs to the Law of God, Enshrined in His Temple

The Hebrew apostle of Jesus Christ urged us in the first century in the year of our Lord to study about what happened to the ancient Israelites and how they were deceived into following the precepts of Spiritualism instead of the precepts of God. Human nature in Biblical times is the same today. The same mistakes and sins the ancient Hebrew Jews committed in the past are the same mistakes and sins modern Christians and modern Jews are committing today. The apostle Paul wrote in 1 Corinthians 10:11, "Now all these things happened unto them for ensamples: and they are written for our admonition, upon whom the ends of the world are come."

The drawing above shows the ancient Hebrews worshipping the sun of whom they addressed as Baal. This terrible apostasy is recorded in Scripture in Ezekiel, Chapter Eight. This apostasy from the God of Abraham, Isaac, and Jacob by God's chosen people of that day led to national ruin for the Creator of the sun, moon, and stars turned His back on the Israelites and removed His protective shield from them, and the Babylonians came and destroyed the first Temple of Solomon and the city of Jerusalem. The Hebrew prophet Ezekiel describes the spiritual fall of Israel in Ezekiel 8:13–18.

"He said also unto me, Turn thee yet again, and thou shalt see greater abominations that they do. Then he brought me to the door of the gate of the Lord's house which was toward the north; and, behold, there sat women weeping for Tammuz. Then said he unto me, Hast thou seen this, O son of man? turn thee yet again, and thou shalt see greater abominations than these. And he brought me into the inner court of the Lord's house, and, behold, at the door of the temple of the Lord, between the porch and the altar, were about five and twenty men, with their backs toward the temple of the Lord, and their faces toward the east; and they worshipped the sun toward the east. Then he said unto me, Hast thou seen this, O son of man? Is it a light thing to the house of Judah that they commit the abominations which they commit here? for they have filled the land with violence, and have returned to provoke me to anger: and, lo, they put the branch to their nose. Therefore will I also deal in fury: mine eye shall not spare, neither will I have pity: and though they cry in mine ears with a loud voice, yet will I not hear them."

UFOLOGY and the New Age Connection

same eight-pointed star has been adopted by the Roman Church to symbolize the Virgin Mary.

Some New Agers who believe in the doctrine of immortality of the soul or transmigration of the soul have been led to kill themselves in the belief that their souls would travel to Sirius to live with their gods. Pagans from both sides of the Atlantic believe that the **star gods were once human beings who are returning from Sirius, their cosmic headquarters, to take over planet Earth again**. Some North American Indian shamans believe that the UFO's may be the Mayan messiah Kulkulcán or the Toltec messiah Quetzalcoatl. Ironically enough, there has been a great revival of the Mayan and Toltec gods among both American and Latin American New Agers, and we shall see why shortly.

To prepare human beings to be accepted by these ancient Mayan gods, a Mexican-based New Age center calling itself the *Mayan Initiation Center* in Merida, Yucatán, is calling for all human beings to receive a **solar initiation**. They claim that an ancient Mayan prophecy which prophesied about the darkness of **Roman Catholicism** forced upon them by the Spaniards **came to an end in 1995**. According to the *Mayan Initiation Center*, it states in its flyer on page two that it was the **ancient Mayans** who built the ancient pyramids which were built in Egypt, Tibet, and other parts of Asia, in addition to the huge pyramids found throughout Latin America. According to these Latin American New Agers, "All of these pyramidal temples were built when mankind lived in the **light of cosmic wisdom**."[3] They also can be quoted on the same flyer on page two as saying, "It is written in time that a brother from a faraway land, way beyond the sea, **will come to awaken** the Maya people, who are to remain asleep during a period of darkness."[4]

At this point, I would like to remind believers of Bible prophecy of 1 John 2:18 and show how New Agers and some Christians are setting themselves up to accept this **great impostor** who shall appear just before the real Jesus of Nazareth returns the second time to gather his elect. "Little children, it is the last time: and as ye have heard that **ANTICHRIST SHALL COME**, even now are there many antichrists; whereby we know that it is the last time." 1 John 2:18.

---

[3] *Mayan Initiation Centers flyer*, Merida 7, Yucatán, Mexico, p. 2.
[4] *Ibid*., p. 2.

The Real Truth About UFO's and the New World Order

Nevertheless, these Latin American New Agers who reject Jesus Christ as Saviour of the world go on to point out on page two of their flyer how Mayan priests used a calendar which they called K'ALTUN which was made up of 13 periods of 20 years each or 260 years. "It was prophesied that two cycles of the K'ALTUN had to be completed in order to bring an end to the darkness brought by Spain. That is, two times 260 years = 520 years." They began this prophecy in 1475 A.D. The two cycles of 260 years or 520 years ended, according to these New Agers, in **1995**. (1475 + 520 = 1995.)

Hence, the year 1995 **marks the year** that the ancient Maya Solar religion is to be **revived and to flourish again**, according to the *Mayan Initiation Center* on page three of their flyer. "Only through the *solar initiation* can the sleeping body of mankind be awakened. The reincarnated teachers of the new age of Aquarius implore for the sacred human race to awaken, so that in this way it can fulfill its sacred destiny, which is to be the true sons and daughters of the cosmic light." The reader may have chuckled at this quote, however, the reader may not be aware of just how many people today are seeking to receive this so-called cosmic light.

Back in March of 1997 **during the spring vernal equinox**, a crowd of about 30,000 New Agers gathered at the ancient pagan temple-pyramid of the Mayan feathered-serpent god Kulkulcán. He was the Quetzalcoatl of the Toltecs who was the equivalent of Adonis to the Greeks and Tammuz to the ancient Babylonians.

During the vernal equinox, ancient pagan religions all over the world had annually celebrated the return of their dead and risen gods in the spring. Like their ancient brethren, **New Agers worship the forces of nature instead of nature's God**. They worship the created things instead of the Creator. Keeping this in mind, let's look at the annual New Age festival held at Chichén Itzá.

In the March 1996 *Sky & Telescope* magazine, E.C. Krupp wrote an interesting article about what he witnessed at Chichén Itzá in Mexico's Yucatán peninsula in the spring of 1987. New Age pagans have revived the ancient Mayan celebration of the vernal equinox to honor Kulkulcán. Krupp points out that to the Mayans, Mexico's Yucatán peninsula was the most important center of power for the northern Yucatán Mayan from the ninth through the 12th centuries A.D. and

UFOLOGY and the New Age Connection

had laid in ruins for centuries. Why are New Agers interested in reviving the worship of Kulkulcán and Quetzalcoatl?

Because this writer has explored the ancient Toltec ruins at Teotihaucan in central Mexico and climbed the huge pyramid to the sun-god of Quetzalcoatl, the feathered serpent, it was not hard for me to figure out back in the 70s that both Kulkulcán of the Mayans and Quetzalcoatl to the Toltecs, whose names mean "***bird serpent***," were nothing less than that **old serpent the Devil** who hid himself in the worship of these gods of Toltec and Mayan mythology.

In the prophecies of the book of Revelation, the serpent and the Dragon are synomynous. We shall study how this Dragon (serpent) not only anciently deceived human beings into worshipping him in the most degrading rites, but also how these UFO's are, indeed, Satan and his evil angels setting up and conditioning the whole world to accept him as Christ by using ancient mythology, science fiction, and the New Age and New World Order planned takeover. Both the New Age Movement and the New World Order derived out of the secret society of witchcraft known as the **Illuminati**, which was founded by an evil genius named **Adam Weishaupt**. This is completely examined in Volume Two of these Time of the End prophecies entitled *The New Age Movement and The Illuminati 666*. I published this book in 1983. In Volume One of this series entitled *Beware It's Coming – The Antichrist 666* which I published in 1980, I point out how the reader can prove for himself that these ancient gods our ancient ancestors were deceived into worshipping were actually demon worship. These same gods can be traced back in history and archaeology to the legends of Nimrod and his evil family. The New Age religion is nothing less than a revival of the **same old pagan ignorance** that was determined to convert the whole world centuries ago.

Again, in this volume we will investigate the New Age and the New World Order's history of over 200 years. However, in this volume we shall discover with documented proof how these occult, revolutionary movements, which were both born in the same stall as the Illuminati, are today revolving around the myths written by **Plato** concerning the mysterious island **Atlantis**. Ancient astronauts (UFO's) supposedly visited the continent of Atlantis and gave its inhabitants supernatural secrets of which produced supernatural races and a utopian form of

The Real Truth About UFO's and the New World Order

government. We shall see with documented proof that the goal of the New Age and the New World Order is to **re-establish** the **ten divisions** of the Atlantean government leaving out, of course, the God of Abraham.

To understand the modern Atlantean plan of the New World Order and how our God foretold it in the book of Revelation, the reader must become knowledgeable about the Scriptures and how they record what the deceptions were that the Dragon used to lure the Israelites into worshipping him as Baal, Ashtoreth, and Tammuz. As I will remind the reader several times throughout the pages of this book, **the gods of mythology are the gods of astrology.**

As revealed in *The New Age Movement and The Illuminati 666*, Satan was symbolized as a seven-headed Dragon in the book of Revelation because ancient Babylonian **astrology** was symbolized as a seven-headed Dragon. The seven heads represented the seven chief gods of astrology which were the Sun, Moon, Venus, Mercury, Jupiter, Mars, and Saturn. We will see more about this as we continue. All cultures of the ancient and modern world have their own version of the religion of astrology.

This cosmic serpent or dragon is pictured in Revelation, Chapter 12, as attacking Christ's bride, who is symbolizing Jesus' true people down through the ages of this present world. It is astonishing to see today how mainstream Christians from both the Roman Catholic and Protestant faiths are connecting themselves with these New Age and New World Order deceptions. It is astonishing, indeed, in how many Christians have left the faith that was once delivered to the saints and have fulfilled the prophecy in Revelation 13:4 – "And they worshipped (followed) the dragon (Satan) which gave power unto the beast."

E.C. Krupp said he first saw New Agers gathered to identify with the cosmic feathered-serpent god Kulkulcán at Chichén Itzá, Mexico, back in March of 1982. It was at the time of the climax of the celebration of the pagan vernal equinox. Annually, on March 21st one hour before sunset, a play of sunlight and shadows causes triangular light patches to appear on the west side of the Kulkulcán pyramid. This shadowy figure looks as if a giant diamondback rattlesnake (a symbol for Kulkulcán) appears. As the sun falls in the west, it causes this shadow to appear as Kulkulcán (the feathered rattlesnake) as if he dropped down from the sky and slithered down the banister of the

UFOLOGY and the New Age Connection

steps of his pagan temple. Then, another play of sunlight causes this serpent-like shadow to return upward back to the cosmos.

Like ancient Old World pagans, modern New Agers believe that this planet was visited by ancient astronauts who were the gods of ancient mythology. New Age advocates believe that the early original Aztecs, Toltecs, Mayans, and the Peruvian Inca Indians are the **descendants** of the Atlanteans who, according to New Age philosophy, had established a Utopian civilization but were forced to eventually migrate to North, Central, and South America via Egypt when their island continent of Atlantis sunk into the Atlantic Ocean. Surviving Toltecs were said to have escaped to Egypt and from there, after establishing a colony in Egypt, migrated to North, Central, and South America. This is the reason for the renewed interest in the cultures and religions of the Aztecs, Mayans, Toltecs, and Incas. The North, Central, and South American Indians are believed to have received the knowledge about the cosmos and how to build their pyramids from the Egyptians. The ancient Egyptians often displayed their cosmic gods such as Ra, their sky god, flying through this planet's skies on a **solar disk**. For centuries, the stellar star Sirius was worshipped by Egyptians as the nocturnal representation of the sun-god Osiris and his mother goddess wife Isis. Today, this star Sirius is the primary focus behind New Age philosophy and UFOlogy for New Agers say it is from Sirius that their modern shamans have been able to contact their **ancient astronauts** a.k.a. extraterrestrial beings which are now hovering or shooting across this planet's skies today.

However, I have discovered in my investigation of the New Age Movement that they do differ in their beliefs. Some New Agers believe that the ancient astronauts (UFO's) are from the Pleiades, an open cluster of stars in the constellation Taurus consisting of several hundred stars of which six are visible to the naked eye.

New Agers **tie in** mythology from the Old World as the origin of the star gods of the ancient Indians of the New World. They point out the similarities between the religions of the Egyptians, Greeks, Hindus, and Babylonians with that of the Aztecs, Toltecs, Mayans, and Incas. New Agers are quick to point out that when the Catholic Spanish conquerors of Central and South America reached Mexico they

The Real Truth About UFO's and the New World Order

not only learned that the Aztecs migrated to central Mexico from what is known today as New Mexico, but they also learned from them that before their migration from North America they originally came from an island in the Eastern (to them) Ocean called **Aztlán**. Early explorers in Wisconsin found a fortified village near Lake Michigan of which its Indian inhabitants called **Azatlán**.[5] In Hindu writings of the Puranas and in the Mahabharata, there is the name **Attala** – "the White Island," – a continent located in the Western (to them) Ocean.[6]

However, the **first mention** of Atlantis is made in the *Timaeus* and the *Critias* of **Plato**, the ancient pagan Greek philosopher which said he learned of his account of Atlantis by Solon, an Athenian lawgiver and an ancient relative of Plato who lived two centuries before Plato in Egypt. Solon had supposedly learned of the Atlantis story from a pagan priest in Sais, Egypt, after which he verbally passed it on among his relatives.

After Plato's written dialogues of the *Timaeus* and the *Critias* had made their way in Greece describing Plato's account of the Golden Age of Atlantis, Plutarch (A.D. 46? - 120?) after the death, burial, and resurrection of our Lord began to circulate the Atlantis myth in his *Lives*,[7] which verified Plato's account of Atlantis.

The myth of Atlantis has had an evolution. The discovery of America by Columbus sparked new speculations during the European Renaissance.[8] The tyranny of the Roman Catholic Church and the Reformation accelerated by Martin Luther helped to stir two main divisions against the power that the Vatican had enslaved upon the people of the Old World. These two divisions were the Protestant Reformation and the Humanist Renaissance Era. While Luther preached righteousness by faith and the coming Kingdom of God, humanist European philosophers who were antichrist **combatted** Christianity by **adopting** Plato's account of the Golden Age of Atlantis and set their faces to **re-establish** this **Socialistic** government in our world today. This became the basis of Thomas Paine's deistic writings of

---

[5]*Atlantis: The Eighth Continent*, Berlitz, Ballantine Books, NY, 1984, p. 10.
[6]Ibid., p. 10.
[7]*The New Age Encyclopedia*, First Edition, Melton, Gale Research Inc., Detroit, MI, 1990, p. 45.
[8]*Ibid*., Melton, p. 45.

UFOLOGY and the New Age Connection

Common Sense and *Age of Reason* of which both sparked the American and French Revolution and gave both Adam Weishaupt, founder of the secret society of the Illuminati, and one of his successors, Karl Marx, ideas to continue this Socialistic revolution. We will see more of the rise and the evolution of the Socialistic revolution behind the New World Order scheme as we continue. But, let's again come back to look at this UFO threat and what the real truth about it is.

As New Age scholars try to sell the world that a new **Galactic Age** is coming in the next century which is known to them as the **Age of Aquarius** or the **Golden Age**, however, Christian Bible-believing brethren are preaching that the coming destruction of this present world is near and this coming millennium will see this world's inhabitants either taken with Christ at His Second Coming or destroyed by the brightness of His coming. The Bible prophecies, which many Protestant pastors are confused over, **do not** prophesy of a secret rapture, of a return of the saints after the great tribulation is over, or of a thousand-year reign of Christ in this present world. The Scriptures foretell the **total destruction** of the rejectors of the Gospel including not only New Age Spiritualists, but also Christians, both Catholics and Protestants, who join this New World Order scheme.

The Author and Finisher of the Christian faith is coming out of His place to punish those who have rejected His salvation. Jesus is the Saviour of the world. Those who have rejected salvation will, indeed, unite themselves with these ancient demons who clothed themselves as the star gods of the Babylonians, Persians, Greeks, Romans, Nordic peoples, Egyptians, Hindus, Phoenicians, Mayans, Incas, Toltecs, Aztecs, and of other North American Indian pagan religions.

Jesus prophesied that just before the end of this present world, "fearful sights and great signs (supernatural miracles) shall there be from heaven." Luke 21:11.

The Spirit of Antichrist found in both the New Age Movement and the New World Order Movement is being guided by modern shamans who are communicating with spirit guides of which they have been fooled into believing are the ancient pagan gods of the past who are ancient astronauts coming to **usher in** a new age of enlightenment. New Agers are also quick to point out how ancient primitive man drew paintings in caves of what appears to be **elves** dressed in

The Real Truth About UFO's And the New World Order

headgear with space suits on. They point to the supernatural wonders found in the Nazca Valley of Peru and the runway there which has the appearance of an ancient runway of an ancient airport and of the huge line drawings of a monkey and a hummingbird which can only be recognized from the air. They point out how astronauts today have discovered and photographed the double star Sirius which used to rise three or four thousand years ago in the east during the summer solstice. This, they say, proves that their learned mahatmas really do exist.

New Agers even have an occult society which was founded in London, England, by a small group of Platonic supporters claiming that one of the familiar spirits named Helio-Arcanophus claimed to have been a high priestess in the lost continent of Atlantis. The name of this secret society of Spiritualism is known as The Atlanteans. Their shaman which this spirit named Helio-Arcanophus used to speak through the voice box of to achieve a hookup with their star gods was former actress Jacqueline Murray.[9] We will examine a little of what part Hollywood is playing in this New World Order scheme. However, in this volume we will focus mainly on their religious powers. In Volume Four of this series of Time of the End prophecies, we will have an in-depth study into how both Hollywood and the Music Industry have been Satan's number-one vehicle to promote propaganda for an Atlantean and global New World Order. The title of my fourth volume is *Ancient Prophecies About Mysticism and Hollywood and The Music Industry*.

Again, it is very important that the reader become acquainted with the myths surrounding the lost continent of Atlantis because both the New Age and the New World Order threats are rooted and grounded in them. When studied carefully, not only will the Christian believer learn how **not** to become a victim of this diabolical plot against the real Jesus found in the Scriptures, but after learning about Atlantis the reader shall surely see how our God foretold in Daniel 2:41-43; Revelation 17:12-14; and Revelation 18:23 of what well-known businessmen and religious leaders in our day shall do against the Prince of Peace.

It was eye-opening, indeed, to me when I first studied about how the Atlantean government was set up and how its Socialist Utopian form of government was divided into TEN EQUAL KINGDOMS[10] for the secret society of the Club of Rome, who are the geographical planners

---

[9]*Encyclopedia of Occultism and Parapsychology*, 3rd Ed., Shepard, p. 114.
[10]*Man, Myth, and Magic*, Vol. 1, Cavendish, p. 188.

UFOLOGY and the New Age Connection

of the New World Order scheme, laid out a sketch of what they hoped the world shall become in the next millennium. This sketch which was presented to the powers behind the New World Order in 1974 showed a division of TEN KINGDOMS OR TEN ZONES! We will study more about this also as we continue to trace this history of the New World Order and its evolution. We shall see that this Socialist federation of the New World Order is nothing less than a reproduction of Plato's account of the Atlantean government. Plato's blueprint for re-establishing the Atlantean federation was laid out in his dialogues *Timaeus* and *Critias* and also in Plato's *The Republic* from which Thomas Jefferson pulled many of his ideas.

This Atlantean scheme for a New World Order on this planet is, according to New Age prophets, a great *cosmic design* of the universe for New Agers believe that there is an **interplanetary confederacy** between other inhabited planets **and that planet Earth is to be the 33rd final linking member**. Modern Spiritualists teach that the UFO's are space brothers who are working for the benefit of humankind and are preparing earthlings for this great and important event. Believe it or not, readers, this is indeed the vision behind this New World Order scheme being promoted today by the most learned politicians and religious leaders who are New Age or New World Order advocates.

In Plato's *Critias*, Atlantis is given a legendary beginning. It is based in Greek mythology. Poseidon, the god of the sea who was Neptune to the Romans later and Vishnu to the Hindu earlier or Dagon to the Philistines, had begotten ten sons from a mortal woman of which the eldest of the ten sons was the god Atlas.

In the myth, Poseidon was the brother of Zeus and Hades and after they overthrew their father Cronos, Zeus divided up the world between himself and his two brothers. Zeus chose to rule the sky, Hades the underworld, and Poseidon the sea. The earth and Mount Olympus, which was the home of the gods, were regarded as common territory.[11] Zeus also had a son from a mortal woman which today has become the great hero of the cartoon fantasies. His name is Hercules, the messiah of Greek mythology.

The ten sons of Poseidon were also known as **Teitans** in Greek transliterations or Titans in Old English; and Poseidon, in the myth, bestowed on the ten sons the paradise of Atlantis. Atlantis, in the myth, had two

---

[11]*The Encyclopedia of Mythology*, Cotterell, 1996, p. 89.

The Real Truth About UFO's and the New World Order

islands. A small island became the Metropolis of the empire and the site of the temple of Poseidon. The rest of the empire is said to be on the adjoining continent and was said to lie beyond the Pillars of Hercules a.k.a. the Straits of Gibraltar.[12]

The evolution of the Greek pantheon of gods, which were in reality Satan and his fallen angels, was clearly well-established in Greece by 750 B.C. Its major figures were featured prominently in the writings of an earlier prophet of Spiritualism named Homer. He exalted and promoted these gods in his *Iliad* and the *Odyssey*[13] of which students today are forced to read from, and the *Odyssey* was made into a television movie. The gospels of Homer and Plato are programming and conditioning the inhabitants of this world to choose the side of the Dragon "which gave power unto the beast ... and cause that as many as would not worship the image of the beast should be killed." Revelation 13:4, 15. It can plainly be seen with spiritual eyesight that these ancient gods of mythology from both sides of the Atlantic were inventions from the **invisible Prime Minister** of the world to blind the spiritual eyesight of "them which believe not, lest the light of the glorious gospel of Christ, who is the image of God, should shine unto them." 2 Corinthians 4:4.

Plato, who was born in 427 B.C. and died in 347 B.C., was not only the New World Order's first original administrator, but also one of its high priests of Spiritualism. Not only did he promote the worship of the Greek gods, but he also accelerated the pagan belief in the **transmigration of souls**. To New Agers, Plato was the most important and influential philosopher who ever lived. Besides his Atlantean plan for a universal Utopian commonwealth to be re-established, he taught his disciples the doctrine of **dualism**, which the believer while under a demonic trance is mesmerized into thinking that he had an out-of-the-body experience. Plato's dualism, his theory of the immortal and immaterial soul, and his scheme of rewards and punishments strongly influenced the most recognized scribes of the Roman Catholic Church, one of whom was Augustine.[14] Much of the philosophies of modern Catholicism can be traced to this ancient apostle of Spiritualism, as well as among New Agers. The basic divorce of

---

[12]*Man, Myth, and Magic*, Vol. 1, Cavendish, p. 188.
[13]*World Mythology*, Willis, Henry Holt & Co., NY, 1993, p. 126.
[14]*The Encyclopedia of Parapsychology and Psychical Research*, Berger, p. 324.

UFOLOGY and the New Age Connection

the soul from the body and living on afterwards, the practice of necromancy and earthbound spirits (ghosts) haunting places where they lived or were buried, the doctrine of **pre-existence** of human beings, and the law of **karma** and **reincarnation** of which he borrowed from ancient Hinduism – all show that Plato can be noted as Spiritualism's chief apostle. In his book, *The Republic*, "Plato reiterated that souls will be reborn," however, "according to what they have learned from previous lives, will be able to determine the conditions of their next lives." [15]

The false doctrine of the soul being able to divorce itself from the body and to reach a state of bliss (nirvana) through the law of karma and reincarnation which was made into a popular belief among ancient Grecians by Plato and among American New Agers is where we can find the origin of the spiritual blindness which led the self-proclaimed New Age messiah Marshall Applewhite, the leader of the Heaven's Gate cult, and 38 androgynous followers to kill themselves in order to hook up with a UFO.

Applewhite, a former music teacher, announced to the world, "PLANET EARTH ABOUT TO BE RECYCLED. YOUR ONLY CHANCE TO SURVIVE – LEAVE WITH US."[16] This terrible atrocity was brought about by the belief in the immortality of the soul. Heaven's Gate's victims were taught that suicide was a way to escape from their earthly containers (bodies) so that their souls could reach a higher level of existence. They define death not as the enemy of life but as life itself. Amazingly, a United Methodist minister J. Gordon Melton, editor of the authoritative *Encyclopedia of American Religions*, agrees. He can be quoted in *Time*, April 7, 1997, on page 32. "In this case they had a positive motive, a great place to go to," Pastor Melton said. "So why hang around here?" Applewhite and his followers chose to kill themselves around the **very time** when New Agers in Chichén Itzá and elsewhere were celebrating their vernal equinox to honor their forces of nature, and when the Hale-Bopp comet was exciting the eyes of onlookers as it lightened up the night skies. Shortly before Heaven's Gate's victims committed suicide in a mansion they rented in Rancho Santa Fe, California, another New Age group calling themselves the Order of

---

[15]*The Encyclopedia of Parapsychology and Psychical Research*, Berger, p. 324.
[16]*Time*, April 7, 1997, p. 31.

The Real Truth About UFO's and the New World Order

the Solar Temple had 74 of their members take their own lives in Europe and Canada in the past three years. They believed that suicide transports them to a new life on Sirius[17] known to ancient Egyptians as the abode of Osiris and Isis. The **symbol** for Sirius is displayed on the front cover of this volume. Applewhite convinced his followers that a UFO was trailing the Hale-Bopp comet, and that this UFO was a shuttle to ferry their departed souls to this same double star. When authorities found the victims of Heaven's Gate, Thomas Nichols, the brother of Nichelle Nichols who was the actress who played the demi-goddess in the original *Star Trek*, was found among them. The cult's work space in the mansion they rented was decorated with posters of alien beings from the *X-Files* and *E.T.* A Heaven's Gate victim on a farewell tape explained that the movies of *Star Trek* and *Star Wars* helped him to make his decision to leave behind his human container and be with the other members on the craft in the heavens.[18] It is eye-opening to learn that much of George Lucas' *Star Wars* **trilogy** was taken from the **doctrines found in mythology and folklore**.

The occult doctrine of becoming stronger after dying and leaving one's container (body) behind to reach a higher level of existence was certainly portrayed by Alec Guinness as the *Star Wars* **shaman** named **Obi-Wan Kenobi** in this occult-exalting movie.

As pointed out earlier, ancient mythology has had its evolution. This mysterious double star Sirius of which much of the New Age theology is centered around was originally worshipped as "***Athtar or Lucifer***."[19] Sirius later evolved as the abode of the soul of Osiris or the star that "***ferries the Phoenix***," which meant the soul.[20]

Again, the double star Sirius that was worshipped by the Egyptians originally as the nocturnal representation of the hidden sun-god was nothing less than Lucifer, whose name means "***day star***" which is the sun and who is the prince of the power of the air who is fooling New Agers and apostate Christians into worshipping him and his demons as the gods (UFO's) of mythology. We will study more about Sirius and the Roman Catholic connection as we continue later.

---

[17]*The Arizona Republic*, March 27, 1997, p. A-17.
[18]*Time*, April 7, 1997, p. 33.
[19]*Mythology of All Races*, Vol. 12, Gray, Cooper Square Pub. Inc., 1964, p. 54.
[20]*Ibid.*, Gray, p. 54.

UFOLOGY and the New Age Connection

Since I wrote my last book about the conspiracy behind the New Age Movement and the secret society of the Illuminati, so much more information about this has come forth during this past decade. So, I thought I should write more volumes about this very serious subject.

Much of what I pointed out in Volume Two, *The New Age Movement and The Illuminati 666*, came to pass! Back in 1983, I pointed out that **Communism** in Russia would **change** into forced international **Socialism**. Again, in 1983 when most Christians had never heard of the New Age Movement or of the New World Order conspiracy, the above book pointed out that multitudes of Protestants and Catholics would be deceived into joining this confederation. This is also history. In 1983 in the same book, it was pointed out how a worldwide confederation of people from the occult would eventually unite the general movement of the Papacy and the mainstream Protestants into a New World Order through the United Nations. This is now becoming history! We shall see that this is true in this volume.

Volume Two, *The New Age Movement and The Illuminati 666* of this series on Time of the End events, is another reference book based on the prophecies of the book of Daniel and the book of Revelation. It dwelt mainly on the political side of this New Age and New World Order conspiracy. This volume – Volume Three – entitled *The Real Truth about UFO'S and The New World Order Connection 666* will, like Volume One entitled *Beware It's Coming – The Antichrist 666*, focus mainly on the religious side. We will discover how the New World Order conspiracy of the occult was, indeed, foretold from the Holy Scriptures, and we will also learn who their prophets and apostles are and what the prophets and apostles of the Bible predicted about them and what shall surely come upon those who follow them. Volume Five of this series of reference books will again show more of the political side of this three-fold union of Lucifer's and what has developed since I published *The New Age Movement and The Illuminati 666* book in 1983.

If the reader would like to receive a copy of Volume Five entitled *Ancient Prophecies About The Dragon, The Beast, and The False Prophet 666*, or if the reader would like all of the volumes I have written on these very important issues, again, they are displayed in

The Real Truth About UFO's and the New World Order

this book. All of the volumes I have written concerning the warnings about this **spirit of antichrist** and how it would engulf the world in our day were written to be read individually. Each volume contains more information for the serious-minded readers who have the love of the truth that they may be saved so they will become more prepared for this coming crisis that shall surely come upon this earth; for it is written that most of the inhabitants of this planet shall be deceived, "and they worshipped the dragon which gave power unto the beast." Revelation 13:4. These Christ-centered volumes were compiled and written and documented to be encyclopedias on Time of the End events. They are written for the readers so they will not only become more intelligent about what this Dragon is doing now in our day but also how to avoid receiving the Mark, Name, and the Number of his Name (666). The book of Revelation is centered around these two main themes – the Dragon, his Mark, Name, and Number (666), and the Lamb of God and His Seal and His Name and His Blood. Volumes One through Five are also centered around these same prophecies. In Revelation 12:9, **it warned that the Dragon deceived the whole world**. This has surely taken place! The reader will see that this is true.

If the reader feels like he or she is 50 years behind in advancing in the things of God, the reader may get caught up on present-day truth by proving and testing these volume's credibility like the Bereans did with the apostle Paul. "These were more noble than those in Thessalonica, in that they received the word with all readiness of mind, and searched the scriptures daily, whether those things were so." Acts 17:11. I also invite my readers to do the same for I have not received any special revelation from God through dreams and visions to bring these amazing facts to you. I learned these truths for today by hard-core study for over a quarter of a century. The Lord of the Sabbath has blessed my ministry tremendously because of these last two volumes I have written to help advance the cause of Christ. I pray He will do the same with these three new volumes. My intentions in writing these reference books are mainly to help the modern Jews, Catholics, Protestants, Buddhists, Hindus, Muslims, and those who follow the philosophies of Confucius or the 17th and 18th century philosophers to see their error in not knowing the Scriptures or misinterpreting them.

UFOLOGY and the New Age Connection

Both the ancient Jewish prophets and the apostles of Christ Jesus foretold that God would **divide** the people of this world today into just **two divisions**. The prophecies of the Holy Scriptures do foretell that there are other sheep that are not of the religion of Jesus who will join Him and His other sheep in these last days. God has His people **scattered throughout all these religious bodies**, and He knows those who will become awakened to the fact that they are called and chosen to be of His fold for there shall be **one fold** and **one Shepherd** and there is only **one door** that leads to this fold. But, the Dragon, the prince of darkness, has opened other doors that lead away from finding the True Shepherd. The prince of darkness has invented this so-called cosmic light that has blinded the minds of the inhabitants of this planet, and he has engrossed the minds of the people of this world in sports and the entertainment industries so that they would become lovers of pleasure more than lovers of God. The people of this world have been robbed of the True Light which comes from above which was written in Scripture as holy men wrote them as they were moved by the Holy Spirit. Today, the Truth is evil spoken of and so are they who proclaim it. However, Babylon the Great **shall be exposed** for everyone to behold and so will the knowledge of the True God and His Christ, Jesus, so all may discern the difference between Christ and **THE** Antichrist. Satan's last effort to completely take over this world began in these last days during the French Revolution.

These Deists **swapped** the coming Kingdom of Christ for Plato's Atlantis and its so-called Golden Age with its government divided into ten divisions. Reader, this is the plan of these successors of Adam Weishaupt's Illuminati out of which this New World Order scheme derived. Instead of promoting the coming Kingdom of Christ, New World Order politicians and businessmen are determined to re-establish a global Atlantean government. The reader will be shocked to find out who were the 18th-century apostles of this giant occult deception today.

However, it was not until 1985, two years after I published my last book about the Illuminati, that I became aware of another plot in the United States which has today united all the six major religions into a one-world religion. It is calling itself the Temple of

The Real Truth About UFO's and the New World Order

Understanding whose headquarters are within the Protestant Cathedral of St. John the Divine in New York City. I have since been there several times showing other astonished eyes how New Agers are using this church in an effort to unite the world under **one common religion**.

We shall be looking into the history of the Temple of Understanding and what their plans and goals are in Volume Five as we continue to study the religious side of this conspiracy of the Illuminati. The reader should find this very interesting because a pamphlet, announcing plans to build a pagan temple to house Hindus, Buddhists, Jews, Muslims, and people in Confucianism with Christianity under one roof, said, "**The leaders of the Temple of Understanding are the Illuminati.**"

Although I wrote about the infamous Aleister Crowley and what part he played in advancing the cause of Illuminism, it was not until after I wrote my last book that I became aware that well-known rock stars such as the Beatles, the Rolling Stones, Jimi Hendrix, Jim Morrison of the Doors, and others were avid followers of Aleister Crowley. I was aware of Charles Manson's connection for I wrote how Manson belonged to the secret society of black magic called Ordo Templi Orientis of which Aleister Crowley became its head after Helena Blavatsky died. I did not know that the late Timothy Leary was also a follower of Crowley and that Elvis Presley was a follower of Helena Blavatsky until recently.

Aleister Crowley, to the followers of black magic, is as the apostle Paul is to Christians. Aleister Crowley, who claimed to be the messiah of the New Age or Aeon, also claimed to be the "Epopt of the Illuminati." He wrote to his disciples how he received telepathic messages from extraterrestrial beings (UFO's) from the double star Sirius. Albert Pike, the "Epopt of Freemasonry" and leader of the Illuminati here in America back in the late 1800s, called Sirius the Blazing Star or Dog Star.[21]

The Dog Star to the people of Spiritualism is the nocturnal representation of the sun because it has a dark companion star. The sun, which is generally worshipped as both a male and female god, was

---

[21]*Morals and Dogma of the Ancient and Accepted Scottish Rite of Freemasonry*, Pike, pp. 14, 15.

UFOLOGY and the New Age Connection

The above photograph shows a New Age center that promotes Theosophy. This center of Spiritualism is located in Sedona, Arizona. My wife and I visited there in the spring of 1997. Sedona, Arizona, like Mt. Shasta, is considered among New Age Spiritualists to be an area in the world that draws ETs (extraterrestrial visitors) which are believed to be ascended masters who gave the Atlanteans supernatural technology. Huge profits are made by modern New Age necromancers who claim to be a channel which these ETs supposedly have chosen to speak through to prepare the people of planet Earth for their visitation. A New Age magazine entitled Sedona: Journal of Emergence!, *which has subscribers from all parts of the country and the world, is published and printed in Sedona. Here some of the most sought-after necromancers (channelers) display their books and compete among themselves for clients. One of the most sought-after channelers of the New Age Movement today is Dr. Joshua David Stone who has authored 13 books about how his readers are to prepare themselves also to become a contactee of this so-called Cosmic Hierarchy of masters, which according to Stone, includes Jesus. Stone holds evangelistic efforts, like Christian pastors do, however, he charges $250 – $300 to attend. On pages 22, 23 in the above magazine, Stone has full-page ads inviting all to attend his Wesak Celebrations, one of which was to be held at Mt. Shasta in California from April 30 to May 2, 1999. Stone promises those who attend that they will be in the presence of Melchizedek, Buddha, Maitreya, Djwhal Khul, Quan Yin, the Divine Mother, Mother Mary, St. Germain, and others who make up this Cosmic and Planetary Hierarchy. Stone states in his ad that Melchizedek told him that he has a number of surprises in store for them if they attend. While spying out their bookstore shown above, we saw not only books promoting the New Age conspiracy, but also of the former pope of Satanism and hero of the heavy metal music culture, the late Aleister Crowley. Multitudes of people in the United States have united themselves with New Age sorcery because of their ignorance of the Holy Scriptures and because Jesus is blended in with their Spiritualistic doctrines. Necromancy has become a multi-billion dollar business, whose teachers, like Balaam among the Israelites, have walked away with the rewards of divination in their hands.*

The Real Truth About UFO's and the New World Order

in Egyptian mythology Isis and the dark god Osiris.

As pointed out in my last two books, all of the ancient gods of Spiritualism are believed today to have once been men who evolved into gods. Spiritualism says these gods are now teaching **a select few** here on earth the secrets of immortality. Occultists believe these gods will be seen in this coming **Galactic Age** known as the Age of Aquarius. Communications from these **spirit guides** are teaching their contactees that this world shall be united into a universal bond of union in the 21st century. The planet Earth, according to the pythonists of the New Age Movement, is about to be ushered into a **Socialist federation** which will establish a Utopian lifestyle for its citizens. To prepare the inhabitants of the world for these ancient gods (UFO's) to return to planet Earth, mankind **must become vegetarian and clean up his environment**. Hence, the origin of the United Nations Environment programs!

All New Age beliefs, like ancient mythology, are centered around the stars and planets as being the homes of the gods of the universe, and that these gods **were once men** who visited this planet in the past and developed a super human race of people and a Utopian society on a continent called **Atlantis**. Some New Agers teach that New England in the United States gave birth to the New Age religion because anciently it was **connected** with the continent Atlantis. One modern-day scribe of ancient pagan thought who helped to promote that the ancient gods were once men is Erich Von Däniken who wrote books trying to prove this theory. He is the author of *Chariots of the Gods?* In his books, Erich Von Däniken takes his readers on a journey through the world showing illustrations from ancient ruins and drawings of how ancient primitive man pictured what their ancient gods looked like. He shows how ancient artists drew on their walls, pottery, sacred edifices, etc., not only their gods flying in chariots, but how they were dressed. He does show pictures of ancient drawings depicting what appears to be gods (UFO's) **dressed in space suits with head gear**. What caught my eye years ago, as I was trying to understand where the origins of these ancient gods came from of which both ancient and modern cultures today are, indeed, centered around, was when I learned about the astonishing remains of what

UFOLOGY and the New Age Connection

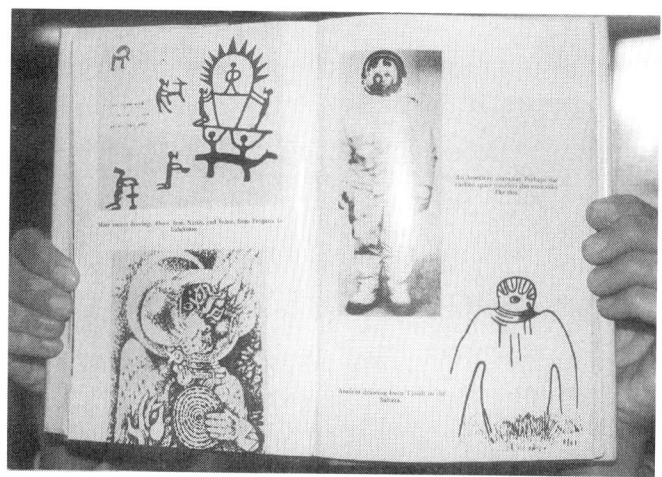

All New Age beliefs, like ancient mythology, center around the stars and planets as being the homes of the gods of the universe and that these gods were once men who visited this planet in the past and developed a super human race of people and a Utopian society on a continent called Atlantis. Some New Agers teach that New England in the United States gave birth to the New Age religion because anciently it was connected with the continent Atlantis of which the name Atlantic *derived, which derived from the god Atlas, the god who holds this planet in its fixed position in our solar system. One modern-day scribe of ancient pagan thought who helped to promote that the ancient gods were once men is Erich Von Däniken who wrote books trying to prove this theory. He is the author of* Chariots of the Gods?. *In his books, Erich Von Däniken takes his readers on a journey through the world showing illustrations from ancient ruins and drawings of how ancient primitive man pictured what their ancient gods looked like. Above, my wife is holding a copy of his book,* Chariots of the Gods?. *He shows how ancient artists drew on their walls, pottery, sacred edifices, etc., not only their gods flying in chariots, but how they were dressed. He does show pictures of ancient drawings depicting what appears to be gods (UFO's) dressed in space suits with headgear.*

The Real Truth About UFO's and the New World Order

appears to be an ancient air strip or runway in the Nazca Valley of Peru. The line drawings of a huge, giant spider, hummingbird, and a monkey that can only be seen from an airplane today because of their sizes were also puzzling to me. The 820-foot trident sign, which I know symbolizes the astrological number 666 on a side of a mountain which seems to be pointing to the ancient runway found in Peru, was also very puzzling and astonishing to me. In one myth found in Egyptian mythology which the author of *Chariots of the Gods?* uses to help give his theory credibility, it talks about Ra, the sun-god of the Egyptians, who was symbolized by the All-Seeing Eye which can be seen over the pyramid found on the back of your one dollar bill. **The Egyptian worship of the sun, moon, and stars shows in their ancient pagan arts solar disks carrying their favorite god, like Ra, directing ancient astronauts in their journeys through the universe.**

As pointed out, the occult doctrines of Atlantis, their gods, and the UFO connection have had their evolutions. The doctrine of the lost paradise of Atlantis can be traced to Plato, then to the European Renaissance of the 15th to the 17th centuries, which was accelerated by Adam Weishaupt's Illuminism, and updated by Karl Marx in his *Communist Manifesto*. As the reader will see, **Marxism in 1848 divided into Leninism/Stalinism on the left and New Age Utopian Socialism on the right.** Illuminism, Marxism, and New Age occultism are all brothers and sisters and are all part of a *red* revolution which is adopting into its family both Catholics and Protestants. Although they have their own paths, they all are heading in the same direction today.

While the prophet of the violent side of Marxism, Nicholai Lenin, was making his debut, a prophet and a prophetess of New Age ethical Marxism began to make known to their brethren the occult side of this Atlantean scheme of the New World Order. It was the writings of H.G. Wells and George Bernard Shaw, besides Karl Marx's writings, which helped accelerate this Atlantean scheme among the atheists a.k.a. humanists. However, in the 19th century it was Ignatius Donnelly and H.P. Blavatsky who accelerated this Atlantean plan among New Agers. Ignatius Donnelly (1831–1901) published in 1882 *Atlantis: The Antediluvian World*, which he begins with Plato's account of the Golden Age of Atlantis and shows similarities between the religions of the Babylonians, Egyptians, and Hindus with

UFOLOGY and the New Age Connection

that of the Toltecs and Mayans. He tries to prove in a scholarly manner the evolution of mankind and how the Toltecs and Mayans are descendants of the Atlanteans. Then, H.P. Blavatsky (1831–1891), a Russian occultist who co-founded the notorious Theosophical Society in New York in 1875, borrowed Donnelly's speculations of the evolution of mankind and its Atlantean connection and in 1889 produced her own book on this subject entitled *The Secret Doctrine*.[22] Blavatsky claimed to have written her book and other volumes under the direct dictation of this secret cosmic brotherhood known among New Agers as the Great White Brotherhood.[23] Blavatasky said her spirit guides told her that there was another advanced race besides the Atlanteans in the Pacific Ocean who were on the lost continent of Lemuria.[24]

Later, a secret society in Germany produced still another lost paradise. They were known as the **Thule Society**.[25] It was a blend of Islamic mysticism, Freemasonry, and Alchemy. Thule was a magical island in Nordic mythology of which the Aryan race produced an advanced civilization. Here we find the Hitler connection with the New Age Movement and how these communications with these so-called spirit guides guided and forced human beings to kill each other during World War II.

Adolf Hitler, who was raised a Roman Catholic but turned from papal Christianity, embraced the Nordic version of these so-called gods (spirits) of mythology. Dietrich Eckart (1868–1923) was the German shaman who introduced Hitler to black magic and the Thule Society. There are two excellent books that expose with documented proof that Hitler himself became a shaman and thought of himself as a christ or messiah to usher in a New Age. They are *The Unknown Hitler*, Schwarzwaller, National Press, Inc., 1989, and *Adolf Hitler*, Toland, Anchor Books, Double Day, 1976.

In the book, *The Unknown Hitler*, its author pointed out how both H.P. Blavatsky and British occultist Aleister Crowley had made their

---

[22]*New Age Encyclopedia*, **1st Edition, Melton, 1990, p. 46.**
[23]*Ibid.*, **Melton, p. 195.**
[24]*Ibid.*, **Melton, p. 46.**
[25]*The Unknown Hitler*, **Schwarzwaller, 1989, pp. 66, 67.**

The Real Truth About UFO's and the New World Order

occult knowledge known in Germany. "There were cross-links," says Schwarzwaller, that connected the occult secret society of the British Golden Dawn, which Crowley once belonged to, with the occultists in Germany.[26]

As pointed out on page 120 of *The New Age Movement and The Illuminati 666*, Aleister Crowley joined in 1912 the secret society of Ordo Templi Orientis which H.P. Blavatsky and Karl Keller founded in 1902 in Germany. Both Blavatsky and Crowley were very well-known among German occultists before the rise of the Thule Society in 1918 and before Hitler and his ban against Freemasonry. Hitler eyed Freemasonry, western capitalism, and Communism as Jewish-backed factions to enslave the world. However, the reader may not realize that both international Communism and Hitler's Nazism, although deadly rivals, planned to enslave the world into a Socialistic form of government. While Communism promised equal rights among the races, Hitler's national Socialism promised the extermination of all races who were not of the Aryan race. Hitler developed his "***Aryan doctrine***" from Dietrich Eckart, a male witch who was also a wealthy publisher, playwright, and poet. Like Aleister Crowley, Eckhart was a drug addict. He was once a Rosicrucian and a Freemason, but had broken off with them because Freemasonry promotes among its members racial integration.

Eckart taught Hitler that there had been another lost paradise like Atlantis in the far north called Thule that had not been completely wiped out like the continent of Atlantis. Those that remained were being guarded by ancient, highly intelligent beings similar to the "*masters*" of Theosophy or the Great White Brotherhood. According to Eckhart, only the truly initiated could establish contact with these beings by means of magic-mystical rituals and if contacted, these supernatural beings allegedly would be able to endow the initiated with supernatural strength and energy.[27] These spirits promised that a new race of supermen were to be created from "***Aryan***" stock who would exterminate all "***inferior***" races.[28] As the reader may know, we still have this doctrine among White Supremacists today.

[26]*The Unknown Hitler*, **Schwarzwaller, 1989, p. 63.**
[27]*Ibid.*, **Schwarzwaller, p. 67.**
[28]*Ibid.*, **Schwarzwaller, p. 67.**

UFOLOGY and the New Age Connection

The origin of the New Age Movement derived from the slogan on the back of the United States dollar bill:

Novus Ordo Seclorum

(New Order of the Ages / Age of Aquarius)

The seven ages of mankind according to astrology:

10000 - 8000 BC	8000 - 6000 BC	6000 - 4000 BC	4000 - 2000 BC	2000 - 0 BC	0 - 2000 AD	2000 AD
THE AGE OF	THE AGE OF	THE AGE OF	THE AGE OF	THE AGE OF	THE AGE OF	THE AGE OF
LEO	CANCER	GEMINI	TAURUS	ARIES	PISCES	AQUARIUS

The Real Truth About UFO's and the New World Order

While the Marxists promoted the **re-establishment** of the Utopian Socialist government of Atlantis, Hitler's National Socialist Party promoted the **re-establishment** of the Utopian Socialist government of the lost paradise of **Thule**; hence, the **Thule Society of Germany** was formed. Here, **two great factions**, which were both **rooted** and **grounded** in **mythology, clashed.** Adolf Hitler was a New Ager, as was H.P. Blavatsky and Aleister Crowley. He caused more destruction of human lives, save his archenemy Joe Stalin. However, both Communism and Nazism originally derived from the occult sciences of **Plato**. Some historians may argue that Marx, Lenin, and Stalin were atheists which is true. However, the Communist goal of establishing a **Utopian** civilization **derived** from Plato's myth about Atlantis. The reader who has learned to put his trust in Bible prophecy needs to remember that New Agers are not united in their doctrinal beliefs. Today, some New Age astrologers do not believe that the Age of Aquarius will take place by the year 2000. They say that the Age of Aquarius is really 300 years away. Yet, many New Agers still contend that the Age of Aquarius is already underway or will begin shortly.[29] They are determined to **replace Christianity** with a new religion as was Adam Weishaupt. This new religion, of course, is the old religion Plato promoted. While Hitler's terrible *red* scourge of Nazism was threatening the world, American and European politicians united with the *red* Communists from the U.S.S.R. to war against Hitler and the Japanese. During this hellish time, another falling star was in the making to replace Aleister Crowley's efforts to promote occult knowledge and how to invoke these "**secret chiefs**" which Hitler was controlled by and used as their instrument of destruction.

There are several other names in history who have helped continue this New World Order scheme, like Gerald Gardner who was another self-proclaimed witch, but Edgar Cayce's name stands out among occultists as one of their best-known psychics. Although Cayce did not receive the public notice during his lifetime as did Blavatsky and Crowley, he certainly can be credited with keeping alive the Atlantean excitement while Hitler was trying to re-establish the Aryan society of Thule. Like Blavatsky and Crowley, Cayce was a **medium** although he was considered to be a Christian. He learned to invoke

---

[29]*New Age Encyclopedia*, **1st Edition, Melton, 1990, p. 26.**

UFOLOGY and the New Age Connection

familiar spirits (spirit guides) **to speak through him** while he was under a **trance**. Edgar Cayce gave thousands of psychic readings during his lifetime. Many of them were about Atlantis. Cayce claimed to have access to a body of knowledge called the **Akashic Record** which supposedly records every sound and thought that any human being has ever had.[30] This diviner and medium learned to **hypnotize** himself. While under a hypnotic trance, demons who he thought were spirits of people that had left their earthly containers (bodies) would channel messages through Cayce's voice box about the history of Atlantis, people's past lives, reincarnation, or give healing remedies for the sick. Cayce was said to have had a thorough knowledge of medicine, but when he was awakened from his trance he remembered nothing.[31] This is the reason Edgar Cayce was coined the "*sleeping prophet*" by occultists.

According to the *New Age Encyclopedia* on page 46, Edgar Cayce was the most important person in the development of the contemporary view of Atlantis. Cayce spoke of Atlantean technology built around **crystals**. From here, the speculations emerged that the Atlanteans had developed a **crystal technology** that powered their cities and transportation systems. This was accelerated by Ruth Montgomery in the book she co-authored – *Ruth Montgomery: Herald of the New Age*. This self-proclaimed prophetess of the New Age Movement who was eclipsed by Shirley MacLaine said that her spirit guides told her that the continent of Lemuria, which Blavatsky said had been located somewhere in the Pacific, was inhabited by gentle, spiritual people while the inhabitants of Atlantis were scientific and technological. Montgomery claimed that air travel was introduced to the Atlanteans by visitors from outer space. These supernatural beings supposedly taught the Atlanteans how to use a **great crystal** which provided means to **power** their aircrafts and ships.[32]

Will these ancient gods like Baal, Ashtaroth, Tammuz, Krishna, Kulkulcán, Quetzalcoatl, etc., display themselves from UFO's as occultists believe? This is the backbone to New Age beliefs today!

---

[30]*Atlantis*, Stein, 1989, p. 44.
[31]*Ibid.*, Stein, pp. 44, 45.
[32]*Ruth Montgomery: Herald of the New Age*, Montgomery/Garland, 1986, p. 185.

The Real Truth About UFO's and the New World Order

They point out how **ancient shamans** knew about Sirius having a companion star centuries before it was photographed by astronomers in our day. New Agers point out how multitudes of sound people, from policemen to astronauts to the Air Force pilots, have seen UFO's and reported sightings. Even President Jimmy Carter says that he saw UFO's.[33] There have been **UFO hoaxes**; however, there is no question in my mind that some of these sightings are true. As pointed out, I have seen with my own eyes, along with three companions that were present with me in 1975, a formation of UFO's. How could we deny this fact!

Again, are the UFO's ancient astronauts? Are they the gods or goddesses of the people of Spiritualism whom Indian medicine men claimed to have been communicating with for centuries? Are these ancient landing sights like those which have been found in Peru going to be where these pagan deities will parade themselves before earthlings? These questions can be answered with authority.

Jesus has his messengers as well. Did He not warn his disciples in the last days we would see "**FEARFUL SIGHTS** and **GREAT SIGNS**" from heaven? (See Luke 21:11.) One champion who wrote against the deceptions of Spiritualism prophesied in the 1800s:

"Fearful sights of **SUPERNATURAL CHARACTER** will **SOON** be **REVEALED** in the heavens, in token of the power of miracle-working demons." *The Great Controversy*, White, p. 624 (Emphasis added.)

Again, this messenger of Jesus wrote over one hundred years ago the following:

"As we near the close of time, there will be greater and still greater external parade of heathen power; **HEATHEN DEITIES** will manifest their **SIGNAL POWER**, and will **EXHIBIT THEMSELVES BEFORE THE CITIES OF THE WORLD**." *Testimonies to Ministers*, White, pp. 117, 118. (Emphasis mine.)

Looking down to our day through the eye of prophecy, Isaiah prophesied, "Who are these that fly as a cloud, and as the doves to their windows?" Isaiah 60:8.

There are, indeed, my New Age reader, extraterrestrial beings

---

[33]*Mysteries of the Unknown-The UFO Phenomenon*, Time-Life Books, Inc., p. 128.

UFOLOGY and the New Age Connection

marshaling their forces and the nations of this world with the intent to take over this planet. There are, indeed, **secret societies** and individuals which have **taken dictation** from them about how to prepare the human beings of this planet for a coming **Galactic Age**.

Again, New Agers, these chariots of the gods (UFO's) are **not** from the silver star Sirius or the Great White Brotherhood as ancient shamans and Blavatsky, Besant, Bailey, Crowley, etc., have written volumes of books about, **but are actually the fallen angels** from Heaven whose commander is Lucifer a.k.a. Satan!

I have written two other volumes about this conflict between Jesus and "*Baalzebub*," whose name means "*Lord of the Fly*." I have shown with documented proof how not only was Satan worshipped as Baalzebub, but how all the ancient gods worldwide were actually demons who **camouflaged** their worship in the legends of Nimrod.

History and the ancient Scriptures point to Nimrod and his evil family as the **ringleaders** and first **adepts** of occultism. Nimrod, who was the world's first king after the Flood, was also the world's **first architect**. It was Nimrod on this side of the Flood who built the first cities. (See Genesis, Chapter Ten.) Nimrod became the first sun-god, known in ancient times as Baal. It shall be shown that all occult knowledge **began** at Babylon on this side of the Flood, **not** at Atlantis. All the North, Central, and South American Indians did, indeed, migrate here from across the Atlantic. However, they started from Mesopotamia, not Atlantis. They learned how to build pyramids at Babylon, not at this so-called lost paradise. Let's look again at some of the names of these ancient gods of mythology.

Nimrod, whose name means "*rebel*," was also worshipped as a god known to the ancient Babylonians as **Merodach**. The name *Merodach* means "*to be bold or to rebel*."[34] To the ancient Romans, Nimrod was the war-god Mars, which also means "*the rebel*." This is where we derive the third month **March** from.[35]

Now Nimrod to the ancient Anglo-Saxon was worshipped as Zernebogus whose name actually means "*seed of the prophet Cush*."[36] Kush or Cush, according to ancient Scripture, was the father of

---
[34] *The Two Babylons*, Hislop, p. 28.
[35] *Ibid.*, Hislop, p. 44.
[36] *Ibid.*, Hislop, p. 34.

The Real Truth About UFO's and the New World Order

Reader, the book of Revelation points back in history to Nimrod's ancient city of Babylon as being the mother of all the various branches of ancient and modern Spiritualism. Spiritualism's gods and goddesses are believed today to have once been humans. However, the gods and goddesses of astrology, which have fooled our ancient ancestors into worshipping them instead of God, were actually Lucifer and his fallen angels. (See Psalm 106:28, 29; 1 Cor. 10:20.) The ancient drawings found on the walls of caves displaying extraterrestrial visitors as gods flying across the sky on their solar disk or crescent have, indeed, been found. Spiritualism's ancient apostle Plato taught his followers that the ancient gods had visited planet Earth and had given the Atlanteans advanced technology in which to build the pyramids and to establish a Utopian Socialist society which became known as the Golden Age of mankind. The effort to re-establish the Golden Age of Atlantis lies at the heart of the New Age and New World Order schemes. As ancient shamans sought their gods for supernatural power and technology which enabled them to build the pyramids, so have shamans of secret societies today sought advanced technology from these same fallen angels who are posing as aliens from other planets. There have been charlatans who have used the UFO excitement to make fast money by producing photographs, films, and even aliens themselves, but turned out to be hoaxes. Nevertheless, Jimmy Carter, astronaut Gordon Cooper, and former Naval Intelligence Agent and Christian Talk Show host William Cooper all publicly announced they have seen UFOs. I would have remained a skeptic today if it was not for seeing them in formation in Hawaii in 1975. Nonetheless, reader, do not be surprised if these UFOs turn out to have been made in the good old USA and that Satan and his fallen angels appear on earth as not only aliens, but as Christ and His apostles! My wife spotted this flyer in the Sahara Public Library in Las Vegas.

UFOLOGY and the New Age Connection

Nimrod, whom the ancient Babylonians worshipped as Hermes. (See Genesis 10:6.) Hermes is actually a Chaldean name, not originally Grecian. **Hermes**, which any learned New Ager knows, is the **father** of all metaphysical sciences. This is where the word *Hermetic* originated from to which occultists and their secret societies identify their crafts. This god of magic a.k.a. Hermes Trismegistus is divided into two meanings. The name "***Her***," says Hislop in his book, ***The Two Babylons***, on page 25: "In Chaldee is synonymous with Ham, or Khem…'The Burnt One,' as 'Her' also, like Ham, signified 'the hot or burning one.' This name formed a foundation for covertly identifying Ham with the sun…"

The word "***Mes***," says Hislop, means "***to draw forth***" or "***son of***." Hence, ***Hermes*** means the "***son of Ham***." Who in Scripture was the son of Ham? It was Cush who begot Nimrod! (See Genesis 10:6, 8.)

Is it by chance that occultists such as the Hermetic Order of the Golden Dawn, which Aleister Crowley once belonged to while it was in its heyday, use this name ***Hermes*** to signify the authority of their origination? My New Age reader, is it by chance that your Epopts (priests) lead their new converts through what they call the ***Hermetic Rites or Hermetic Degrees***? Isn't it interesting to know that the Freemasons trace all of their crafts to **Hermes** and **Nimrod**? We will see this shortly from their own words.

People of high I.Q. and intellect today, especially the Hollywood crowd, as well as Mormons, some Roman Catholics, and mainstream Protestants, have received a fable as fact that **mankind originally came from the stars**. The belief in spirit guides, ascended masters, reincarnation, astrological charts, necromancy, etc. has from Hollywood's birth been promoted by its most well-known citizens.

Most of the early actors and actresses kept their interest in the sciences of witchcraft or metaphysics or parapsychology low key. However, since Hollywood's reigning high priestess of metaphysics, Shirley MacLaine, boldly promoted New Age witchcraft through her books and movies, closet Spiritualists are boldly doing the same. New Agers who have been well-known entertainers from the Music and Movie Industries have made the sins of Babylon, Egypt, and Sodom reappear in the large cities in the United States and all over the world. The abominations that these three nations practiced are

The Real Truth About UFO's and the New World Order

recorded in Scripture, and are being promoted by not only famous movie and rock stars, but by famous politicians and businessmen as well. Is it by chance that one natural disaster after another is falling upon our wicked cities? Fires, floods, hurricanes, tornadoes, freezes, and earthquakes have torn at the heart of America recently. Now, we are beholding what terrorists can do in the land of the free.

While holding lectures about the New World Order in Los Angeles in January 1994, we experienced what it was like to ride a 6.6 earthquake in our Bounder motor home. However, these judgments of God are nothing to what has been prophesied to come shortly.

While New Age disciples and politicians are prophesying the soon coming of the "**Age of Aquarius**" a.k.a. the "**Galactic Federation**," sudden destruction will come upon those who believe and promote this lie. There will never be a Golden Age of Atlantis established in this present world. New Ager, the God who dwells between the two cherubims foretold an attempt to divide this world into a confederacy having ten divisions, however, they shall turn against each other. Complete **anarchy will develop** in the midst of them, and they will **destroy** themselves.

Nevertheless, there are two gospels today which are gathering the whole world into two distinct camps. There are two ecumenical movements. There are two main focuses of thought today – New Age thinking and Christian thinking **OR** the re-establishment of Atlantis and the establishment of the Kingdom of Christ.

"And the ten horns which thou sawest are ten kings, which have received no kingdom as yet; but receive power as kings one hour with the beast. These have **one mind**, and shall **give** their power and strength unto the beast. These shall make **war** with the **Lamb**, and the Lamb shall overcome them: for he is Lord of lords, and King of kings: and they that are with him are called, and chosen, and faithful. And he saith unto me, The waters which thou sawest, where the whore sitteth, are peoples, and multitudes, and nations, and tongues. And the ten horns which thou sawest upon the beast, these shall **hate** the whore, and shall make her **desolate** and naked, and shall eat her flesh, and burn her with fire. For God hath put in their hearts to fulfil his will, and to agree, and give their kingdom unto the beast, until the words of God shall be fulfilled." Revelation 17:12–17.

UFOLOGY and the New Age Connection
THE TEN DIVISIONS OF ATLANTIS PLANNED WORLDWIDE IN THE 21ST CENTURY BY NEW WORLD ORDER ADVOCATES

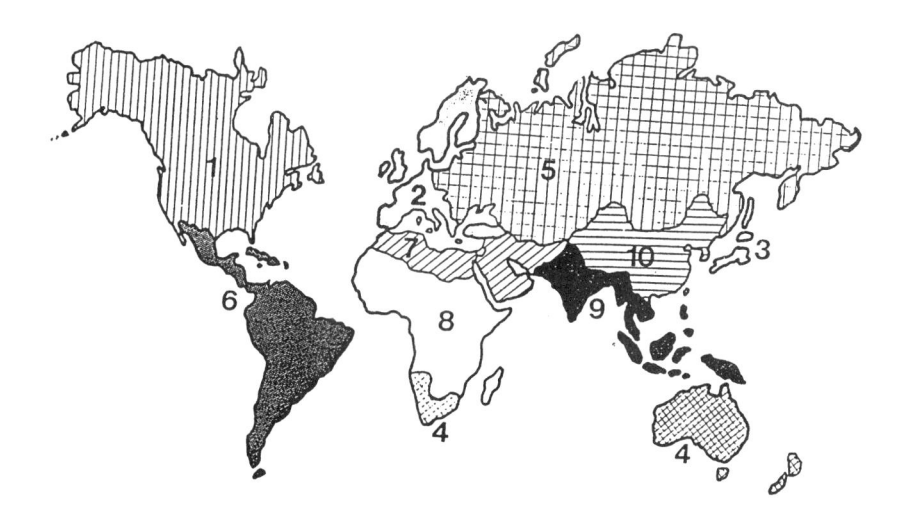

New World Order advocates calling themselves the Club of Rome planned back in 1974 to divide the whole world into **TEN ZONES**. *The Club of Rome was organized by merchants, scientists, educators, and politicians in 1968 for the purpose of bringing financial and political unity throughout the world. The Club of Rome is the geographical planner for this New World Order scheme. However, little do these merchants (businessmen) who are behind this world alliance realize that this division of the world was foretold in Bible prophecy. This shall be studied in Volume Four,* Ancient Prophecies About Mysticism and Hollywood and The Music Industry, *and in Volume Five,* Ancient Prophecies About The Dragon, The Beast, and The False Prophet.

The Real Truth About UFO's and the New World Order

Nevertheless, the reader will be shocked to know how many Christians have crossed over and joined the New Age Movement. To begin to show how Christians have been drawn into New Age beliefs, let's look into an encyclopedia.

According to *The New Age Encyclopedia* on page 291, it says Brad Steiger's book, *Revelation: The Divine Fire* (1973) "became a **virtual encyclopedia** of New Age mysticism as it was emerging in the early 1970's." Three years later Steiger, a New Age writer, produced a book called *Gods of Aquarius: UFO's and the Transformation of Man*. This book not only focuses on the claims of people who have contacted these **extraterrestrial beings** or **higher intelligences**, but it also made popular the belief that humans were inhabitants of other planets in past lives.

It was very eye-opening to discover why the wise God of Abraham chose to use the **seven-headed Dragon** as a symbol for Satan. In Revelation 12:3, 4, 17, we read: "And there appeared another wonder in heaven; and behold a great red dragon, having seven heads and ten horns, and seven crowns upon his heads. And his tail drew the third part of the stars of heaven, and did cast them to the earth: and the dragon stood before the woman which was ready to be delivered, for to devour her child as soon as it was born.... And the dragon was wroth with the woman, and went to make war with the remnant of her seed, which keep the commandments of God, and have the testimony of Jesus Christ."

As already established, the **seven-headed Dragon** was the ancient Babylonian **symbol for astrology**. Its seven heads represented the **seven chief gods of mythology**[37] which were worshipped in Mesopotamia, Egypt, Greece, Rome, India, Scandinavia, and among the North, Central, and South American Indians. One early Babylonian tradition had Sin, a male god, as the moon and Ishtar as **Sirius**, the **eight-pointed star**. Then, later, the five-pointed star (the pentagram) became identified with Venus after the double star Sirius stopped appearing at dawn in the east about three or four thousand years ago. The religion of astrology and its spread from Mesopotamia has certainly had an evolution with various traditions and offshoots. However,

---

[37] *Origins of Astrology*, Lindsay, Barnes & Noble, Inc., 1971, p. 233.

UFOLOGY and the New Age Connection

Hermes in Greek mythology was borrowed from Babylonian mythology. In the Greek tradition, according to Greek Gods and Heroes, *Graves, Doubleday & Co., NY, 1960, p. 21,* **HERMES WAS THE GOD OF MERCHANTS, BANKERS, THIEVES, FORTUNETELLERS, AND HERALDS.** *One of his signs was the swastika which was engraved on his throne that was made of a single piece of solid gray rock. Hermes was also the god who invented the alphabet. He has also been worshipped as the god of mathematics, medicine, and the occult sciences. According to* The New Encyclopaedia Britannica, *Micropaedia, Vol. 5, p. 875, he is especially worshipped as the god of fertility, and his images were ithyphallic. He was and is known among ancient and modern pagans as the messenger of the gods and often appeared with his kérykeion or herald's staff which was another sign that would invoke him among those who wore it. This sign is the caduceus that even Christian physicians proudly display on their hospital attire.*

According to The New Book of Knowledge, *Grolier Inc., 1982, p. 208-b, the popular wand of Hermes was also known as the wand of Aesculapius who was also worshipped as a god of healing or medicine. Again, just to prove who these ancient gods really are, look at Genesis, Chapter Three. What was Satan's agent that he used to deceive Eve? It was the serpent, perhaps a python, for the root of the word* "**divination**" *derived from it and also the word* "**fortuneteller**," *for they are also known as a pythonist. We will investigate more of this later.*

In astrology, the serpent in the spiritual realm represents the sun, but in the physical realm the sun-god was symbolized in Egyptian mythology as a bull because the dead god Osiris, the sun-god and husband of Isis, died and his soul transferred into Apis, according to Bulfinch's Mythology, *Thomas Bulfinch, The Modern Library Random House, pp. 234, 235. Apis was a bull. This is why bulls were worshipped with the greatest reverence by the Egyptians and where the Israelites got the idea in molding their golden calf. It is also where the New Agers may trace their doctrine of transmigration of the soul.*

In Genesis, Chapter Three, the serpent was not the Devil, but the Devil spoke through him. How? He did this by what is now called in New Age beliefs, channeling. By the occult science known and accepted today as ventriloquism, Satan threw his voice to the serpent and he said, "Ye shall not surely die." He also promised her immortality if she did not obey the Gospel of God. What else did the Father of Lies say to Eve? "Then your eyes shall be opened, and ye shall be as gods." Satan promised Eve that great spiritual enlightenment would come to her if she disobeyed God. Sound familiar, New Ager?

49

The Real Truth About UFO's and the New World Order

Bible prophecy points to Lucifer a.k.a. Satan as the father of the gods of mythology (astrology), and those who worshipped these gods were actually worshipping Lucifer whose name means "*day star*." In Revelation 12:4, it says that the Dragon's "tail drew the third part of the stars of heaven." These stars of Heaven symbolize angels who once worshipped God, but turned to follow Lucifer. A parallel can be seen here among the human race. Multitudes who have once claimed to be Christians have also turned from Christ to follow the Dragon by accepting and practicing doctrines that have derived out of the pages of astrology. The apostle Paul foretold that latter-day brethren would do this in 1 Timothy 4:1: "Now the Spirit speaketh expressly, that in the latter times some shall depart from the faith, giving heed to **seducing spirits**, and **doctrines of devils**."

Latter-day Christians must have a knowledge of the Scriptures and have their faith in Christ rooted and grounded in them for this Antichrist who began his rebellion against Christ in Heaven will appear as Jesus Christ during these days of the Time of the End. The world shall worship this great deceiver because they had not the love of the Truth which is found written on the pages of the Bible. Jesus warned in John 5:43: "I am come in my Father's name, and ye receive me not: if another shall come in his own name, him ye will receive."

Today, Spiritualism, which derived out of the precepts of astrology, teaches that mankind originated from the stars, and that the **UFO's** are their ancient brethren who are coming back to take over this planet. Those who have been conditioned to believe this are being conditioned to receive this Antichrist when he personates this planet's real Creator and Lord. Jesus predicted, "**HIM YE WILL RECEIVE**."

The world, as a whole, rejected the real Messiah who was Christ Jesus. Jesus warned in Matthew 24:5: "For many shall come in my name, saying, I am Christ; and shall deceive many." However, **the last false christ will be Satan himself**, and his fallen angels shall not only personate Jesus' disciples, but also these ancient gods of mythology which pagans both in ancient and modern times have worshipped.

It is interesting to note that Hermes (who was really Cush) was the messenger of the gods of mythology to both the Babylonians

UFOLOGY and the New Age Connection

The above photograph I took as I visited the Unarius Academy of Science in August of 1997 in El Cajon, California. According to its co-founder, the late Ruth Norman, 40,000 years ago UFO's (Superbeings) from the Pleiades visited the island continent of Atlantis and gave its inhabitants advanced technology.[38] These UFO's were, according to the Normans, the ancient gods of mythology who have been reincarnated many times. Gautama Siddhartha (563–479 B.C.), who became the Buddha, the Enlightened One, said: "I have been Indra, the ruler of the gods, thirty-six times, and many hundred times was I a world-monarch."[39] The Normans, like Buddha, claimed to be reincarnated many times. Ruth Norman claimed to have been Socrates, Peter the Great, Charlemagne, Queen Elizabeth I, Queen Maria Theresa, Hatshepsut, Akbar of India, Quetzalcoatl of Mexico, and Atahualpa, the last Inca of Peru in her past lives.[40] She taught her disciples that planet Earth shall be visited by UFO's in 2001 and planet Earth is to be united into an interplanetary confederation with other inhabited planets this same year. As avatars and cosmic visionaries, the Normans claimed to be leading their disciples into a New Age Spiritual Renaissance.[41] The age of modern interest in UFO's actually began with two supposed sightings in 1947: one in Boise, Idaho, and the highly-published Roswell incident *near Roswell, New Mexico.*

---

[38]*Pathway To Light*, **The Unarius Academy of Sciences, El Cajon, CA, p. 44.**
[39]*A Dictionary of World Mythology*, **Cotterell, G.P. Putnam's Sons, NY, 1979, p. 66**
[40]*Pathway To Light*, **The Unarius Academy of Sciences, El Cajon, CA, pp. 7, 8.**
[41]*Ibid.*, **p. 8.**

The Real Truth About UFO's and the New World Order

and to the Greeks. He was Mercury to the Romans and is also the god of bankers and merchants. Hermes was Nebo to the ancient Canaanites. Jesus warned through His faithful apostle John that it would be the **merchants** (businessmen – Revelation 18:23) that would lead the world into the deceptions of **sorcery** which also derived out of astrology. It is also very interesting to discover that a mural painting in the **United Nations Meditation Room**, which this writer has taken many to see for themselves, displays the symbol of this god of bankers and merchants. One of Hermes' symbols was the caduceus that the A.M.A. adopted. The caduceus of Hermes is painted in abstract art with a symbol of the sun and the moon. We will study more about this and the United Nations and of the shocking discoveries of who actually founded this modern Tower of Babel as we continue.

Again, the doctrine of transmigration of souls that Plato promoted in his writings has led to the belief that human beings are originally from the stars or planets and once the body is divorced from the soul, this soul returns to where it originated if the believer has reached nirvana which comes after being reincarnated several times. Most Catholics, Protestants, and Muslims have also adopted a similar belief among them. Most Christians teach that at death they go immediately to Heaven. However, if you are a bad person, you will go to hell or purgatory. New Agers call this **bad karma**. They teach they will be reincarnated into an animal or something until they learn to be good. Nirvana is the final goal in the Eastern religions of Hinduism and Buddhism for nirvana means a peaceful state of blissful existence.[42] This is what has led some to **shed** their earthly containers.

I have discovered in my research that mythology has had its special religious orders among its believers and tribes to keep its traditions alive and well. Just as the Levite tribe from the twelve tribes of Israel were chosen to preserve and perpetuate the sacred oracles of God, so did Satan have him a select few to preserve and perpetuate the unholy doctrines of astrology. Among the Celtic peoples, they were the Druids who are alive and well today. Among the ancient Babylonians, they were the Chaldeans. Among the Greeks, they believed that their lives and destinies were governed by a great number of divinities called the Olympians. Hermes, whose symbol was the

[42]*Man, Myth, and Magic*, Vol. 7, Cavendish, p. 2004.

UFOLOGY and the New Age Connection

wheel of the sun or swastika, was the Olympian's chief messenger. The pagan Greeks believed that their sacred **Delphi** was one of their most religious sites and was the focus of the worship of Apollo, the sun-god and son of Zeus, for in the myth Apollo established his sanctuary in Delphi and handed down his law (oracles). The priests of this law of Apollo were known as Pythians of which derived out of the name *Pytho*,[43] which was a **python** snake that Apollo in the myth slew. Again, it is interesting to note that it was a serpent, probably a python, that Satan used to give Eve his first oracles of lies that "**ye shall not surely die**" and "**your eyes shall be opened**, (become clairvoyant) and ye shall be as gods, knowing good and evil." Genesis 3:4, 5. All the beliefs today found among the various religions and schools within the New Age Movement hang on these two oracles. New Agers today consider the **oracles of Delphi** and its site sacred as the Jews and Christians view the city of Jerusalem.

In Ezekiel 18:4, the Creator says the soul dies: "Behold, all souls are mine; as the soul of the father, so also the soul of the son is mine: the soul that sinneth, it shall die."

Nevertheless, those who believe in the doctrine of immortality of the soul among New Agers believe humans originated from the stars and that the gods themselves were once human beings.

According to *The New Age Encyclopedia*, page 291, it was Brad Steiger who helped make popular the idea that humans had a previous life on another planet. He called them "*star people*." He says that the women who believe they have come from another planet he has coined "*star maidens*."

According to Steiger, *star maidens* are those women who have interacted with these UFO's since childhood. He said he discovered during the course of his travels holding lectures and meetings that these human *star people* share certain characteristics. All are physically attractive, have great magnetism and intelligence, and are usually found in the counseling and teaching professions! Nearly all of them, says Brad Steiger, have Rh negative blood type, and some have extra vertebrae. He went on to say that some men matched these characteristics similar to that of the women. He subsequently

---

[43]*World Mythology,* Willis, Henry Holt & Co., NY, 1993, p. 138.

The Real Truth About UFO's and the New World Order

devoted his attention to his concept of *star people*[44] showing equal opportunity. Aleister Crowley also taught his disciples that they originally came from the stars. Bible-believing people may have chuckled at this a bit upon learning of this popular New Age belief, but are you aware that Elvis Presley and other famous entertainers believe(d) this lie? Presley's involvement in the New Age Movement was confirmed recently by his best friend, Larry Geller, who was his New Age spiritual adviser and guru. We will study Presley's involvement in Spiritualism later in Volume Four as we study into other well-known rock star's histories. Before we study how Spiritualism has especially been promoted through the Music Industry, let us take a look at the Movie Industry.

Brad Steiger is the author of more than one hundred books. Steiger's books not only promote Spiritualism, but also biographies about movie careers of Valentino, Judy Garland, and Jim Thorpe. Steiger's book about Valentino was made into a movie.

Brad Steiger's wife, Sherry Hansen Steiger, not only claims to be an expert on the paranormal, UFOlogy, and of the Hollywood scene, but also claims to be a Christian. Sherry Steiger who promotes Spiritualism is, ironically enough, a licensed, ordained, Protestant minister and former staff member at the Lutheran School of Theology in Chicago.

The Steigers co-authored a book on the dark and secret history of Hollywood's most famous citizens and how they were involved in Satanism and white magic. Their book, *Hollywood and The Supernatural*, published in 1990 by St. Martin's Press, "presents compelling evidence that **Hollywood's fixation** with the occult and supernatural is not just fiction," so says a statement found on the back of their book.

The Steigers pointed out in their above book how Valentino never made a movie without first consulting his own spirit guide for guidance. Rudolph Valentino and his wife Natacha were both mediums or channelers as the modern term today applies.

The Steigers, writing positively, point out in their book how Hollywood stars, writers, directors, and producers have always had a deep interest in spirit guides, ascended masters, secret doctrine, past-life

---

[44]*The New Age Encyclopedia*, Melton, p. 291.

UFOLOGY and the New Age Connection

explorations, astrological charts, tarot cards, etc. They also point out how these occult practices have been very fashionable among the citizens of the Hollywood hills. However, amazingly enough, Sherry Steiger who is an ordained Protestant minister failed to show her readers a warning from Scripture of what shall come upon all who practice these things. **MULTITUDES** have been led to believe that metaphysics is from God. However, the Scriptures plainly show that this is an abomination to the Almighty. These sciences are listed in the below Scriptures:

"There shall not be found among you any one that maketh his son or his daughter to **pass through the fire**, or that useth **divination**, or an **observer of times**, or an **enchanter**, or a **witch**. Or a **charmer**, or a **consulter with familiar spirits**, or a **wizard**, or a **necromancer**. For all that do these things are an **abomination** unto the Lord: and because of these abominations the Lord thy God doth drive them out from before thee. Thou shalt be perfect with the Lord thy God. For these nations, which thou shalt possess, hearkened unto observers of times, and unto diviners: but as for thee, the Lord thy God hath not suffered thee so to do." Deuteronomy 18:10–14.

Later, we shall study each one of these sciences of the occult and see how UFOlogy is connected with them. Now, according to astrology, which is the basic foundation to all of the practices of witchcraft, the sun-god is the chief god of the zodiac, and everything on earth which is first is dedicated to him. Everything which is first is sacred because he is the first god in the hierarchy of the gods. Hence, the first day of the week, **Suns-day**, the first day of the month, the first day of the year, the first of the harvest, the first of the flocks, and the first-born child were generally dedicated in ancient pagan history to the sun-gods.

To ensure fertility, the pagans often sacrificed their first-born child in fire to their heathen deities. Fire to ancient pagans, as well as to modern pagans today, was sacred because the sun-god is made of fire. The ancient Israelites, who blended occult beliefs into the sacred things of God, were led to practice the same things. However, they were not sacrificing their children to gods, as they were led to believe by their religious leaders, but to **demons posing as the gods**.

The Real Truth About UFO's and the New World Order

"They joined themselves also unto Baalpeor, and ate the sacrifices of the dead. Thus they provoked him to anger with their inventions: and the plague brake in upon them. But were mingled among the heathen, and learned their works. And they served their idols: which were a snare unto them. **YEA, THEY SACRIFICED THEIR SONS AND THEIR DAUGHTERS UNTO DEVILS**, And shed innocent blood, even the blood of their sons and of their daughters, whom they sacrificed unto the idols of Canaan: and the land was polluted with blood." Psalm 106:28, 29, 35–38.

Throughout this book, we will examine just what Spiritualism is from the Scriptures and how metaphysics led the Israelites to commit many abominations; then, we will compare what these philosophies are doing to the minds of the human race today.

There is hardly a day that goes by where we do not hear somebody from the world promoting the **New World Order** or **Global 2000**. I often wonder how many of the politicians or those from the entertainment field who are promoting this New World Order really understand what they are promoting? How many well-known personalities of the world have ever taken the time to explain to us what they actually mean when they say, "New World Order" or how many of the common people of the world ever think to ask these great men of the earth just what they mean when they say, "There is coming a New World Order?"

I do believe that not one in a hundred thousand people who are promoting this popular slogan, New World Order, actually understands what they are saying or doing. I do believe that not one in one hundred thousand Christians who have joined in with them understands that the book of Revelation foretold and warned that it would be the **GREAT MEN** of the world (the most famous) that Satan would use to unite the whole world against the true followers of Christ Jesus in these last days. "For thy **merchants (businessmen)** were the great men (religious and political leaders along with the celebrities) of the earth; for by thy **sorceries** (witchcraft) were all nations deceived." Revelation 18:23. (Emphasis mine.)

Reader, what are politicians, generally, before they become political candidates? They are businessmen! The sure Word of prophecy warns it will be the well-known personalities of the world in these

UFOLOGY and the New Age Connection

last days who will bring about the last scenes in the conflict between Christ and Satan!

What will these great men of the earth try to do to Christ's true followers? "And he causeth all, both small and great, rich and poor, free and bond, to receive a mark in their right hand, or in their foreheads: And that **no man might buy or sell, save he that had the mark, or the name of the beast, or the number of his name.**" Revelation 13:16, 17.

The businessmen of the world are predicted from prophecy to have such a grip on the world's economy that they will keep those who refuse to bow to their dictates and who refuse to receive the Mark, Name, or Number of the beast (666) from being able to buy or sell. These things we will study into more as we continue.

The book of Revelation is very plain that Satan (the Dragon) "deceiveth the **WHOLE WORLD**." (See Revelation 12:9.) Most of us would shrink back at the very thought of worshipping Satan, but we do not have to join Satan's army to be on his side. All that is needed to be enlisted in his army is to be found following his precepts instead of Christ's!

"Know ye not, that to whom ye yield yourselves servants to obey, his servants ye are to whom ye obey; whether of sin unto death, or of obedience unto righteousness?" Romans 6:16.

Christians and my New Age readers who are presently caught up in this tidal **wave of Spiritualism** that is sweeping the world into its foaming swells, are you aware that this so-called ancient cosmic light of the Maya and Aztecs led them to eat the heart of their human sacrifices? Are you aware that this revival of the Maya and Aztec religions that you are perpetrating anciently sacrificed thousands of human beings annually?

CHAPTER II

HOW THE NEW AGE AND THE NEW WORLD ORDER BEGAN

"To the law and to the testimony: if they speak not according to this word, it is because there is no light in them."

Isaiah 8:20

How the New Age and the NWO Began

It is generally believed in our society that if the majority are doing it, it is right. This is just the opposite of what Jesus taught. "Enter ye in at the strait gate: for wide is the gate, and broad is the way, that leadeth to destruction, and many there be which go in threat: Because strait is the gate, and narrow is the way, which leadeth unto life, and few there be that find it." Matthew 7:13, 14.

The majority of the people of the world were predicted almost 2,000 years ago to be used by Satan in promoting a worldwide effort to unite the whole world with him and his fallen angels.

Reader, the Scriptures are very plain! Do not follow the majority of Christians today, much less the philosophies of the world. "These shall make war with the Lamb, and the Lamb shall overcome them: for he is Lord of lords, and King of kings: and they that are with him are called, and chosen, and faithful." Revelation 17:14.

Today, there is a worldwide Luciferian conspiracy to take this world for Lucifer before the year 2000 A.D. For over a quarter of a century now, I have been researching its history. This modern-day Spirit of Antichrist is not only uniting pagan nations with it today, but Roman Catholics, Jews, Muslims, and Protestants as well!

Not much further into the future will the prophecy be fulfilled in Revelation 17:13: "These have **ONE MIND**, and shall give their power and strength unto the beast."

However, Jesus of Nazareth will have Him a small remnant of disciples that will not bow their knee before the Dragon – "that had gotten the **victory** over the **beast**, and over his **image**, and over his **mark**, and over the **number** of his **name** (666), stand on the sea of glass, having the harps of God." Revelation 15:2.

Very few are there today who call themselves Christian pastors who teach their congregations the warnings and reproofs which are written from the book of Revelation. Very few, indeed, have any knowledge about it so they can intelligently preach about it.

I remember the first Christian church I joined and their attitude towards that last great book of the Bible. I used to ask my church leaders, "What is the Mark of the Beast?" or "What does the number 666 mean?" When I brought these reasonable questions to them, I was

The Real Truth About UFO's and the New World Order

always quickly told, "Don't worry about the book of Revelation. All you need to know is Jesus and His salvation."

I also remember being told in 1970 when I initially became a Christian and first became aware of the Antichrist that the saints won't go through the coming tribulation. I was told that Christians will be raptured out of this world; therefore, Christians do not have to worry about studying the book of Revelation. I was also informed that Christians will not receive the mark because they will not be here when it is enforced.

This sounded reasonable at first, I thought, because the people who taught me this appeared to me then to be very religious and knowledgeable about the Scriptures. For a time, I left this puzzle alone.

Then, I was shown a book about the prophecies of the book of Revelation that was written by someone outside the church that I belonged. This again sparked my interest in finding out just what all this meant in Revelation 14:6–12:

"And I saw another angel fly in the midst of heaven, having the everlasting gospel to preach unto them that dwell on the earth, and to every nation, and kindred, and tongue, and people, Saying with a loud voice, Fear God, and give glory to him; for the hour of his judgment is come: and worship him that made heaven, and earth, and the sea, and the fountains of waters. And there followed another angel, saying, Babylon is fallen, is fallen, that great city, because she made all nations drink of the wine of the wrath of her fornication. And the third angel followed them, saying with a loud voice, If any man worship the beast and his image, and receive his mark in his forehead, or in his hand, The same shall drink of the wine of the wrath of God, which is poured out without mixture into the cup of his indignation; and he shall be tormented with fire and brimstone in the presence of the holy angels, and in the presence of the Lamb: And the smoke of their torment ascendeth up for ever and ever: and they have no rest day nor night, who worship the beast and his image, and whosoever receiveth the mark of his name. Here is the patience of the saints: here are they that keep the commandments of God, and the faith of Jesus." Revelation 14:6–12

After reading Revelation 14:6–12, which is the most solemn warning ever given to God's people and the people of the world, I just

How the New Age and the NWO Began

could not understand how any Christian church could tell its members not to study the book of Revelation, especially when it clearly says: "Blessed is he that readeth, and they that hear the words of this prophecy, and keep those things which are written therein: for the time is at hand." Revelation 1:3.

It was not until I started prayerfully searching on my own that I began to understand these astonishing truths from the book of Revelation. After I found out there were many books written about the Antichrist and his number 666, I began to search and search the Scriptures, Bible commentaries, and other Bible-related books on this most important subject.

Jesus warned over and over again that the biggest deceptions Satan will use to pull Christians into his confederacy against Jesus will come in the name of Jesus!

"For many shall come in my name, saying, **I am Christ**; and shall deceive many... For there shall arise **false Christs**, and **false prophets**, and shall shew great signs and wonders; insomuch that, if it were possible, they shall deceive the **very elect**." Matthew 24:5, 24.

After diligently searching for years to know the difference between the Christ and the Antichrist and how there are multitudes of false interpretations and beliefs about the prophecies of the book of Revelation, I can really appreciate what Jesus meant when he said: "Take heed that no man deceive you." Matthew 24:4. But, I also thank God for the promise, "**And ye shall know the truth, and the truth shall make you free**." John 8:32.

Our Lord does not want us to immediately believe everything we hear or read about Him. "Prove **ALL THINGS**; hold fast that which is good." 1 Thessalonians 5:21.

A diligent seeker of God will have to meet error every step of the way while traveling towards the Heavenly Canaan. Today, especially, there are false prophets coming in the name of Jesus and false shepherds galore. We must have our own experience in seeking and proving Scripture and learn to be an expert in being able to take the truth and extract the error. God wants us to have the ability to separate the precious seeds of truth from the chaff of it. God wants us to be able to show others the difference between the Christ and the Antichrist!

The Real Truth About UFO's and the New World Order

Needless to say, I was not a bit surprised to hear former President George Bush seven years after I published my last book say, "There will be a New World Order." I was, however, startled to see how vividly correct I was in my last book about the Roman Catholic Church's involvement with Communism and the New Age Movement when the famous Jesuit, Malachi Martin, publicly admitted this in the same year of 1990 in his book, *The Keys of This Blood*. (See pages 243–274.) Something even more startling was when John Paul II admitted that he is against capitalism[1] and, like New Agers and Communists, denies the literal truth of the Bible and accepts the theory of evolution[2] instead of the Bible record of creation. The prophecies pointing to the fusion of Spiritualism, the Papacy, and the apostate Protestants is especially studied in detail in Volume Five entitled *Ancient Prophecies About The Dragon, The Beast, and The False Prophet*.

As discussed previously, *The New Age Movement and The Illuminati 666* was published in 1983 before most Christians became aware of this conspiracy. At that time, there was only one other Christian writer exposing both the religious and political sides of this conspiracy. It was Constance Cumbey. The name of her book was *The Hidden Dangers of the Rainbow*. Ironically enough, her book was printed at the very same time my book was and by the very same printer!

Although I still do not agree at all with Constance Cumbey's interpretation of Revelation, Chapter 13, she did help me see from her book the religious label that these determined people of Spiritualism use to sell their ideology to unsuspecting Christians. Religiously, this worldwide threat of the occult is coming at us as the New Age Movement, but, politically, as the New World Order.

However, in the past there have been several Christian and non-Christian authors who have tried to expose the political side of this New World Order. The first was John Robison back in the 18th century. His book is called *Proofs of a Conspiracy*. He tried to show Freemasons that there was a worldwide revolution being orchestrated within the Masonic Order. John Robison, a Freemason, exposed to other Freemasons that the dangerous secret society

---

[1] *Newsweek*, December 2, 1996, p. 47.

[2] *Time*, November 4, 1996, p. 85.

How the New Age and the NWO Began

of the Illuminati, which had become the highest order of Freemasonry in Munich, Germany, in the year 1777,[3] was using their Order for a worldwide Luciferian revolution. However, this warning fell on deaf ears, and so will it be with most today!

Not one in a hundred thousand people of the world have heard of the Illuminati. What is the Illuminati? For those who have not read my last book, *The New Age Movement and The Illuminati 666*, the Illuminati were and are today schools of ancient witchcraft. Just as the God of Abraham, Isaac, and Jacob had schools established for men to attend to learn the oracles of God, so did Lucifer have him schools to teach the arts of witchcraft. These schools which were called the Illuminati were not only to teach the crafts of the occult, but were also to be a worldwide revolutionary force to take this world for Lucifer before the year 2000.

Adam Weishaupt, the original founder of the Bavarian Illuminati, was a male witch, and I must say an **apostle** of Lucifer. Weishaupt wrote a plan of the occult to take this world for Lucifer before the last age of astrology which is known in religious circles of the occult as the **Age of Aquarius**.[4] Synonymous names for the Age of Aquarius are the **Golden Age**,[5] **Utopian Age,** or the **Galactic Age**. Ashkenazi Jews from Europe and Russia called Illuminism the **Haskalah**[6] (Enlightenment). Weishaupt borrowed his ideas from Plato's Atlantean scheme as did the earlier European philosophers of the Renaissance Era. Here, the reader may understand why Spiritualism was so accepted by many Germans before Blavatsky and Crowley made their debut for the Illuminati had been established long before the Thule Society of which Hitler became a member.

This chapter shall reveal why the United States is now looked upon today by the people of Spiritualism as the birthplace of the New Age Movement, and why the American Revolution was not only the model for the French Revolution, but also for the Russian, Chinese, Cuban, and other Latin American revolutions as well!

---

[3]*Encyclopedia of Freemasonry*, Vol. 1, Mackey, p. 346.
[4]*The Occult Illustrated Dictionary*, Day, p. 57.
[5]*Finding Your Place in the Golden Age*, Chaney, p. 2.
[6]*Encyclopaedia Judaica*, Keter Publishing House, pp. 1433, 1434.

The Real Truth About UFO's and the New World Order

Very few there are, indeed, today who know that both Thomas Jefferson and Benjamin Franklin were not only members of the dangerous secret society of witchcraft calling itself Freemasonry, but both of them were "expert astrologers." They helped design the seal of the All-Seeing Eye on the back of the dollar bill.

According to *The Occult Illustrated Dictionary*, page 56, the reason why the occult sign on the reverse of the great seal of the United States is found on the back of the American one dollar bill is "Because more than 50 of the signatories of the Declaration of Independence were either Masons or Rosicrucians and were much concerned with the esoteric sciences, such as astrology, numerology, tarot, Kabalah, etc. Benjamin Franklin and Thomas Jefferson were expert astrologers."

Again, from the same *Occult Illustrated Dictionary*, page 57, we can find the origin of Novus Ordo Seclorum which Freemasonry, who were cells of the Illuminati, used as their motto to overthrow Christianity in the 18th century. This book says, "Novus Ordo Seclorum means 'New Order of the Ages,' referring to the Gold, Silver, Bronze, and Iron Ages which comprise 26,000 years. The **AQUARIAN AGE** in astrological terms." (Emphasis mine.) As shown earlier, there are some New Agers who no longer hold this view. They say that that popular song in the 60s, "***This is the Dawning of the Age of Aquarius***," was wrong, yet others say this Galactic Age is already beginning to materialize.

I first became aware of the seven ages of astrology by reading the book, *The Compleat Astrologer*, written by Parker on page 44. This book shows that these seven ages known as Leo, Cancer, Gemini, Taurus, Aries, Pisces, and Aquarius began in the year 10,000 B.C. and extended to the year 2000 in which supposedly the Age of Aquarius was to begin. In Bible prophecy, this universal attempt to unite this world under one banner was called in symbolic language "Babylon the Great," and can be found in Revelation 17:5. The word "***Babylon***" means "***confusion***." Hence, Jesus pointed to the state of spiritual confusion that this world confederacy would be in just before He comes to rescue His people. We certainly can see this today, not only among New Agers, but also among mainstream Christians.

Just to show how serious the times are in which we live, I would like to point out to you that it was not only George Bush who used

How the New Age and the NWO Began

this occult slogan (the New World Order), but, as many of you know already, also Bill Clinton! On the front page of *The Los Angeles Times*, Thursday, January 21, 1993, was an article written by David Lauter about the new president. Writing positively about Clinton, David Lauter wrote the following:

"**WASHINGTON** – In 1782, with the Revolution safely won, Congress took a moment to adopt a design for the Great Seal of the United States and with it a motto for the nation still to be created: Novus Ordo Seclorum – A New Age Now Begins."

This slogan, **Novus Ordo Seclorum**, which means Age of Aquarius to the New Agers in which the gods of astrology will take over this planet was also heralded by the humanist Enlightenment Movement of the French Revolutionists during the 18th century. Today, this Novus Ordo Seclorum is heralding enforced international enslavement by uniting everyone into Atlantean Socialism.

About four years after I published *The New Age Movement and The Illuminati 666* warning Christians about this dangerous movement of Spiritualism, on August 16–17, 1987, New Age sun-worshippers met in different parts of the world to bring in and greet the new Age of Aquarius. This age had to be ushered in by 144,000 believers. Again, this New Age phenomenon was based in Mayan and Aztec Spiritualism.

This sacred event to those modern pagans of the New Age Movement was known as the **Harmonic Convergence**. It was as sacred to them as Yom Kippur is to the Jews. Those who worship the forces of nature instead of nature's God believed that at least **144,000** New Age believers had to meet in various "sacred places" or "power points" in the world; or a 25-year period of increasing earthly catastrophes would ensue and by 2012 AD, if the Harmonic Convergence fails, the people of the earth will be destroyed.[7]

This urgent appeal to gather New Age believers to the 350 sacred power points to rescue the earth from destruction was promoted by Shirley MacLaine, the late John Denver, the late LSD guru Timothy Leary of the 60s, and José Argüelles, a wizard, medium, and bestselling New Age author.[8] José Argüelles is the actual father of the

---

[7]*Newsweek*, August 17, 1987, pp. 70, 71
[8]*Discover*, January 1988, p. 90.

The Real Truth About UFO's and the New World Order

Harmonic Convergence and claims he holds seances with a ***star person*** named Treadwell of the system Actara who phones him at home.[9]

José Argüelles, also an art historian, studied deeply into the astrological beliefs of the Mayan and Aztec cultures and religions. Sharing the similar religious beliefs of astrology, Argüelles authored a book on the astrological prophecies of the Mayans and Aztecs. The title of it is *The Mayan Factor Path Beyond Technology*. Argüelles argued that his studies of the ancient Aztec astrological calendar showed a chronological phenomenon would occur on August 16 and 17 of 1987. The Aztec calendar, with its 13 cycles of heaven and nine cycles of hell, would come to an end 25 years after August 16, 1987.

The Aztecs believed the end of the ninth hell cycle would mark the second coming of Quetzalcoatl, the pagan messiah of peace, and he would revisit the earth. The Hopi Indian legend has it that on August 16, 1987, 144,000 sun-dance enlightened teachers will help **awaken** the rest of humanity to these gods a.k.a. extraterrestrial beings.[10]

New Agers, as well as the Aztecs, Mayans, Incas, American Indians, Egyptians, and Babylonians believe(d) that these gods of their ancestors were once famous **Adepts** or teachers on earth. They believe(d) that these teachers reached **Christ consciousness** or became a god while they were on earth. Then, when they died, their spirit went to take possession of one of the planets or stars in the universe, and, eventually, became gods in the universe. As pointed out, Spiritualism has had an evolution. Mahatmas are not spirits. Today, New Agers teach that man is God and that these Mahatmas are **advanced humans** living in Tibet.

Spiritualism also advocates they will be made fit to live with their gods (these UFO's) by being translated or receiving a **transformation** while experiencing this so-called cosmic light. This is the basic promise to all who become diligent students and followers of astrology of which their so-called cosmic light is based on. However, here lies the basic lie of the Devil from the very beginning of his efforts to deceive and destroy man. Again, I would like to remind the reader:

"And the serpent said unto the woman, **YE SHALL NOT SURELY DIE**: For God doth know that in the day ye eat thereof, then your

---

[9]*People Weekly*, August 31, 1987, pp. 26-29.
[10]*Time*, August 31, 1987, p. 63.

How the New Age and the NWO Began

eyes shall be opened, and ye shall be as gods, knowing good and evil." Genesis 3:4-5.

This is, indeed, how humans are uniting with fallen angels which are demons as foretold in 1 Timothy 4:1:

"Now the Spirit speaketh expressly, that in the latter times some shall depart from the faith, giving heed to seducing spirits, and doctrines of devils." I Timothy 4:1.

Those who ignorantly **reject** sound Bible doctrine to follow the precepts of astrology are again, like Eve, **eating forbidden** fruit that will rob its victim of receiving vital spiritual life from God. "Thereof thou shalt surely die." Genesis 2:17. **"But, except ye repent, ye shall all likewise perish."** Luke 13:5.

Nevertheless, the modern diviner of the occult, José Argüelles, pointed out that after the cycle of the ninth hell, August 16 and 17 marks the beginning of the end of the Aztec calendar and a turning point, he says, of historic magnitude excluding anything we have ever known. August 16 and 17, 1987, would also **mark** the second coming of Quetzalcoatl, the god of the Toltec Indians.[11] As pointed out, New Agers believe that the Toltec and Mayan Indians are the **descendants** of the lost continent of Atlantis.

The Toltec Indians were believed to have built the huge pyramids in central Mexico which this writer has explored. However, back in 1980 I pointed out in *Beware It's Coming – The Antichrist 666* how the Mayan and Aztec gods can be traced through the Bible, history, and archaeology to be nothing less than the original ancient Babylonian gods which derived from the worship of Nimrod, Semiramis, and Tammuz.[12] The names were different because of the different languages. This is why the Scriptures point back to Babylon as being the cradle to all false religions. "Babylon the Great, the Mother of Harlots" spread false religion in this part of the world as well. "And they worshipped the dragon which gave power unto the beast." Revelation 13:4. This can clearly be seen in the worship of Quetzalcoatl.

As pointed out, Quetzalcoatl is also two names combined into one. The name *"Quetzal"* is the name of the beautiful bird that was seen

---

[11]*Newsweek*, August 17, 1987, pp. 70, 71.
[12]*Beware It's Coming – The Antichrist 666*, Sutton, pp. 9-108.

The Real Truth About UFO's and the New World Order

in the days of Moctuzuma. The name *"Coatl"* in Indian means *snake* or *serpent*. Hence, the name *"Quetzalcoatl"* means *"bird serpent,"* which is the symbol of Quetzalcoatl. Serpent heads with feathers are protruding out from the pyramid down in central Mexico. This huge Toltec pyramid was built to honor Quetzalcoatl, but later used by the Aztecs to **sacrifice humans** to their gods. For this, other Indian tribes drove the Aztecs out of that area to a salt lake which became Mexico City.

This Quetzalcoatl, the bird serpent god of the Toltec and Aztec Indians, was nothing less than "that old serpent, called the Devil, and Satan, which deceiveth the whole world." Revelation 12:9.

The Mayan bird serpent god was named Kulkulcán, not Quetzalcoatl. Like in the name Quetzalcoatl, Kulkulcán is two names made into one. *"Kulkul"* means *"bird,"* and the word *"can"* or *"kan"* in the Mayan language means *"serpent."* Hence, Kulkulcán, the pagan messiah to the Mayans, was also **nothing less** than **"that old serpent, the Devil**, which deceiveth the whole world." As we saw earlier, New Agers gather at the Chichén Itzá pyramid during the vernal equinox to honor this Mayan god today.

According to *The New Age Encyclopedia*, page 28, José Argüelles said that the Maya believed in a 5200-year "great cycle." According to José Argüelles, the Mayan's great cycle runs from 3113 B.C. to A.D. 2012[13] and is nearing its end also.[14] Argüelles says August 16 and 17, 1987, was exactly 25 years before the end of the Mayan calendar, and nine of our planets will be aligned on those dates in a configuration called a grand trine. This allows for an unprecedented amount of energy to converge in one place and harmonize with itself, creating an energy greater than any experienced on earth to date.[15]

August 16 and 17 is a cosmic trigger point in history, according to Argüelles. He believes these dates mark the beginning when the world is to shift gears, as he called it. He says in A.D. 2012 we will pass out of this beam,[16] which astrology calls the Age of Pisces, into the Galactic Age, known as the Age of Aquarius.

---

[13]*Discover,* **January 1988, p. 90.**
[14]*Newsweek*, **August 17, 1987, p. 70.**
[15]*Ibid.*, **August 17, 1987, p. 70.**
[16]*Ibid.*, **August 17, 1987, p. 70.**

How the New Age and the NWO Began

Hence, Quetzalcoatl and other **extraterrestrial beings**, who were once men but have reached godhood, will visit the earth again. Some are believed to be Jesus or His disciples and still another is **Maitreya**.

In Hinduism, these human beings who were once great men of the earth that died and became heavenly Adepts or teachers are known as Mahatmas. These so-called Mahatmas or spirits that communicate knowledge to humans are also known to witches and mediums as spirit guides. This Cosmic Hierarchical body of Mahatmas (masters) is also known in the occult as the **Great White Brotherhood**.

These extraterrestrial beings (ETs) are the UFO's that people have sited, New Agers claim. José Argüelles said on August 16 and 17, 1987, "There will be anything from mass UFO sightings to actually receiving communications from them."[17]

Argüelles prophesied that if there was not a worldwide effort of at least **144,000** believers stationed on 350 sacred places in the world, holding hands and humming the sacred syllable "OM…," all life forms on this earth will be heading for extinction.

Hence, thousands of people of the occult participated in preparing for the Harmonic Convergence at dozens of so-called power points around the world. They met at the great pyramids of Egypt, the Temple of Delphi in Greece, Machu Picchu in Peru, Mount Fuji in Japan, Stonehenge in England, Mount Shasta in northern California, Central Park in New York City, Cartersville, Georgia, Palo Alto, California, the Black Hills of South Dakota, etc.[18]

More than 144,000 New Agers did show up on this weekend of August 16 and 17 to help ward off 25 years of catastrophe, as prophesied by Argüelles, by outstretching their arms and humming their sacred "OM…"

At 5:00 a.m. on Sunday, August 16, on Sagaponack Beach on Long Island, New Agers spread their blankets, then sat down, crossed their legs, closed their eyes, lifted palms upward and waited intensely facing the east for the sunrise. When the first blush of the light of the sun appeared, the New Agers unleashed a high-velocity "OM…" that *Time* magazine, August 31, 1987, said "would rival a swarm of yellow jackets."

---

[17]*Newsweek*, **August 17, 1987, p. 70.**

[18]*Time*, **August 31, 1987, p. 63.**

The Real Truth About UFO's and the New World Order

Woodstock, New York, was another sacred meeting place of the 350 sacred New Age locations around the world. Woodstock, known as the cradle of the Hippie Movement in the 60s which drew one-half million drug users and fornicators to wallow in the mud, did not draw the crowd to this Harmonic Convergence in numbers as the rock concert did. But, Nathan Koenig, film maker and an organizer of the Woodstock festivities of 1969, said, "The magic is back," according to *People Weekly*, August 31, 1987.[19] To tuned-in and learned New Agers, the "**Aquarian Art Festival**" held in August of 1969 a.k.a. Woodstock was a model for this coming New World Order a.k.a. the **Golden Age of Atlantis**.

Indeed, the New Agers today are reminiscent of those of the Hippie Movement of the 60s with the hand-holding, hugging, and smiles. However, Woodstock 1994 was another disappointment to those who are lovers of pleasure more than lovers of God, and so will this New World Order scheme be a disappointment.

Going back to the year 1987 on Mount Shasta, Gerry Bowman, a medium, claimed to channel the spirit of the apostle John during the weekend of August 16 and 17 before thousands.[20]

Time magazine on August 31, 1987, page 63, recorded that 75 New Agers met at an Indian burial site in Cartersville, Georgia, to help ward off destruction and bring in the new age. "They sat in small groups and burned incense and sage. One man produced a tortoise shell on which he arranged some amethysts. As the darkness dissolved, Yoga practitioners began a series of alarming bird-like maneuvers.

"On Mount Shasta in northern California, 5,000 pilgrims shivered on the rocky fir-covered slopes. Before the sun's rays warmed the night, a solitary woman, crouching on a sheepskin, began to beat a drum. Sounds of flutes and songs filled the air, and tears streamed down the faces of three women wrapped in Indian blankets. They passionately believed the solemn intonation of participant, Shirley Stanfield: Expect to be changed forever."[21]

However, the sacred Sunday came and went. *People Weekly* on

---

[19]*People Weekly*, August 31, 1987, pp. 26-29.
[20]*Ibid.*, August 31, 1987, pp. 26-29.
[21]*Time*, August 31, 1987, p. 63.

How the New Age and the NWO Began

August 31, 1987, said, "And the dead were not raised. The UFO's did not land. Mother Earth was not racked by devastating quakes. Quetzalcoatl, the Aztec god, did not reveal himself. And the world as we know it did not end – Amen."

After August 16 and 17 passed, *Discover* says, "To be fair, Argüelle's ideas weren't without some particles of real science. According to the U.S. Naval Observatory, seven of the nine planets were in grand trine configuration on August 16. But, what this has to do with energy and harmony is unclear."[22]

José Argüelles, the prophet of the New Age, was asked about the great disappointment of August 16 and 17, and he simply said, "All I said was that something was going to happen on those dates, and it did happen, in a grassroots way, with no PR."[23]

I guess José Argüelles can point out that 144,000 had their pilgrimage to their power points, and other prophets and prophetesses claimed to have had communication with extraterrestrial beings which they believed to be once famous teachers here on earth. However, what he did not point out are the warnings about how to detect a false prophet which are found in the Christian Bible.

"But the prophet, which shall presume to speak a word in my name, which I have not commanded him to speak, or that shall speak **IN THE NAME OF OTHER GODS, EVEN THAT PROPHET SHALL DIE**. And if thou say in thine heart, How shall we know the word which the Lord hath not spoken?

"When a prophet speaketh in the name of the Lord, if the thing follow not, nor come to pass, that is the thing which the Lord hath not spoken, but the prophet hath spoken it presumptuously: thou shalt not be afraid of him." Deuteronomy 18:20–22.

Before the August 16 and 17 pilgrimage of the New Agers to their sacred power points, *American Health*, Jan./Feb. 1987, said Andrew Greeley, a Roman Catholic priest, sociologist, and professor of sociology at the University of Arizona, took a scientific survey. He found nearly half of American adults (42%) claimed to have been in contact with the dead. Still higher percentages of Americans reported having had psychic experiences such as extrasensory perception (ESP).

---

[22]*People Weekly*, **January 1988, p. 90.**
[23]*Ibid.*, **January 1988, p. 90.**

The Real Truth About UFO's and the New World Order

Greeley said two-thirds of all American adults (67%) now claim to experience ESP. These surveys were done by Andrew Greeley and his colleagues at the University of Chicago's National Opinion Research Council (NORC).

Andrew Greeley, who authored the book, *Confessions of a Parish Priest*, said he became interested in what psychologists call "paranormal" experiences back in the 70s when he began to realize how many people have them. Nevertheless, being a sociologist, novelist, and a parish priest never having had an ESP experience or contact with the dead, like his church, he said he doubts that the paranormal phenomena will ever be scientifically validated.[24] However, he goes on to say on page 47 in *American Health*, "But even though I've never had a psychic or mystical experience myself, most Americans have. We saw this in our first study in 1973 and in data from a repeat survey we have just analyzed."

Greeley goes on to say in his survey that 59% of Americans have experienced **déjà vu**, that eerie sense of going to a new place and feeling sure you've somehow been there before. Other Americans reported being very close to a powerful, spiritual force that seemed to lift you out of yourself. Five percent of the American population claimed to have been literally **bathed in light** as the apostle Paul was. He points out what used to be considered in the past as paranormal is now normal. "It's even happening to **elite scientists** and **physicians** who insist that such things cannot possibly happen," says Greeley. His studies show that these people are not nuts or psychiatric cases. They are, he says, "for the most part, ordinary Americans, somewhat above the norm in education and intelligence and somewhat less than average in religious involvement."

P. Richard Olson, an associate professor of Family Medicine at the University of North Carolina, reported that nearly two-thirds (64%) of widows at two Asheville nursing homes had at least "once or twice felt as though they were in touch with someone who had died."[25] Greeley said "surprisingly, that many widows who experienced these visitations had not previously believed in life after death."

Greeley believes these encounters with the paranormal may be

---

[24]*American Health*, Jan./Feb. 1987, p. 47.
[25]*Ibid.*, Jan./Feb. 1987, p. 48.

How the New Age and the NWO Began

health-giving, and his data which he has compiled about it since 1973 shows that those who have had these encounters with the dead have changed their belief into a loving God, rather than a judgmental one. He said contact with a dead relative could certainly change one's mind about God. He went on to say that these experiences "could even change the nature of our society."

Greeley also pointed out in his survey that millions have undergone religious moments of **ecstasy**. Millions have reported out-of-body trips, being bathed in light, or other encounters which he said have transformed lives.[26]

There is hardly a day that goes by in which Americans are not being bombarded with the mystery of iniquity today. *Unsolved Mysteries* and the *X-Files* and other popular television talk shows are ever busy promoting the sciences and experiences of metaphysics.

The movie, *Out on a Limb*, starring Shirley MacLaine on ABC-TV encouraged millions to explore into the occult, and those who have to come out of the closet. This popular movie actress is most known today as one of the most strongest supporters and promoters of New Age witchcraft. She played herself in the television movie which was based on her book, *Out on a Limb*.

In the same issue of *American Health*, there was found a story written about Shirley MacLaine and her New Age religion. It states on page 57 of this article that Shirley MacLaine believes that the spirit world has selected her to **"channe**l" the world of a new/old enlightenment to a skeptical age.

This medium's book, *Out on a Limb*, describes her experiences of mystical encounters, out-of-body trips, past lives, and spirit guides. All this she portrayed in her movie. It is not hard to see how far America has **fallen away** from the basic Christian beliefs on which this country was founded when a professed medium or channeler can go before millions and promote the sciences of witchcraft. Fifty years ago, they would not have dared to do such things for fear of ridicule and harm.

MacLaine believes that America is the New Spiritual Republic, the **New Atlantis**, and the New Jerusalem, where the **New Age** would be

[26]*American Health*, Jan./Feb. 1987, p. 49.

The Real Truth About UFO's and the New World Order

conceived or born.[27] She points out how many of the founding fathers of this country were aware of the teachings of the occult that reach as far back as Egypt of the pharaohs. She states that is the reason they put the pyramid with the **third eye** (which symbolizes clairvoyance) on the back of the dollar bill.[28]

Unfortunately, what Shirley MacLaine said about many of our founding fathers of the United States is true. However, the original Europeans that were the first to step ashore on this land of America in the 15th and 16th centuries were **Christian pilgrims**, not New Agers, fleeing persecution from the Roman Catholic Church.

However, later, many of our founding fathers fell victim to three great errors that came forth out of the mouth of the Dragon (Revelation 16:13) from England in the early days of British rule. The three great errors were **Illuminism**, **Deism**, and **Freemasonry**.

The principal meaning of Deism signifies the belief in a single God and in a religious practice founded **solely on natural reason** rather than on **supernatural revelation**.[29] Thus, Deists **reject** the Bible as being given by the **inspiration** of the **Holy Spirit** and the **Deity of Christ**. While Deists profess belief in God as Creator of Heaven and earth, they reject **Jesus Christ** and **His doctrines**.[30] Today, Deism is **Unitarianism**.

The Scriptures warn, "Hereby know ye the Spirit of God: Every spirit that confesseth that Jesus Christ is come in the flesh is of God: And **EVERY SPIRIT THAT CONFESSETH NOT** that Jesus Christ is come in the flesh is **NOT** of God: and this is that **SPIRIT OF ANTICHRIST**, whereof ye have heard that **it should come**; and even **now** already is it in the world." 1 John 4:2, 3.

Deists, while professing to believe in a Supreme Being, teach that God does not have a personal role in governing the affairs of men, and they reject the resurrection and future life of Christians. Some deists go as far as to completely reject the New Testament as

---

[27]*American Health*, **Jan./Feb. 1987, p. 52.**

[28]*Ibid.*, **Jan./Feb. 1987, p. 52.**

[29]*The Encyclopedia of Religion*, **Vol. 4, p. 262.**

[30]*Ibid.*, **p. 262.**

How the New Age and the NWO Began

a fabrication and impostor;[31] therefore, to them so was Jesus.

However, there were some who called themselves Christian Deists in England who accepted both the Christian religion and Deism. They tried to blend the belief of supernatural revelation of God with the belief of natural reason, but were independent of any divine authority.

Deism was most prominent in England. The powerful influence of Deism grew there in England, but it was met with vicious persecution and was branded as blasphemy by the Church of England. Blasphemy in those days of church persecution was punishable by forfeiting civil rights, fines, even imprisonment, and, lastly, the possibility of being burned at the stake.

An antichrist, Francois-Marie Arouet a.k.a. Voltaire, as well as Immanuel Kant, Thomas Paine, Benjamin Franklin, and Thomas Jefferson, were **all** recorded in history and on the books in Heaven as being **Deists**.[32] Like their European brethren of the Renaissance, they also promoted **Plato's Utopian Atlantean** form of government. Jefferson, Franklin, and Paine all **rejected Jesus as Saviour** of the world, and **all** had a part in **overthrowing Christianity in France** during its revolution. Did not Jesus tell the apostle John in Revelation 18:23 that these conspirators who would make war with the Lamb (Revelation 17:12-14) would be "**the merchants**?" Who are the politicians today? Are they not known as "**the great men of the earth**?"

I know for some this information hurts as it did when I first found out these facts. I have seen the magnificent Jefferson Memorial in Washington, D.C. to honor him for his great achievements which he contributed in the founding of the United States. I have been to the little house in New Rochelle, New York, where Thomas Paine lived and worked for the American Revolution. Thomas Paine's book, *Common Sense*, **triggered** the American Revolution. Thomas Paine was very close friends with Voltaire and shared the same beliefs.

Again, I want to remind you of something that I will be revealing to the reader throughout this entire book. The Scriptures are very clear about who Satan would use to promote his number-one religion that would deceive billions.

---

[31]*The Encyclopedia of Religion*, Vol. 4, p. 262.
[32]*Ibid.*, p. 263.

The Real Truth About UFO's and the New World Order

The above photograph I took while visiting the site of Thomas Paine's cottage where he spent his last remaining years in poverty and in obscurity. His cottage is located in New Rochelle, New York. This was my second visit there. Thomas Paine was anti-christ and his book, Common Sense, sparked the American Revolution. Later, his book, Age of Reason, sparked the French Revolution. Paine worked hard to bring about a social change and a New World Order. However, Paine's books later ended up being responsible in causing millions to be shackled to an equal or worse enslavement than that of King George III or of the Roman Catholic Church. Just 14 years later, another enemy of Christ was born and raised to carry on this world revolution against all religions and all governments. His name was Karl Marx. Marx drew out of this 18th century Enlightenment Movement ideas to write his 40-page Communist Manifesto. He is responsible for untold millions, nea, perhaps billions to lose their lives in the name of social change. This Deism or atheism which was especially inspired in France by Paine and Voltaire during the French Revolution developed into Communism later in the 19th century.

How the New Age and the NWO Began

The Masonic magazine entitled The New Age Magazine, *April 1986, pp. 54, 55, published monthly by The Supreme Council, 33rd°, Ancient and Accepted Scottish Rite of Freemasonry, freely states that Thomas Jefferson was not a Christian, but a Deist. This Masonic magazine also states that Jefferson helped bring about the French Revolution. "On the basis of the available material the author presents the evidence and concludes that Jefferson was a deist. Although Jefferson was a member in good standing in the Episcopal Church, he did not subscribe to all the beliefs of the Christian religion.* **HIS WERE BASED ON REASON.** *He did not accept those concepts attributed to revelation or miracles….*

"He was in France as a representative of the American government before and after the Fall of the Bastille, when a mob stormed that prison and the French Revolution with all its violence and excesses began. He had first-hand information about the unholy alliance of church and state leaders in France that helped bring about this revolution….Jefferson's three heros of the Enlightenment were Bacon, Newton, and Locke."

According to Coil's Masonic Encyclopedia, *Coil, 33rd°, p. 100, Johann Joachim Christopher Bode (1730–1793), who was a member of the Illuminati, translated into German* The Jesuits Driven From Freemasonry and Their Weapons Broken by the Freemasons. *This had been published in 1788 to gain adherents against papal Christianity.*

The Real Truth About UFO's and the New World Order

"For thy **merchants** were **THE GREAT MEN OF THE EARTH; for by thy SORCERIES were ALL NATIONS DECEIVED.**" Revelation 18:23.

As pointed out earlier, the plan of the occult to take this world for Lucifer (Satan) by the year 2000 A.D. was called **Novus Ordo Seclorum** which in Latin means **New Order for the Ages** OR **New World Order**. In astrological terms, it means the **Age of Aquarius**.

Adam Weishaupt's plan to destroy Christian influences would commence in France where the Papacy had, since Clovis in A.D. 508, the power to dictate their Canon Law. Those who refused to obey the Papacy, like in England, had to meet persecution. Actually, the citizens of France were the first nation to feel the cruel wrath of the Roman Catholic popes, and Adam Weishaupt was at one time a professor of Roman Catholic Canon Law. However, he turned from Catholicism to explore the sciences of the occult of which he became an expert. French Illuminists, who were posing as religious reformers before the French citizens and pointing out the cruel persecution of the French Huguenots and fanaticism of the Roman Catholic Church, caused the citizens which had been in bondage and at the mercy of papal bishops immediately to join Weishaupt's efforts to overthrow the power of the Roman Catholic supremacy. To accomplish this goal, these conspirators had to overthrow the present government. At that time, King Louis XVI was a very staunch Roman Catholic, and plans were made to infiltrate his government. These conspirators would accomplish this by becoming **members** of the French Parliament. The French citizens, oppressed by papal tyranny and hungry for a change, began to promote these Jacobin Club members. Headed by Robespierre, these French Illuminists a.k.a. Jacobins became members of Parliament.

The Jacobin Club was the name these conspirators were using in France because their headquarters were located in an empty Roman Catholic convent on Jacobin Street in Paris. Their German brethren were the Illuminati.

Jacobinism, which promoted a form of Deism, threw out God altogether. This hammer, which broke up the power of the Papacy, was known as the religion of Reason. It was also known as **Jacobinism** in the third quarter of the 18th century in France. In Germany, it was

How the New Age and the NWO Began

looked upon as Illuminism. Both of these atheistic movements were coming from the same stall. The notorious **Jacobin Clubs**,[33] which were a secret society of the elite in France, were nothing less than **cells of the Illuminati**, republican freethinkers patterned after the lodge of the Illuminati which Adam Weishaupt founded.

Voltaire and Thomas Paine were both Freemasons and advocates of Illuminism. They promoted **Illuminism** as the **Enlightenment**, and this dark era of history is today looked upon as something wonderful. It is also known as the **Age of Reason**. Reader, history records that the greatest war Satan waged against Christ and His people was surely waged during the history of the French Revolution of which will again be revealed in our day!

During this Age of Reason in France, they too had their popular entertainers, like Shirley MacLaine, and politicians promoting the New World Order. The philosophies of Illuminism eventually led to call the Bible an impostor, and a call by the French Revolutionists was imposed among the French citizens to publicly burn all their Bibles. A comedian, similar to that of George Burns, by the name of Monvel, who, as a **priest of Illuminism**, said, "God! If you exist…avenge your injured name. I bid you defiance. You remain silent; you dare not launch your thunders; who, after this, will believe in your existence?"[34]

This Illuminism that popular politicians and entertainers were promoting through their legislative halls of France and among its citizens helped cause the French Revolution. The infidel Voltaire said, "I am weary of hearing people repeat that twelve men established the Christian religion. I will prove that one man may suffice to overthrow it."[35]

Another entertainer during the French Revolution, a dancer with similar views as that of Shirley MacLaine, started claiming that she was the reincarnation of the Goddess of Reason or Liberty. This Goddess of Wisdom was Athena to the Greeks.

This entertainer, who was well-known as a popular dancing girl of the opera as Shirley MacLaine is today, was exalted by the National

---

[33]*Encyclopaedia Britannica*, Vol. 12, p. 837.
[34]*Daniel and The Revelation*, Smith, pp. 284, 285.
[35]*The Great Controversy*, White, pp. 288.

The Real Truth About UFO's and the New World Order

Assembly of France to be worthy of worship. The orator who introduced the worship of Reason said: "Legislators! Fanaticism has given way to reason. Its bleared eyes could not endure the brilliancy of the light. This day an immense concourse has assembled beneath those gothic vaults, which, for the first time, re-echoed the truth. There the French have celebrated the only **TRUE WORSHIP**, – that of **LIBERTY**, that of **REASON**. There we have formed wishes for the prosperity of the arms of the Republic. There we have abandoned inanimate idols for Reason, for that animated image, the masterpiece of nature." [36] (Emphasis added.)

This **dancer**, who was pretending to be the **Goddess of Reason**, after being accepted by the President of that assembly, was mounted on a portable throne and conducted amid an immense crowd to the Cathedral of Notre Dame, where she was seated to take the place of God. Shortly afterwards came the command of these Illuminists to burn their Bibles in the streets.[37] While the citizens of France replaced Christ with the worship of this lewd woman of the entertainment field, **they grieved away the Spirit of God** which keeps in check demons from totally taking control of people. This national departure from the Word of God in France was followed by national ruin. This so-called **Age of Enlightenment or Age of Reason** led these poor deceived people into the **Reign of Terror** which lasted three and one-half years. Complete anarchy broke out! During this horrible time between 1793 and 1797, history cries out what will happen to a nation who rejects God and our Saviour.

During the Reign of Terror in France, no one was safe. The police protection of that nation ceased to exist. The laws that protected its citizens from murder, rape, and theft were ignored and thrown out as the Bible was. Family against family, soldier against soldier, and politician against politician was the daily scene over France. The people turned in on each other and tried to exterminate each other by the guillotine or by any other means possible. Here from *The Great Controversy* on page 284, it records what the **Jacobins** did to the French citizens once they overthrew Christianity:

---

[36]*The Great Controversy*, White, p. 275, 276.
[37]*Daniel and The Revelation*, Smith, pp. 284, 285.

How the New Age and the NWO Began

" ' Then came those days when the most barbarous of all codes administered by the most barbarous of all tribunals; when no man could greet his neighbors or say his prayers …without danger of committing a capital crime; when spies lurked in every corner; when the guillotine was long and hard at work every morning; when the jails were filled as close as the holds of a slave ship; when the gutters ran foaming with blood into the Seine…. While the daily wagon loads of victims were carried to their doom through the streets of Paris, the proconsuls, whom the sovereign committee had sent forth to the departments, reveled in an extravagance of cruelty unknown even in the capital. The knife of the deadly machine rose and fell too slow for their work of slaughter. Long rows of captives were mowed down with grapeshot. Holes were made in the bottom of crowded barges. Lyons was turned into a desert. At Arras even the cruel mercy of a speedy death was denied to the prisoners. All down the Loire, from Saumur to the sea, great flocks of crows and kites feasted on naked corpses, twined together in hideous embraces. No mercy was shown to sex or age. The number of young lads and of girls of seventeen who were murdered by that execrable government is to be reckoned by hundreds. **BABIES TORN FROM THE BREAST WERE TOSSED FROM PIKE TO PIKE ALONG THE JACOBIN RANKS**.' In the short space of ten years, multitudes of human beings perished." (Emphasis mine.)

Reader, the events that led to the French Revolution are being **repeated again**, **this time worldwide**! As pointed out in *The New Age Movement and The Illuminati 666*, published in 1983, this Goddess of Reason is nothing less than the Statue of Liberty in New York today! No? Who gave this pagan goddess to us over one hundred years ago? It was France!

Ironically enough, it was Shirley MacLaine, the **popular dancer** today who says in her book, *Dancing in the Light*, that **each individual is a god**, who led America in the televised tribute to a born-again Statue of Liberty, which was originally named **Liberty Enlightening the World**.[38]

Adam Weishaupt, the founder of the Illuminati conspiracy, united his secret society with the Freemasons in Munich in 1777.[39] As pointed

---

[38]*American Health*, **Jan./Feb. 1987, p. 52.**

[39]*Encyclopedia of Freemasonry and Its Kindred Sciences*, **Mackey, p. 346.**

The Real Truth About UFO's and the New World Order

out in *The New Age Movement and The Illuminati 666* book, over 50 names who signed the Declaration of Independence were either Freemasons or Rosicrucians.

However, it was God in Heaven who took this confusion of the third quarter of the 18th century and molded it according to His will. It was the wisdom of God, not mere man, that produced the wonderful Constitution of the United States which protects its citizens from what happened during the Dark Ages of papal rule and of the French Revolution. It became known as the "*Miracle of Philadelphia*." It is a historical fact that George Washington and John Adams were **not** in the same political camp with Jefferson, Franklin, and Paine. Even though they **all** were Freemasons, **not all** Freemasons were supporters of the Illuminati's plans. **Washington and Jefferson were rivals.**

Slowly but surely, that shield protecting us from civil and religious oppression is stealthily being removed little by little today. We will see that this is so as we continue in the coming chapters.

In *The San Juan Star*, Sunday, June 30, 1991, on page 21 appeared a historical account of Benjamin Franklin's connection with not only the American Revolution, but the French Revolution as well. Charles Toth, the author of this article, retired from the University of Puerto Rico and authored several books on the history of both revolutions.

Charles Toth, writing positively about the wonderful achievements and inventions which Franklin contributed to the world, also pointed out how Franklin arrived in France just six months after the signing of the Declaration of Independence in 1776. Benjamin Franklin, who was a Deist and an expert in astrology, lived in France before their revolution. Remember, the American Revolution began on July 4, 1776; the French Revolution was over ten years later.

Benjamin Franklin, six months after July 4, 1776, became the new ambassador to France from the newly-formed United States. As an inventor, philosopher, and statesman, his popularity in France was exceedingly high. France and England were on opposite sides in the 18th century, and Franklin's influence with France helped in receiving both military and financial aid from France to assist the American Revolution.

However, Charles Toth in this same article brings out something very disturbing that loyal followers of Christ may not appreciate.

How the New Age and the NWO Began

FRANKLIN, BENJAMIN

FRANKLIN ON HIS WAY TO FRANCE.

Like Thomas Jefferson and Voltaire, Benjamin Franklin was a Deist and was, indeed, an apostle of the New World Order conspiracy. Although Franklin professed a belief in God and wrote about Him, he quietly rejected Jesus as God manifest in the flesh (1Timothy 3:16) and as Saviour of the world. While professing godliness, Jefferson, Voltaire, Paine, and Franklin denied the power thereof.

It was both Thomas Jefferson and Benjamin Franklin (who are considered among the Great Men of the Earth – Revelation 18:23), who helped design the seal with the pyramid and the **ALL-SEEING EYE** with Novus Ordo Seclorum written under it. This seal was placed there on the back of the American one dollar bill during the Franklin D. Roosevelt administration. "For by thy sorceries were all nations deceived." Revelation 18:23.

The word "Dragon" in the book of Revelation is mentioned just 13 times. To the people of Spiritualism, the number 13 is a magical number in astrology of which Jefferson and Franklin were experts. It is not by chance that there are sets of 13 found in both seals.

1. *13 leaves on the olive branch*
2. *13 berries on the olive branch*
3. *13 bars and stripes in the breast plate of the eagle*
4. *13 arrows in the eagle's left talon*
5. *13 letters in "E Pluribus Unum"*
6. *13 letters in "Annuit Coeptis"*
7. *13 pentagrams forming the hexagram over the eagle's head*
8. *13 levels of the pyramid with Novus Ordo Seclorum (New World Order)*

According to The International Encyclopedia of Secret Societies & Fraternal Orders, *page 224, the Shriners were founded by a group of 13 Master Masons.*

The Real Truth About UFO's and the New World Order

Toth quotes from a book about Franklin's journeys in Europe and what he was promoting. Quoted from *The San Juan Star* on page 21 is the following:

"Perhaps Franklin's arrival in France was best described by Antonio Pace in 'Benjamin Franklin in Italy': It stirred wild speculation in Europe… [He] seemed nothing less than **THE APOSTLE** come to make his revelations to the Europeans in the name of a society arisen in answer to the **ILLUMINISTIC** prayer for a **NEW WORLD ORDER** based upon rational principles." (Emphasis added.)

Charles Toth quotes John Adam's comments regarding Franklin's ideas which he promoted among the French before the French Revolution.

"John Adams reported from Paris, not without a touch of envy, 'His reputation was more universal than that of Leibnitz, or Newton, Frederick the Great or Voltaire, and his character more beloved and esteemed than any or all of them… When they spoke of him, **THEY SEEMED TO THINK THAT HE WAS TO RESTORE THE GOLDEN AGE'.** "

Charles Toth says: "That Franklin was accepted as the **HERALD** of a **NEW AGE** to come was greatly fostered by his conscious efforts…. Appearing to fuse the *l'esprit humain* of a Voltaire with *la sensibilité* of Rousseau, Franklin was embraced in the salons of Paris as the perfect *philosophe*." (Emphasis added.)

As shown, this New World Order we hear religious and political leaders promoting today actually began in the third quarter of the 18th century, not the 20th century. It was started by Adam Weishaupt, the founder of the original occult secret society called the Illuminati, on May 1, 1776. Here from *The Encyclopaedia Britannica*, Macropaedia, Vol. 9, pp. 1154, 1155, we read the following:

"**Not all** the **FREEMASONS** became **supporters** of the Revolution and of the French, but many of them did so. The moderate and constitutional demands of the **MASONIC LODGES** began to be accompanied by more democratic demands, and there were in Milan, Bologna, Rome, and Naples **CELLS OF ILLUMINATI**, republican freethinkers, after the pattern recently established in Bavaria by **Adam Weishaupt**." (Emphasis added.)

How the New Age and the NWO Began

Here, from *The American Heritage Dictionary* on page 656, we can read some more historical facts about this conspiracy. It is quoted:

"**ILLUMINATI** – 1. Persons claiming to be unusually enlightened with regard to some subject. 2. a. The Illuminaten (see). b. Persons regarded as **ATHEISTS**, libertines, or radical republicans during the 18th century (such as the French Encyclopedists, the **FREEMASONS**, or freethinkers): '*THE DOCTRINES OF THE ILLUMINATI AND PRINCIPLES OF JACOBINISM.*' "(Emphasis mine.)

How few Christians who are members of the Masonic Order know that it is a historical fact that it was the Freemasons, cells of the Illuminati, who made war on the Bible during the French Revolution! How few Christian pastors know that this Illuminism (or atheism) that was used as a tool to combat Christianity during the French Revolution also forbade the worship of Christ through their National Assembly!

Since my last book, *The New Age Movement and The Illuminati 666*, which was published in 1983 and has a comprehensive study into the doctrines of Freemasonry, I am privileged to say that the Lord has used me to bring high-ranking Masons to see their error. These men have now renounced Freemasonry and have resigned!

At least **one out of 12 American men** in the United States has fallen victim of this snare of Satan's and has wrapped himself **unwittingly into the fold of our enemy.**

Defenders of Masonry often accuse me as once being a Freemason because of my knowledge about their order and their secret oaths and beliefs. Therefore, they try to pawn me off to their brethren as once being a Mason, but, for some reason, Sutton left the order or was disfellowshipped and became disgruntled. That is why, they say, I am attacking the Masonic lodges. This I have heard over and over again.

However, reader, I was never connected at any time in my life with Freemasonry or with any secret organization. I was never a scholar of the occult sciences, but I will admit being a scholar for Jesus! I received my knowledge of the doctrines of Spiritualism by a diligent study of the Scriptures, along with a diligent study of history. Not until then was I equipped enough spiritually to later compare Masonic doctrines from their own books with that of Baal worship from Scripture and history. I have found it to be the same thing.

The Real Truth About UFO's and the New World Order

This volume will study the reason for the prevailing ignorance of the general masses of Masons which I did not bring out in my last book, *The New Age Movement and The Illuminati 666*.

The Encyclopaedia Britannica and *The American Heritage Dictionary* clearly record that the Freemasons caused the French Revolution. Any Roman Catholic writer who knows 18th-century history will verify this. The Freemasons guillotined multitudes of Catholic bishops and priests during the French Revolution. If a Roman Catholic in the 18th and 19th centuries was found to be a Mason, he was automatically excommunicated. **Nevertheless, attitudes have changed.** In the 20th century, it was a Catholic Freemason that helped design the Capitol building in Washington, D.C. after the similitude of what is at the Vatican! His name was **James Hoblin**. It is also interesting to note that this pagan Goddess of Liberty is standing on top of the Capitol of the United States.

The first thing the Masonic order will shout in America is that they are a Christian organization. I believe God has some of His people in these lodges who are Christian, but **Freemasonry is not** a Christian organization. However, a defender of Masonry will say, "Freemasons are not atheists!" Today, that is true in part. However, during the 18th century they were not hiding under the cover of Christianity, but Illuminism which today is being promoted as secular humanism. This era of evil in the 18th century, as already pointed out, was known as the Age of Reason or the Age of Enlightenment. Like the Illuminists of the 18th century who promoted a revival of the Renaissance of France which promoted the Atlantean Plan of Plato, so are those of the New Age Movement today ushering in what they call a New Age of understanding and intellectual revival.[40]

It is not by chance that the Masonic Order's magazine for the thirty-third degree published by the Supreme Council, 33rd Degree, Ancient and Accepted Scottish Rite of Freemasonry of the Southern Jurisdiction of the United States, until recently was sent out under the title of *NEW AGE*.

It is not by chance that Adam Weishaupt, the founder of the dangerous secret society of the Illuminati, was also a Freemason. This freethinker, Adam Weishaupt, began to **replace** Christianity in France

---

[40]*The Cincinnati Enquirer*, Saturday, October 18, 1986, p. D-10.

How the New Age and the NWO Began

with the **religion of Reason** by using the Masonic lodges to cover his conspiracy. The secret society of the Illuminati became a secret society **within** the secret society of Freemasonry.[41]

Today, the Masonic lodges in America are known as **Blue Lodges**. Freemasonry is **divided into two mainstreams**. European Masonry and American Masonry, which is known as the Blue Lodge. The European or ancient Masonry is real Masonry. **The Blue Lodge is pseudo-Masonry**. Albert Pike, 33rd Degree, past Grand Commander of the Supreme Council, 33rd Degree, Ancient Scottish Rite of Freemasonry, says the **American Blue Lodge in America is a hoax**.

In his book, *Morals and Dogma, Ancient and Accepted Scottish Rite*, which I have in my own possession, Albert Pike, one of Freemasonry's most recognized scholars, says the following on page 819:

"**The Blue Degrees** are but the outer court or portico of the Temple. Part of the symbols are displayed there to the initiate, but **HE IS INTENTIONALLY MISLED BY FALSE INTERPRETATIONS**. It is not intended that he shall understand them; but it is intended that he shall imagine he understands them. (Emphasis mine.)

"Their (the symbols) true explication is reserved for the Adepts, the Princes of Masonry.... It is well enough for the mass of those called Masons, to imagine that all is contained in the Blue Degrees; and whoso attempts to undeceive them will labor in vain, and without any true reward violate his obligations as an Adept."

Do the Adepts and Princes of Masonry look down upon those of the Blue Degrees as being vulgar? Pike again answers this question on page 819 of *Morals and Dogma*:

"The symbols of the wise are the idols of the vulgar, or else as meaningless as the hieroglyphics of Egypt to the nomadic Arabs. There must always be a commonplace interpretation for the mass of Initiates, of the symbols that are eloquent to the Adepts."

In another authorized Masonic publication called *Magic Black and White* we read: "FORTUNATE IS THE MASON OR PRIEST WHO UNDERSTANDS WHAT HE TEACHES. BUT OF SUCH DISCIPLES THERE ARE ONLY A FEW."[42] (See *The Masonic Report*, McQuaig, p. 5.)

---

[41]*The Encyclopedia of Freemasonry and Its Kindred Sciences*, **Mackey, p. 368.**
[42]*Magic Black and White*, **Hartman, p. 62.**

The Real Truth About UFO's and the New World Order

It has been my experience by talking to Freemasons that the general membership of Freemasonry has absolutely no knowledge of the deceptions which have been cleverly hidden from them. It should be understood by the reader that most American Freemasons are loyal Americans, and they know not the slightest about the New World Order conspiracy which has its genesis during the French Revolution.

As pointed out earlier, at least one out of 12 men in the United States are Freemasons. Multitudes of famous men in the past and present have been deceived by this wonder-working power called Freemasonry.

Some of the distinguished Americans who have been members are George Washington, Henry Clay, Thomas Jefferson, John Adams, Davey Crockett, Jim Bowie, Henry Ford, Charles Lindbergh, Wil Rogers, J. Edgar Hoover, Chief Justice Earl Warren, Barry Goldwater, Red Skelton, and Gerald Ford, just to name a few.

Again, it should be understood that most American Freemasons believe they are in a Christian organization and do not think they are bowing their knee before Baal. They look at Shriner's Hospitals and the community work they do as proof of their Christian character. However, deception is never without some truth mixed with it. Multitudes of decent, law-abiding, Christian gentlemen have been **used** to **camouflage** this **anti-Christian worldwide fraternity**.

The familiar Biblical names so often used in Freemasonry, such as Solomon and Solomon's Temple, actually have nothing to do with the great king of Israel. American Freemasons are told in the lower ranks that ancient Freemasonry dedicated their lodges to King Solomon because he was the first Most Excellent Grand Master. However, nothing could be further from the truth. The higher orders of Masonry are told:

"This name Solomon **IS NOT THE ISRAELITISH KING**. It is the name in form, but different in its meaning," says Martin Wagner in his Masonic book, *An Interpretation of Freemasonry*, on page 97.

"This name is a composite, **SOL-OM-ON**, the names of the **SUN** in **LATIN**, **INDIAN**, and **EGYPTIAN**, and is designed to show the unity of several **God-ideas** in the ancient religions, as well as those

How the New Age and the NWO Began

of Freemasonry."[43] **Freemasonry is an international interfaith organization.**

The Masonic lodges are looked upon by worldly eyes as great Christian centers of the great men of the earth. This elite fraternity boasts of the many great politicians and businessmen Freemasonry has produced. However, the Great I AM warns it will be **THY MERCHANTS** (Businessmen) of the earth that Satan will use to deceive all nations. "For thy **MERCHANTS (BUSINESSMEN)** were the **GREAT MEN OF THE EARTH**; for by thy **SORCERIES (WITCHCRAFT)** were all nations deceived." Revelation 18:23.

"For we wrestle not against flesh and blood, but against principalities, against powers, against the rulers of the darkness of this world, against **SPIRITUAL WICKEDNESS IN HIGH PLACES**." Ephesians 6:12.

In the Blue Degrees of Freemasonry, there is found the legend of the Third Degree. Hiram Abiff was slain by one Jubelum who was one of the three ruffians that was trying to force the Grand Master Hiram Abiff to reveal the secrets of a Master Mason. The other two ruffians were Jubela and Jubelo. As Hiram Abiff tried to flee out of the South Gate of Solomon's Temple, he was met by the ruffian Jubela. He was struck by Jubela with a 24-inch gauge across the throat. Then, he attempted to retreat by the West Gate where he was met by the second ruffian Jubelo. After refusing to reveal the secrets of a Master Mason, Hiram Abiff was struck by Jubelo with a square across the breast. He now attempted to make his escape by the East Gate where he was met by the third ruffian Jubelum who struck him on the forehead with a maul which killed him on the spot.

This legend of Hiram Abiff is too lengthy to go into detail, but this legend is really the legend of Osiris, the sun-god of the Egyptians, who was killed by Typhon, the god of darkness. The legend of Osiris the sun-god and Typhon says that the sun and darkness kill each other and are reborn each day.

James D. Shaw, a former 33° Freemason and **past Master to all Scottish Rite bodies** who became a Grand Master after a long coveted desire to do so, was awakened to the fact that Freemasonry's god is not Christ, but Lucifer. James D. Shaw says:

---

[43]*The Masonic Report*, McQuaig, p. 13.

The Real Truth About UFO's and the New World Order

" 'Oh, it's all in fun,' I was told as I impersonated a character named Hiram Abiff in the initiation of the Third Degree. Little did I know that I would have to renounce and leave the institution of Masonry before I would find out just who this 'Hiram Abiff' actually represented!

"I didn't know, and neither does one in one hundred thousand candidates for the Third Degree know that they are impersonating Osiris of Egypt, or Baal of the pagan Canaanites and Phoenicians, or Bacchus sun-god of the Greeks, who is slain annually by the principle of darkness represented by the three winter signs of the Zodiac. And is portrayed in the Masonic Lodge by three ruffians, called Jubela, Jubelo, and Jubelum. How Satan must have laughed at me as I served him diligently as priest of the Lodge for so many years. I was not willing to be just a ' card carrier,' I was too eager for that. So I served in all the chairs and ultimately became Worshipful Master of the Lodge. I pursued the degrees of the Scottish Rite and joined the Shrine in my quest for pre-eminence in the eyes of men. In time I became Past Master to all Scottish Rite Bodies. And finally was selected for the coveted 33rd Degree, and was made a 33rd Degree Mason in House of the Temple in Washington, D.C."

James D. Shaw became a Christian pastor. His testimony, in part, was taken from the Introduction of *The Masonic Report* written by C.F. McQuaig.

Like James Shaw, who was a Past Master to all Scottish Rite Freemasonry, most American Freemasons, although they are led through these initiations, **do not realize** they are representing the **day star** in the American lodges. In the Blue Lodge to cover the fact that Freemasonry is Baal worship, the new initiate is told he is impersonating Hiram Abiff, a supposedly murdered Grand Master of ancient Freemasonry and a Tyrian artist that was helping to build Solomon's Temple.

Here, from the pen of Edmond Ronayne, **past Grand Master of Masonry**, the following is stated from his book, *The Master's Carpet*, on pages 359–360:

"Now to understand all this, let us remember that the candidate represents Osiris, or Baal, or Hiram which are all one and the same principle, and that that principle is 'the fertilizing and fecundating

How the New Age and the NWO Began

powers of the sun' – 'the sun-god'. Let us also bear in mind that there is supposed to be a constant, unceasing conflict going on between this sun-god and night or darkness." (See *The Masonic Report*, p. 31.)

In heathen sun worship, the sun-god is worshipped as a triad god. For instance, in Hinduism, when the sun rises from the east he is Brahma; when he rises to his highest point in the sky at noon, he becomes Siva. When he sinks into the western ocean, he becomes Vishnu. In Freemasonry the Candidate is symbolically representing the sun-god traveling to his three positions (east, south, and west) daily. While the Candidate represents the sun-god, the Worshipful Master, the Junior Warden, and the Senior Warden represent darkness fighting against light (the sun). (See *The Masonic Report*, pp. 33, 34.)

"**MY PEOPLE ARE DESTROYED FOR LACK OF KNOWLEDGE**: because thou hast rejected knowledge, I will also reject thee, that thou shalt be no priest to me: seeing thou hast forgotten the law of thy God, I will also forget thy children." Hosea 4:6

"O Israel, thou hast destroyed thyself; **but in me is thine help**." Hosea 13:9

In *The General Ahiman Rezon* by Daniel Sickles on page 75, we read the following:

"Lodge meetings at the present day are usually held in **upper chambers**," and the reason for this custom is that "before the erection of temples the celestial bodies were worshipped on hills and terrestrial ones in valleys." (See *The Masonic Report*, p. 15.)

The Masonic lodges are a symbol of the universe, and the lodge buildings (temples) are built as the pagan temples are, **facing east and west**. The Mason's initiations, ceremonies, and rituals are always held at night, (just like the Baal worshippers), on the highest area around, (the second floor of Masonic buildings). In the Rite of Secrecy, the Candidate is led in the lodge room from the west to face the east (the rising sun), places his hand on the square, compass, and whatever sacred book is found on their altar, (depending on what nation you are in), and takes an oath carrying horrible penalties if violated.

In the Temple Legend of the Third Degree, the Candidate has to impersonate Hiram Abiff, the supposed Grand Master of Solomon's

The Real Truth About UFO's and the New World Order

Temple who was persecuted and killed by three ruffians. In the Blue Lodge (pseudo-Masonry), the Candidate is told that the three ruffians were Jubela, Jubelo, and Jubelum. However, in real Masonry, they represent the sun's three daily positions and the three winter signs of the zodiac.

In real Freemasonry, these three ruffians represent Typhon, the Egyptian god of darkness, delivering a blow to the brightness of the sun-god (Hiram Abiff) in his daily struggle from east to west. The three principle officers of a Masonic lodge are the Worshipful Master, the Senior Warden, and the Junior Warden. In the initiation into the Third Degree, the Candidate is led to the south, west, and east where at each station he is met by the Worshipful Master in the east, the Junior Warden in the south, and the Senior Warden in the west. First, the Candidate is led to the south (Jubela) and is pricked with a compass by the Junior Warden; then, he is led to the west side of the lodge where he meets the Senior Warden (Jubelo) and receives a blow to his chest from a square by the Senior Warden. Then, he is led to the east (Worshipful Master or Jubelum) where he receives a controlled blow from a mallet in the forehead. The Candidate then falls backwards into a large canvas or sheet and is wrapped in it. Then, he is covered by chairs. This represents the death of the sun-god (Hiram Abiff); hence, the origin of the symbol of Freemasonry, the compass and the square. In the First Degree, the Candidate is deceived into believing that the *"G"* in the middle of the compass and square represents God. Later, in the Second Degree, he is told it represents geometry. However, in reality it represents **G.A.O.T.U.** (Great Architect of the Universe) or the god of nature, the sun-god! Hence, here we find the origin of the compass and the square which is one of the most prominent symbols in Masonry.

Albert Pike, 33rd Degree, and one of the most recognized scholars of Freemasonry, admits that **"THE MASONIC LODGE REPRESENTS THE UNIVERSE."** (See *Morals and Dogma*, page 209.) Edmond Ronayne, past Grand Master of Lodge 639 in Chicago, says in his Masonic book entitled *The Master's Carpet* on pages 301 and 302:

"The lodge room then is brought before us as a symbol of the Universe, governed by the sun-god, and its cubical form expressed

How the New Age and the NWO Began

in the language of the ritual is made to represent the united power of light and darkness, and the constant conflict which is supposed to be always going on between them. In other words, the lodge room is the real heaven (in miniature), where the 'god of nature,' – 'G.A.O.T.U.' – always presides, where his symbol is always displayed, where his worship is always practiced, and when the 'good Mason' (?) dies he is simply transferred from this lower heaven or this 'lodge below,' to the Mount Olympus of the craft, called the 'Grand Lodge above.' " (See *The Masonic Report*, p. 15.)

Reader, the Blue Lodge Mason in America is told that the "*G*" represents God. However, it should be noted from the above quote that the "*G*" in the middle of the square represents the *G.A.O.T.U.*, the sun-god. These letters in Freemasonry mean the Great Architect of the Universe.

Freemasons are required to take an oath from the very first degree of Masonry. Here is the oath the new initiates must take to become an *Entered Apprentice Degree* as quoted from *The Masonic Report* on page 11:

"I do most solemnly and sincerely promise and swear, without the least equivocation, mental reservation, or self evasion of mind in me whatever; binding myself under no less penalty than to have my throat cut across, my tongue torn out by the roots, and my body buried in the rough sands of the sea at low watermark, where the tide ebbs and flows twice in twenty-four hours; so help me God, and keep me steadfast in the due performance of the same."

Nevertheless, the Bible warns: "But above all things, my brethren, **SWEAR NOT**, neither by heaven, neither by the earth, **NEITHER BY ANY OTHER OATH**; but let your yea be yea; and your nay, nay; lest ye fall into condemnation." James 5:12.

My Christian brother or sister of these secret societies and of the Order of the Eastern Star, the Bible warns us not to take oaths and to swear not, which you had to do to be initiated into a lodge. Additionally, Jesus who is the Author and Finisher of Christianity says, "But be not ye called **Rabbi**: for one is your **MASTER**, even **CHRIST**; and all ye are brethren." Matthew 23:8.

Jesus said plainly here that we are not to call anybody Master. What do Masons call the leaders of your lodges? What do New Agers call their spirit guides? Both Masons and New Agers call them masters.

The Real Truth About UFO's and the New World Order

"Be ye not unequally yoked together with unbelievers: for what fellowship hath righteousness with unrighteousness? and what communion hath light with darkness? And what concord hath Christ with Belial? or what part hath he that believeth with an infidel?

"Wherefore come out from among them, and be ye separate, saith the Lord, and touch not the unclean thing; and I will receive you, And will be a Father unto you, and ye shall be my sons and daughters, saith the Lord Almighty." 2 Corinthians 6:14, 15, 17, 18.

Just to show how dangerous it is for Christian pastors and laymen to belong to any of these secret societies, here from one of the most recognized scholars of Freemasonry are listed below the founders of their order.

Like all metaphysical schools, Freemasons can trace their origin to Nimrod, the great rebel and enemy of God, and to his father Cush, who was worshipped as Hermes among the Babylonians and Greeks. (See Genesis 10:6-12 and 11:1-9.) Here are some astonishing statements from Albert G. Mackey, 33rd Degree and past Grand Master of Freemasonry.

"**HERMES**. In all the old manuscript records which contain the Legend of the Craft, mention is made of Hermes as one of the founders of Masonry."[44]

"**NIMROD**. The Legend of the Craft in the Old Constitutions refers to Nimrod as one of the founders of Masonry."[45]

Here are some more shocking facts about how this New World Order scheme has caused world revolutions. This will be of special interest among Latin American Christian brethren.

Among the anti-Christian Enlightenment Movement, which was truly founded and established by Adam Weishaupt at age 28, there was another Freemason, like Benjamin Franklin, Voltaire, Thomas Jefferson, and Thomas Paine, who at the age of 27 began his mission to overthrow the power of papal Christianity. This most famous personality of the **Enlightenment Movement** was Simón Bolívar. This Freemason and military dictator was born in Caracas, Venezuela, in 1783 into an aristocratic upper class family, but was orphaned at

---

[44]*The Encyclopedia of Freemasonry and Its Kindred Sciences*, **Mackey, p. 322.**
[45]*Ibid.*, Mackey, p. 513.

How the New Age and the NWO Began

age nine. His uncle sent him to Madrid in 1799, just one year after Napoleon's General Berthier marched into the Vatican and dethroned Pope Pius VI, to complete his education.[46]

Bolívar also traveled and studied in other parts of Europe[47] while the stormy winds of the **Age of Reason** were still blowing. This most famous Latin American revolutionary and liberator from the tyranny of the pope and his Jesuits received his **transformation** from Christian thought to Enlightenment thought from the help of one Simón Rodríguez. He introduced Bolívar to the writings of another antichrist named Jean Jacques Rousseau[48] who also helped Adam Weishaupt and Voltaire to receive their transformation earlier.

While in Rome, Bolívar vowed publicly to free South America from the Vatican and today he is looked upon as the George Washington of South America. However, reader, George Washington was not involved with the Illuminati nor was John Adams, even though they were deceived about Freemasonry. Not all Freemasons took part in this New World Order scheme. However, Bolívar is, indeed, honored in the *Coil's Masonic Encyclopedia*, Vol. A-Z, on page 100 as a Freemason who was inspired by the French Revolution and by the example of the United States, which he visited in 1809.

However, Simón Bolívar, who spent his entire fortune to liberate the South Americans from the papal and Spanish tyranny, had his own self-interest in mind. He wanted to swap the papal chains they had on the South Americans for a pair of his own devising for he was determined to become the Napoleon of all of South America. However, rival ambitions were producing outbursts of rebellion and defiance against Bolívar's authority. Narrowly escaping assassin's daggers, combined with the deterioration of his health because he had tuberculosis, Bolívar as dictator of Columbia stepped down in the spring of 1830.[49] On December 17, 1830, this Illuminist, Simón Bolívar, who was already an exhausted man from the failure of his political and revolutionary plans, died of tuberculosis.

[46]*Encyclopedia of World Biography*, Vol. 2, 1973, p. 50.
[47]*The World Book Encyclopedia*, Field Enterprises Educ. Corp., 1959, p. 864.
[48]*Academic American Encyclopedia*, Vol. B, 1993, p. 365.
[49]*Encyclopedia of World Biography*, Vol. 2, 1973, p. 52.

The Real Truth About UFO's and the New World Order

As we continue to study this New World Order conspiracy, the reader shall see that we, indeed, have multitudes of **modern-day Nimrods**, great rebels, who have united with fallen angels against the God of Abraham, Isaac, and Jacob. They are determined, like Nimrod, to overthrow the worship of this planet's Creator by building a society leaving God out; and, like Nimrod, those who will not join them will be thrust out as well. However, Jesus, who is Christ, has other plans. He spoke from ancient days these words:

"I have long time holden my peace; I have been still, and refrained myself: now will I cry like a travailing woman; I will destroy and devour at once." Isaiah 42:14.

Reader, it is estimated that one out of 12 men in the United States is indeed a member of Freemasonry. Most congressmen, senators, and even presidents have been, or are, members of Freemasonry. However, most of these members **do not really understand what they are involved in**. It is a most terrible mistake by those talk show hosts and authors of books who are exposing this dangerous New World Order scheme to promote the use of physical force and violence upon these conspirators who are working within the United States government. The bombing at the World Trade Center in New York City and at the Federal Building in Oklahoma City should show the reader who claims to be a follower of the Good Shepherd that this kind of action is from the Evil One and not from God. All who advocate the overthrow of this New Age/Marxist revolution by force are voicing the words of the Dragon. The final triumph of the Kingdom of Christ will come through the preaching of the Gospel. "**For all they that take the sword shall perish with the sword.**" Matthew 26:52. "And they **overcame** him by the blood of the Lamb, and by the word of their testimony; and they loved not their lives unto the death." Revelation 12:11.

This battle between good and evil is to be fought by God Himself. It is His battle, not ours. We are called to use nonviolent means to make those who are victims of this New Age deception to become aware of their error. It is the goodness of God that turns evil people from their wickedness, not by trying to force people to do so or die. "For the weapons of our warfare are not carnal, but mighty through God to the pulling down of strongholds." 2 Corinthians 10:4.

How the New Age and the NWO Began

Nevertheless, Christians are not to be ignorant of Satan's devices. They are not just to stand still and do nothing. Jesus warned that this conspiracy to unite human beings with the Devil would even "deceive the **VERY ELECT if possible**." It is the duty of every born-again Christian to warn others of these things; but, how can a Christian warn others when he or she has no knowledge? Such is the condition of multitudes of Christian pastors who claim to be feeding and protecting God's sheep.

Satan is today demonstrating his supernatural character and power in the heavens. Heathen deities, which Bible rejecters have been fooled into worshipping, are manifesting themselves before astonished human eyes!

The most learned occultists, and even scientists and astronauts, are claiming to be communicating with extraterrestrial beings a.k.a. UFO's. These contactees are teaching the world that these UFO's are the ancient gods who were once men which were worshipped among the ancient Babylonians, Egyptians, Hindus, Romans, etc. As I have tried to point out many times, these so-called **higher intelligences** or **extraterrestrial visitors** are not extraterrestrial beings from other planets, but are, in actuality, Satan and his fallen angels! This is how multitudes are being fooled into uniting with demons as Revelation 16:13, 14 clearly foretold! The **backbone** of the worldwide movement of Spiritualism today is **ALL** centered around this doctrine! These voices that modern necromancers, pythonists, and parapsychologists are communicating with are receiving instruction that the gods are going to revisit the earth and take it over. Therefore, there must be a **transformation of human intelligences** and also a **cleansing** of both the body and the world in order that Mother Earth and Father Sky and its inhabitants are pure enough to receive their deities. It is these same spirits who are using human contacts to **re-establish the ten divisions of Atlantis** and the cleansing of this planet in preparation for this illusion.

Hence, here lies the basic foundation of the United Nations environmental programs in which thousands of voices from politicians, religious leaders, entertainers, and the media are projecting to the inhabitants of this planet. Hence, here lies the foundation of "Holistic Medicine" and **New Age vegetarianism**. Most of the health food

The Real Truth About UFO's and the New World Order

stores in the United States are New Age! They are using the truth about how this planet's natural resources are polluted and depleting and how it is not safe to eat meat any longer as a recruiting station to bring unsuspecting people into the sciences of metaphysics, whose author is Lucifer himself. This we shall see is true as we study in Chapter Three, *The New World Order and the Promotion of Metaphysics*.

As we continue to study the prophecies about the rise and evolution of modern Babylon the Great as it was predicted from Chapters 16, 17, and 18 of The Revelation of Jesus Christ, we will also learn what part modern Israel will play in the coming great battle of God Almighty. In Chapter Three, it will be shown with documented proof that Zionism also became a victim of this New World Order scheme to take this world for Lucifer by the year 2000. This **Illuminism** or the **Enlightenment Movement** a.k.a. **Utopianism**, which intoxicated French citizen's minds and led to the overthrow of Christianity in France during the revolution, also at the same time intoxicated multitudes of European Jews. This era of the 18th-century Enlightenment Movement, as we shall learn from a Jewish encyclopedia, was known as the **Era of the Haskalah**.[50] It will also be shown with documented proof that this Era of the Haskalah changed Jewish thinking to embrace **Marxism**,[51] which led to the overthrow of Christianity in Russia!

While the Russian leaders were led to repeat the scenes of horror of the **Reign of Terror** in France, Mohandas Gandhi in India became a convert of Illuminism out of which Marxism derived and helped lead the overthrow of Christianity in India. Now, gullible American Christians are unwittingly embracing this deadly *red* plague from these *red* revolutionaries today! No? Wait until the reader sees how Marxism (Illuminism) infiltrated mainstream Christianity, and how it is especially being promoted by the rich and famous from the Movie and Music Industries!

---

[50]*Encyclopaedia Judaica*, Vol. 16, p. 1047.
[51]*Ibid.*, p. 1047.

CHAPTER III

THE NEW WORLD ORDER AND THE PROMOTION OF METAPHYSICS

"There shall not be found among you any one that maketh his son or his daughter to pass through the fire, or that useth divination, or an observer of times, or an enchanter, or a witch,

"Or a charmer, or a consulter with familiar spirits, or a wizard, or a necromancer.

"For all that do these things are an abomination unto the Lord: and because of these abominations the Lord thy God doth drive them out from before thee."
Deuteronomy 18:10–12

The Real Truth About UFO's and the New World Order

"And I saw three unclean spirits like frogs come out of the mouth of the dragon, and out of the mouth of the beast, and out of the mouth of the false prophet. For they are the spirits of devils, working miracles, which go forth unto the kings of the earth and of the whole world, to gather them to the battle of that great day of God Almighty." Revelation 16:13, 14.

Jesus warned through the apostle John that **three general movements of devils** would unite humans into the ranks of modern Spiritualism. These demons have appeared to humans in many different forms among initiates of this so-called cosmic light. Believe it or not, demons do appear as ancient Hindu gods, Pan, or devas to these people.

Many times in my experience I have come face to face with those who have been learning forbidden knowledge of witchcraft. These people generally have been in their early 20s to 40s, very intelligent and attractive, and seemingly levelheaded people, not at all like the witch of Endor. It has also been my observation to learn that many of these intelligent human beings caught in the snare of the Devil have believed the whole time that the mysterious power to perform supernatural wonders which they had been diligently seeking was the power of God, not the power of Satan.

Today, there are two mainstreams found among the people of the occult. This was not heard of in ancient witchcraft which deceived the Israelites down through their history. Today, the two mainstreams which divide the people of the occult are known as **white magic** and **black magic**.

As I showed in my last book, the people of the occult that practice white and black magic distinguish themselves by displaying their symbols. While white magic uses the pentagram star with one point up to represent them, the reverse pentagram that Anton LaVey displays with its two points up represents black magic or Satanism. They do not worship Satan in white magic, they say. **They do not believe Satan exists**. They are taught by their prophets or through books they have written to worship the forces of nature and a mother goddess. Satanists worship themselves.

In *The St. Petersburg Times* newspaper, October 30, 1990, was displayed a photograph of young witches practicing their craft. Generally,

The NWO and the PROMOTION of METAPHYSICS

witches congregate under trees in the forest at night to worship their gods. In this article of *The St. Petersburg Times*, it said a feud over witchcraft went public in Pasco County, Florida, in the summer of 1990. A witchcraft church, or coven, by the name of Coven Lothlorien sued four New Port Richey residents, accusing them of disrupting a June 17, 1990, ritual.

In the **civil lawsuit**, the Coven Lothlorien accused the four New Port Richey, Florida, residents of trespassing, destroying religious artifacts, and disrupting ceremonies they were holding at night on June 17, 1990. The residents were quoted as saying that the coven held animal sacrifices and worshipped Satan. Later, the same residents told *The St. Petersburg Times* that their accusations were exaggerated, and that their only complaint was that the witches were noisy late at night.

These little covens can be found everywhere. They are divided into little splinter groups with each coven generally consisting of **13 members or less**. Some covens include men and women while others only allow women. The general name of this worldwide revival of pagan abominations is known as **Wicca**. They claim their religion was before Christianity ever came into history. Therefore, they argue, it is older and more credible.

Just like Christianity is divided into many various denominational sects and has a diversity of beliefs, so is Wicca divided into many different covens and has a diversity of beliefs. Today, in the United States alone, there are multitudes who belong or identify with Wicca, which is an old English name that simply means witch. Two-thirds of the followers of Wicca, however, are women who have had bad marriages or have been disappointed with mainstream Christianity.

Wicca is a pagan European religion akin to both the ancient **Druids** who believe that Stonehenge was built by the Atlanteans. They have the doctrine of reincarnation and their goal is to become one with divinity by attaining personal perfection. Their expressions of reverence for nature with its focus on the changing seasons, the elements of the environment, and the movements of the sun, moon, and stars lead these nature worshippers to Baal instead of Jesus who created all things.

Nevertheless, Diane Stein, the author of the book, *The Women's Spirituality Book*, and **who is a witch herself**, says the goal of her

The Real Truth About UFO's and the New World Order

practice of Wicca is the empowerment of women.[1]

Wicca is also a **feminist spiritual trap** to entangle women who have been badly abused by men or resent men or have had bad experiences in Christian faiths. Besides the **pentagram star**, their primary symbol of Wicca is a **mother goddess**. While Christianity's Author and Finisher of the faith is Jesus, a masculine deity, in Wicca witchcraft they prefer to worship a more feminine deity, a mother goddess, who has both male and female attributes.[2]

In Wiccan circles, Laurie Cabot is considered a high priestess and leader of the religion. I saw her on a talk show a few years back around Halloween, dressed in her black robe, with her wild mane of teased black hair, exaggerated makeup, and silver jewelry. Halloween, by the way, is one of the most sacred festivals of Wicca for October 31 is Holy-Eve. October 31 is New Year's Eve to witches. They begin their year on **November 1 as do the merchants** of the earth, along with world governments.

Witches believe that the deceased relatives revisit them on October 31 or Halloween, which means Holy-Eve. Like their Baal worshipping ancient brethren before them, pagans believe that they are obligated to feed the wandering spirits of the dead. If they do not, something bad may happen. This is the **origin of Trick or Treat** which mainstream Christians **ignorantly teach** their little ones to do as they dress up as ghosts, skeletons, goblins, etc.

Around Halloween, Laurie Cabot and others like her take advantage of the Halloween tradition and try to gain sympathy for their cause by appearing on television and radio talk shows and being interviewed by newspaper reporters, etc. Laurie Cabot tries to promote a better image of witches today. Wicca witches complain that they are victims of thousands of years of bad PR. How would you feel, they say, if you had to hide your Star of David or your cross under your shirt or if you were constantly portrayed in the media as a green-faced, wart-encrusted nosed old woman? Laurie Cabot says they have no Devil or Satan in their religion. Wicca is often associated with Satanism, and Wicca followers are protesting that their religious and human rights have been violated.

[1]*The St. Petersburg Times*, **October 30, 1990.**
[2]*The Boston Herald*, **Massachusetts, October 27, 1991.**

The NWO and the PROMOTION of METAPHYSICS

They point out that the witch trials of Salem, Massachusetts (which Salem became noted for), because of the court system of that day and the hysteria of that day by Christians, actually did not execute witches, but ended up executing people who were not witches.

Witches in the past were afraid to come out publicly and admit to being a witch for fear of public ridicule and harm of losing their jobs. However, Kerry Ruane, daughter of Mike Ruane, Salem's state representative when the following article was written, says she is not worried about being publicly identified as a witch. She told *The Boston Herald*, October 27, 1991, "I've worn my pentacle outside for years. It's something I've always proudly displayed."

Dave Condren, news religion reporter, in *The Buffalo News*, May 18, 1991, stated, "High priestess among host of participants at interfaith forum."

Tamarra James, a high priestess of the Wiccan Church of Canada (like Laurie Cabot and King Ahab's wife), is determined to make witchcraft acceptable to the general public. According to *The Buffalo News*, May 18, 1991, Tamarra James attended the first conference of the North Atlantic Region Interfaith Forum held at Buffalo's Hyatt Regency. Most participants were leaders of **Interfaith organizations**, theologians, and speakers representing 12 world religions. We will investigate more about these Interfaith movements later.

According to *The Buffalo News*, May 18, 1991, Tamarra James was not on the roster of participants to speak in behalf of Wicca during the Interfaith Forum. In addition, Wicca was not represented officially at the Interfaith Forum. It states that Tamarra James demanded a voice which was granted.

At the Interfaith Forum, Tamarra James explained how Wicca is trying to undo several hundred years of bad press and how the public mistakenly confuse Wiccans with Satanists. She said Wicca does not have a saviour or a dammer; it is a pagan European religion akin to Native American Indians spiritually. She went on to say it has numerous gods and goddesses, believes in reincarnation, and the Wiccan Church of Canada has about 500 members.

According to the article, *Witches, the Real Story*, by Diane Mason seen in *The St. Petersburg Times*, October 30, 1990, Wiccans say they trace their roots to a time long before the advent of Christianity,

The Real Truth About UFO's and the New World Order

and they take their inspiration from mythology, folklore, and ancient rituals of goddess worship. The goddess, symbolized by the moon, is, according to Diane Mason writing positively about Wicca, "the essence and source of all life and nature." Mason goes on to say that this pagan religion also includes the worship of the **horned god of animals (PAN).**

In Isaiah 13:21, it foretold that **satyrs** dance at the ruins of ancient Babylon. In ancient mythology, satyrs are often pictured as being **part man and part goat** and usually having horns and a hairy body. Again, they are really Satan's angels. Those who have been initiated in cosmic light claim to be able to see them and converse with them.

Sometimes, Satan or his angels will appear in a human form and appear to his subjects as a Mahatma or as an angel as he did when he appeared to Jesus in Matthew, Chapter Four. **Those who have been baptized into the religion of God have the promise of protection from such things.**

However, both in white and black magic, **Pan is the god of nature, music, sex, and revelry**. Pan, according to *Mythology of All Races*, Volume 1, page 195, was the son of Hermes. In *The Houston Chronicle*, Sunday, July 28, 1996, the article *Some Unitarians Aren't Moonstruck with Pagans' Beliefs* written by Richard Stewart was seen. **Unitarians are an Interfaith denomination** whose membership is made up of people from different religious faiths and backgrounds such as Christianity, Judaism, Buddhism, paganism, and humanism. In the 18th century, the Unitarians were the Deists of Europe who were foremost in promoting this Atlantean Plan. However, today, Richard Stewart brought out in his article how Unitarians pride themselves on religious tolerance, but a schism within the Spindletop Unitarian Church in Beaumont, Texas, **over the worship of Pan** has developed. Pagan worshippers of Pan who are **members** of the above church "meet at the changing of the moon to pay homage to nature and a host of harvest, fertility, and other gods. They sprinkle fairy dust and dance around a campfire surrounded by a terra cotta statuette of the Greek god Pan, a ceramic fairy that looks like Tinker Bell, and an Oriental wise man cast in concrete."

Richard Stewart goes on to say, "The pagans said they were fairies and could change their shapes into animals." Michael Thompson,

The NWO and the PROMOTION of METAPHYSICS

the pastor of the above church can be quoted as saying, **"It's perfectly legal and within the structure of the Unitarian Universalist religion."**

Again, the reader may have chuckled upon reading this as well. However, New Agers claim they can see fairies a.k.a. devas in their vegetable gardens helping them grow their produce. The Hopi Indians call them **kachinas**, and the Navajos call them **yeis**. Some Christians call them **elves or leprechauns**. New Agers call them **devas**.

Reader, just to show how dangerous this religion of Jezebel is gaining more and more ground in the United States, I would like to bring out a couple of more appalling things that Diane Mason's article in *The St. Petersburg Times*, October 30, 1990, brought out. "Pagans are, for the lack of a better term, nature worshippers. They consider the earth sacred," says Tony Guagliardo, a former Catholic priest and chaplain for the Air Force. Tony Guagliardo also says in this article that they do not worship Satan, but Wiccans "can take every teaching of Jesus and apply it to their religion and make it wonderful and good."

When the news broke about Nancy Reagan's involvement in the occult, she simply said, according to *People Weekly*, May 23, 1988, on page 113: **"She has never stopped her perfectly harmless pastime of seeking guidance in the stars and has no plans to."**

It is the Dragon's plan to unite all humans **under one banner** which is **Spiritualism**. Satan or his agents appear to their human contactees who learned how to invoke them as benevolent aliens or Mahatmas (teachers) who claim not to be spirits, but rather highly evolved living men who have reached **Christ consciousness** and are sent to guide humans into a New Age and a new religion.

Among New Agers, **Jesus** is thought of as being **one** of these great Mahatmas, as is Buddha, Krishna, Muhammad, and this coming Maitreya. Billions of dollars are spent by the ignorant of Scripture to pay people (psychics) to help them contact these so-called spirit guides, or how they can invoke them themselves. We will study into the history of such schools shortly.

However, King Saul of Israel lost not only his life for seeking advice from an ancient astrologer, the "witch of Endor," but he lost his chance to be forgiven of sin and raised again to see the salvation of the Lord. He ended up committing suicide.

The Real Truth About UFO's and the New World Order

"So Saul died for his transgression which he committed against the Lord, even against the word of the Lord, which he kept not, and also for asking counsel of **ONE THAT HAD A FAMILIAR SPIRIT**, to inquire of it;

"And inquired not of the Lord: therefore he slew him, and turned the kingdom unto David the son of Jesse." 1 Chronicles 10:13, 14.

So will it be with us, today, if we connect ourselves with modern-day witches of Endor. However, Tanya Beck, an Episcopal priest at St. John's Episcopal Church in Clearwater, Florida, shockingly said in the same article written by Diane Mason in *The St. Petersburg Times*, October 30, 1990, "She thinks it is possible for Christians to embrace the idea of God as having both a male and a female essence, a view she personally holds. But, she regards God not as a force 'up there...but a very personal God, a god of community.'" In her weekly services, Tanya Beck uses the hands-on healing techniques and speaks of father/mother god during her sermons. Tanya Beck, who claims to be a preacher of the Gospel of Jesus Christ, can be quoted as saying, **"The witchy stuff is biblical. This is what Christ did; this is what Ghandi did."**

Another spiritual feminist, who is a professed witch and belongs to the Coven Avalon in Clearwater, Florida, says she was raised in a Christian family. She questioned, "How could people talk about our Father which art in Heaven" without wondering, if we have a Father who art in Heaven, surely we must "also have a Mother." Hence, this is the reason for the term **Mother Earth and Father Sky** used so often to get across the New Age environment programs which are being promoted by the United Nations. New Agers teach that God is both male and female. Spiritual feminists, of course, are drawn to the female aspect of their divine rulers rather than the male. Ancient Egyptians worshipped their divine beings as Sirius, the double star, which was, as I pointed out, Isis and Osiris.

Let's look again at this mysterious eight-pointed star Sirius and see how both New Agers and Roman Catholics are, indeed, **finding common ground so in the very near future they can fuse together**.

My New Age readers, as you know, modern shamans claim to have received their knowledge about the occult from this silver star Sirius. They claim this knowledge was given to them by their ascended

The NWO and the PROMOTION of METAPHYSICS

masters of the Great White Brotherhood located on this stellar star. They proudly say that the recent discovery of this stellar star proves that they have been receiving telepathic messages from these gods, a.k.a. UFO's a.k.a. ascended masters, for they boast, "How did ancient shamans from all over the world know about this star for centuries before it was recently discovered?" It was because their ancient brethren saw it when it used to appear 3,000 or 4,000 years ago and then handed this fable down through the centuries to their modern brethren in their writings. The origin of the gods being once men began in the fable about Nimrod and Semiramis, his wife and mother, who were deified and worshipped as Beltus and Beltis, Tammuz and Ishtar, or as Shamash and Inanna, etc., etc. When this Babylonian religion, symbolized in the book of Revelation as a red Dragon, made its way to Egypt, Ishtar became Isis, Nimrod became Osiris, and Tammuz their god-child became Horus. Fallen angels have personated them.

All religions based in star worship originated from Babylon. This is why the various religions of astrology are called Babylon the Great, the Mother of Harlots and the abominations of the earth (Revelation 17:5), for all the religions outside of the worship of the God of Abraham, Isaac, and Jacob have their roots in these fables.

Now, this mother goddess, this Queen of Heaven, has made her worship to be practiced and perpetuated by the Roman Catholics. Mary, the mother of Jesus who is in her grave resting until the first resurrection, has been **swapped to take the place of Isis, Ishtar, Diana, etc., etc**. No? Well, let's see the facts.

To the New Ager, Sirius is the emblem of the mother goddess who was Isis to the Egyptians. However, according to *The Encyclopedia of World Mythology*, p. 123, *Larousse World Mythology*, p. 67, and *The Compleat Astrologer*, p. 13, this double silver star represented the goddess Ishtar (Inanna), the **Queen of Heaven**, and most powerful goddess to the pagan ancient Mesopotamian peoples. The eight-pointed star was used to invoke this good/evil beautiful goddess of sex and fertility who would cause **fear** to come upon her subjects **if not venerated** and **honored** by causing natural calamities or wars. When this worship of the Queen of Heaven made its debut in ancient Egypt and developed into the worship of Isis, she became

The Real Truth About UFO's and the New World Order

the most powerful goddess of the Egyptian pantheon of goddesses who also had good/evil attributes. Isis became the **Patroness of the Sea**, and many of sea-faring men have seen her **emblem** on their maps as shown on the front cover of this volume.

According to Sir James Frazer in his book, *Adonis Attis Osiris*, page 34, this double star was seen by the ancient shamans, New Agers, once a year during the summer solistice between July 16–22 depending on where the worshipper lived in Egypt about 3,000 or 4,000 years ago. As pointed out, it has **disappeared** in our solar system as far as being able to see it with the naked eye; but, when it appeared it was the brightest star in the night skies, and it is about twice the size of the sun. It is now about 8.7 light years away from planet Earth.[3]

According to *The New Columbia Encyclopedia*, page 2528, Sirius has been **rediscovered** and **observed** by modern astronomers, and it is located in the constellation Canis Major. The star behind Sirius who was worshipped as Osiris was also confirmed by observation. The Egyptians worshipped the bright star in front as Isis and the lesser lighted star behind as Osiris. However, to the ancient Babylonians it was Shamash and Ishtar (Inanna), etc.

My Christian Catholic reader, have you ever taken the time to study the similarities of the **personalities** and **characters** found in the epics of the worship of the Egyptian goddess Isis and that of the papal Virgin? What was Isis' symbol? It was the stellar star Sirius, the double star. What is one of the symbols that your church so commonly uses to symbolize Mary? It is the **Stellar Maris** which is the same eight-pointed star that your religious leaders, according to the book, *La Popessa*, on page 81, call a retreat house in the Swiss Alps by a religious order of the Sisters of the Holy Cross. Are you aware that this Stellar Maris symbol which is actually Sirius, the emblem of the Egyptian Isis, is also known in Catholic religious circles as the Star of the Sea and, like Isis to the Egyptians, Mary is exalted as the Patroness of the Sea? This knowledge about Sirius was lost in history after the double star stopped appearing in the East about 3,000 or 4,000 years ago. This is why some occultists are confused about Venus being the emblem of their goddess, which is sometimes the pentagram, because

---

[3]*The New Columbia Encyclopedia*, **Harris/Levey, p. 2528.**

The NWO and the PROMOTION of METAPHYSICS

the planet Venus eventually took the place of Sirius after the double star stopped appearing once a year in the East during the summer solistice. Today, this eight-pointed star Sirius has been adopted by the Catholic Church and has angered pagan New Age feminists because they know it was originally the emblem of their mother goddess.

My Christian Catholic brethren, did you know that the pagan **Queen of Heaven** warned about in Jeremiah 18:17–19 also had in Babylon a clergy of priestesses called **NUNS** before the Roman Catholic Church came into history? Are you aware that one of the exalted titles in ancient Babylon for Ishtar or Inanna of whom Buddhists and Hindus had their own version of was known as the Queen of Heaven? What does the Papacy call the Virgin Mary? The Queen of Heaven! Did you read the cover story in *Time* magazine, December 30, 1991, starting on page 62, why more and more people around the world are worshipping Mary and about the blasphemous exaltation given to this idol today? I will quote from page 62 their incredible words:

"Among Roman Catholics, the Madonna is recognized not only as the **Mother of God** but also, according to modern Popes, as the **Queen of the Universe, Queen of Heaven, Seat of Wisdom, and EVEN THE SPOUSE OF THE HOLY SPIRIT**."

Another attribute found in the worship of this idol called Mary today in the Catholic Church, which proves its real identity and is nothing less than that demon worship of the old pagan goddess Ishtar or Isis idol, is her **seemingly warm and loving character** which Isis was noted for **but could change suddenly if not venerated and honored** among her subjects! Ishtar was both a goddess of fertility and of war and would use her powers in the myth to cause violent storms or terrible wars.

What about the message of Fatima and what took place there? Is this not a repeat of what these ancient goddessess did to their subjects written in their myths? Did not the Virgin Mary prophesy when she supposedly appeared at Fatima and made the sun to spin in the sky to show her power over nature? Did she not prophesy at Fatima on October 13, 1917, according to Roman Catholic sources, that if the hierarchy of the Roman Catholic Church **did not publicly consecrate her before the world to Russia that Russia would cause a great scourge on the world and the faith of the Catholic Church would**

The Real Truth About UFO's and the New World Order

suffer a spiritual decline?[4] However, because John Paul II obeyed the voice of Mary which the previous popes before him ignored, the fall of Communism in 1989 supposedly came. *Time* magazine, page 65, states again: "The world will recognize in due time that the defeat of Communism came at the **intercession of the mother of Jesus**."

The world may believe this, but those who know their Bibles know that these gods of the New Age Movement and that of the Virgin Mary are **devils personating them** and working miracles as it was foretold by the apostle Paul in 1 Timothy 4:1: "Now the Spirit speaketh expressly, that in the latter times some shall depart from the faith, giving heed to seducing spirits and doctrines of devils."

Another pagan custom similar to what the Israelites were deceived into practicing, which led them to give heed to seducing spirits which were personating gods of astrology and promoted through their human agents these doctrines of devils, is the custom of honoring gods and humans **BY MAKING CAKES**. Spiritual feminists in Jeremiah's day who preferred to worship the Queen of Heaven rather than a male Deity said: "Did we make her **CAKES** to worship her, and pour out drink offerings unto her, without our men?" Jeremiah 44:19. This pagan practice was strikingly condemned by God, but, like the ancient Israelites, this custom is socially accepted among modern Christians today.

According to *The Standard Dictionary of Folklore, Mythology, and Legend*, Vol. 1, page 181, the pagan custom of making cakes to honor the gods and humans was a very common custom as it is today. To feed the dead, the Hindus placed cakes beside the corpses upon which were piled boiled rice, sugar, and ghi (melted butter). The Veddas of Ceylon also fed their demon god Siva by means of rice cakes, while in Japan they honored their gods with two flattened spherical cakes and laid them on their shrine – a male cake to represent the sun and a female cake to represent the moon. Cakes of various shapes were used in Greece as sacrificial and propitiatory offerings to Helios in the form of arrows or of girls; to Artemis cakes and honey were placed as an offering, while for Zeus in Athens they used barley cakes in the mysteries of the Eleusinians. In Athens in a ritual called the "Supper of

---

[4]*The Keys of This Blood*, Martin, pp. 47–54.

The NWO and the PROMOTION of METAPHYSICS

Hecate," circular cakes topped with candles were placed at crossroads by the rich at the time of a new or full moon.

Cakes were also given away by pagans at the New Year or used as a magical means to drive evil away. Just as those who worship the Lord of the Sabbath pray to Him for protection from evil, so do pagans pray to their gods for protection against evil gods or evil spirits. However, to show their deities that they are their children, they would either wear the symbol of their god on them or display it on their houses, temples, boundary stones, etc., and it was also placed on their cakes. Did you ever wonder where the origin of making the white, circular cakes with candles came from?

A textbook used in schools to teach our children these things is allowed; but if a Christian teacher began to show from the Bible in schools that these customs are forbidden by the Lord, he or she could suffer some kind of punishment. It is against the law to teach from the Bible and to pray in the name of Jesus, but it is perfectly legal to promote the worship of Zeus or Isis to our children because mythology is not looked upon as a religion.

According to *Child Craft, The How and Why Library*, Vol. 9, page 12, it says the following: "For thousands of years, people all over the world have thought of a **birthday** as a very special day. Long ago, people could be helped by good spirits or hurt by evil spirits. So, when a person had a birthday, friends and relatives gathered to protect him or her. **And that's how birthday parties began**.

"The idea of putting candles on birthday cakes goes back to ancient Greece. The Greeks worshipped many gods and goddesses. Among them was one called Artemis (Ahr tuh mihs).

"Artemis was the **goddess of the moon**. The Greeks celebrated her birthday once each month by bringing special cakes to her temple. **The cakes were round, like a full moon, and because the moon glows with light, the cakes were decorated with lighted candles**."

The Hebrew prophet Jeremiah wrote how there were spiritual feminists among the Jewish women of history who were worshipping a pagan mother goddess whose name was Ashtoreth to the Jews, but to the Egyptians it was Isis. To honor this pagan moon goddess, these women would make her cakes. (See Jeremiah 44:19.)

The Real Truth About UFO's and the New World Order

During my years of research into finding the origin and cause of ancient Israel's apostasy from our Lord, **for "all these things happened unto them for ensamples: and they are written for OUR admonition"** (1 Cor. 10:11), I have discovered other doctrines of devils concerning the sacred cakes which have their origin in the abominations found in the ancient religion of astrology. As pointed out in Volume One, *Beware It's Coming – The Antichrist 666*, cakes were made by Babylonian women to not only honor their goddess Ishtar, but also her pagan son who was the messiah of not only the ancient Babylonians, but also to the Israelites. However, as these doctrines of devils slowly blended into the culture and religion of the Jews, Satan was able eventually to **swap** the hope of a coming Deliverer and Saviour promised as was foretold in the Holy Scriptures for Tammuz, the god of fire and vegetation. "Then he brought me to the door of the gate of the Lord's house which was toward the north; and, behold, there sat women weeping for Tammuz." Ezekiel 8:14.

The word *"antichrist"* means *"instead of Christ."* The great red Dragon has constantly tried to rid the world of the religion of Christ by **counterfeiting** the precepts of God or by **swapping** his false doctrines for doctrines which were written in the Scriptures or by **blending both** which is an **abomination** unto the God of Abraham, Isaac, and Jacob. Here in Ezekiel 8:14, it states that these Israelites were worshipping Tammuz at the gate of the Lord's house!

The Israelites were instructed by their apostate religious leaders, who mixed the religion of astrology with the religion of God, to weep for the return of Tammuz who annually, as this myth teaches, died in the fall and would resurrect in the spring. These cakes were round to symbolize the moon goddess and a cross (tau) was drawn to represent the first letter of Tammuz, which became the sacred symbol of fertility to the Egyptians known as the Ankh. These cakes are very popular among the Roman Catholic women today. These same cakes have just been given a different name. These sacred cakes are called today **Hot Cross Buns**!

Here from *The MaryKnoll Catholic Dictionary* on page 278, we read the following:

"Hot Cross Buns: Small buns decorated with a glazed sugar cross and eaten on Ash Wednesday and Good Friday. It is not known how the custom arose although it is of fairly recent origin."

The NWO and the PROMOTION of METAPHYSICS

If the Catholic writers would study the Scriptures instead of Catechism, he or she would find the origin of not only the hot cross buns they use at Easter, but also of the wafer (cake) they use with **IHS** inscribed on it while practicing the sacrament of their mass. Why do Catholics **face the east** early on Sunday morning and hold **Sunrise Services** as their Protestant brethren do on the most holy day of the pagan religion of astrology – **Easter** – of which both ancient and modern pagans celebrate at the vernal equinox. Do not Christians during their celebration of Easter face the east as the sun rises? This was an abomination to the Lord when the ancient Israelites adopted this pagan festival.

"He said also unto me, Turn thee yet again, and thou shalt see **greater abominations** that they do. Then he brought me to the door of the gate of the Lord's house which was toward the north; and, behold, there sat **women weeping for Tammuz**.

"And he brought me into the inner court of the Lord's house, and, behold, at the door of the temple of the Lord, between the porch and the altar, were about five and twenty men, with their backs toward the temple of the Lord, and **their faces toward the east; and they worshipped the sun toward the east.**" Ezekiel 8:13, 14, 16.

It is very eye-opening, indeed, to learn that New Agers who worship their space goddess Isis or Diana also today make cakes to honor her. A New Age center, the Wainwright House which is located in Rye, New York, claims it is a Judeo-Christian non-sectarian educational organization and sends out invitations to join them in celebrating the changing of the seasons in ceremonies which honor this goddess.[5] They celebrate the divine as equally female and male and, according to the *Wainwright House Fall/Winter 1990 Guide*, on page 32, Evaleon Hill is teaching a course called *Cakes for the Queen of Heaven*.

Volume Five of this series of reference books on Time of the End events studies in-depthly into these pagan doctrines plus a lot more including the arguments Protestants give in trying to justify their continued disobedience to the Fourth Commandment of the Ten Commandments of which some pastors in their ignorance of Scripture say were done away with.

---

[5]*Wainwright House Fall/Winter 1990 Guide*, p. 10.

The Real Truth About UFO's and the New World Order

Volume One, *Beware It's Coming – The Antichrist 666*, I wrote especially for Roman Catholics to help them see what happened down through the history of their church. It shows how the sacrifices and religion of Isis, which was Ashtaroth to the Israelites, became the religion of Mary. It shows how the sacrifices and religion regarding the pagan messiah Tammuz, who was Molech to the Ammonites, became confused with the religion of Jesus. The pagan customs and symbols are the same; only the faces of the gods were changed to Jesus and Mary. This is why, New Ager, many of the women of Wicca witchcraft are jealous and outraged at the Catholic Church in their promotion of the worship of Mary with her star, the Stellar Maris (Sirius), dangling from her graven image because pagan New Age women know that the worship of the Virgin Mary is really Isis their **space mother** and that the Catholics **stole their goddess from them**. Therefore, they say their religion is more credible because it was in existence before Christianity. This is true, but the worship of both of them, my Catholic and New Age reader, is an abomination unto the Lord, and so are the gold and silver ornaments (jewelry) that originally symbolized the sun and the moon to invoke the gods of which both Christians and New Agers bravely wear today. The God of Abraham, Isaac, and Jacob calls this confusion of the people of Spiritualism, the Catholic Church, and the Protestant Church – Babylon the Great.

"Her priests have violated my law, and have **profaned** mine holy things: they have put **no difference between the holy and profane**, neither have they shewed difference between the unclean and the clean, and have **hid their eyes from my sabbaths**, and I am profaned among them." Ezekiel 22:26.

"Woe be unto the **pastors** that **destroy** and **scatter** the **sheep** of my **pasture**! saith the Lord. Therefore thus saith the Lord God of Israel against the pastors that feed my people; Ye have scattered my flock, and driven them away, and have not visited them: behold, I will visit upon you the evil of your doings, saith the Lord. And I will gather the remnant of my flock out of all countries whither I have driven them, and will bring them again to their folds; and they shall be fruitful and increase.... For the land is full of adulterers; for because of swearing the land mourneth; the pleasant places of the wilderness are dried up, and their course is evil, and their force is not right. For both prophet

The NWO and the PROMOTION of METAPHYSICS

and priest are profane; yea, in my house have I found their wickedness, saith the Lord. Wherefore their way shall be unto them as slippery ways in the darkness: they shall be driven on, and fall therein: for I will bring evil upon them, even the year of their visitation, saith the Lord…. The anger of the Lord shall not return, until he have executed, and till he have performed the thoughts of his heart: **IN THE LATTER DAYS YE SHALL CONSIDER IT PERFECTLY**." Jeremiah 23:1–3, 10–12, 20.

"For the wrath of God is revealed from heaven against all ungodliness and unrighteousness of men, who hold the truth in unrighteousness; Because that which may be known of God is manifest in them; for God hath shewed it unto them. For the invisible things of him from the creation of the world are clearly seen, being understood by the things that are made, even his eternal power and Godhead; so that they are without excuse: Because that, when they knew God, they glorified him not as God, neither were thankful; but became vain in their imaginations, and their foolish heart was darkened. Professing themselves to be wise, they became fools, And changed the glory of the uncorruptible God into an image made like to corruptible man, and to birds, and fourfooted beasts, and creeping things. Wherefore God also gave them up to uncleanness through the lusts of their own hearts, to dishonour their own bodies between themselves: Who changed the truth of God into a lie, and worshipped and served the creature more than the Creator, who is blessed forever. Amen. For this cause God gave them up unto vile affections: for even their women did change the natural use into that which is against nature: And likewise also the men, leaving the natural use of the woman, burned in their lust one toward another; men with men working that which is unseemly, and receiving in themselves that recompence of their error which was meet." Romans 1:18–27

"Know ye not that the unrighteous shall not inherit the kingdom of God? Be not deceived: neither fornicators, nor idolaters, nor adulterers, nor effeminate, nor abusers of themselves with mankind, Nor thieves, nor covetous, nor drunkards, nor revilers, nor extortioners, shall inherit the kingdom of God." 1 Corinthians 6:9–10.

One of the last messages that the God of Abraham is sending to those who are wrapped up in the false religions of this world is to

The Real Truth About UFO's and the New World Order

turn themselves from the religion of the Dragon (astrology) and their sins, "and worship him that made heaven, and earth, and the sea, and the fountains of waters." Revelation 14:7.

This worship of the mother goddess, the papal Madonna, certainly does trace back before the birth of Jesus. The pagan mother goddess worship can be traced to Semiramis, the wife of Nimrod. As pointed out, this pagan goddess, commonly worshipped today by Wiccans as Diana or Isis, was worshipped and adorned by the ancient Israelite women as Ashtaroth when they rejected the Word of God and fell victim to this lie of Lucifer's (Satan's). The ancient Israelites worshipped the mother goddess Ashtaroth as the "*Queen of Heaven*," says the prophet of God, Jeremiah.

The prophet tried to show the ignorance of these Israelitish women in worshipping the moon, the symbol of this so-called queen of heaven, and the attempt to blend the mother goddess Ashtaroth with the worship of the God of Israel. Subsequently, later the Lord punished Israel by allowing King Nebuchadnezzar to come and destroy Jerusalem and its magnificent temple. Jeremiah tried to reason with them, but this is why the survivors of the destruction of Jerusalem were led to enslavement by the Babylonians for 70 years. After warning the Israelite women not to blend the worship of God with paganism, the Israelite women said:

"But we will certainly do whatsoever thing goeth forth out of our own mouth, to burn incense unto the **queen of heaven**, and to pour out drink offerings unto her, as we have done, we, and our fathers, our kings, and our princes, in the cities of Judah, and in the streets of Jerusalem: for then had we plenty of victuals, and were well, and saw no evil.

"But since we left off to burn incense to the queen of heaven, and to pour out drink offerings unto her, we have wanted all things, and have been consumed by the sword and by the famine. And when we burned incense to the queen of heaven, and poured out drink offerings unto her, did we make her **cakes to worship her**, and pour out drink offerings unto her, without our men?

"Then Jeremiah said unto all the people, to the men, and to all the women, and to all the people which had given him that answer, saying, The incense that ye burned in the cities of Judah, and in the

The NWO and the PROMOTION of METAPHYSICS

streets of Jerusalem, ye, and your fathers, your kings, and your princes, and the people of the land, did not the Lord remember them, and came it not into his mind?

"So that the Lord could no longer bear, because of the evil of your doings, and because of the abominations which ye have committed; therefore is your land a desolation, and an astonishment, and a curse, without an inhabitant, as at this day." Jeremiah 44:17–22.

In verse 17 of Jeremiah, Chapter 44, it is interesting to note that the reason why the Israelite women would not turn from their worship of the mother goddess was because when they worshipped this goddess "for then had we plenty of victuals (bread), and were well, and saw no evil."

As there are indeed blessings from God, so are there blessings from Satan. Satan will prosper some just to keep them under his power. There must be something good involved or his worshippers whom he uses to bring others to him would leave him.

The **prince of the power of the air** will extend blessings to those who diligently seek him through paganism, through which he hides himself and his wonder-working power. Feminists are especially vulnerable to being drawn into the deception of worshipping a pagan goddess. *The St. Petersburg Times* article, *Witches, the Real Story*, continues to record other words of another defender of Wicca, "Probably one of the most compelling reasons women are drawn to Wicca is to revolt against traditional religion, which offers only a male god figure," says Judith Ochshorn, believe it or not, a professor of women's studies at the University of South Florida. Ochshorn says, "Men have always mediated between women and God."

Spiritual feminists also lure women into Wicca by the seemingly wonder-working power of "cast a circle," a ritual. As established, our apostle Paul warned, "Now the Spirit speaketh expressly, that in the latter times some shall depart from the faith, giving heed to seducing spirits, and doctrines of devils." 1 Timothy 4:1.

These doctrines that the apostle of Jesus Christ said that many Christians would be lured into in these last days are clearly defined in Deuteronomy, Chapter 18.

Reader, I do not know how to write in words how serious it is that we understand the warnings God has given us in this chapter.

The Real Truth About UFO's and the New World Order

It has been over a quarter of a century now since I began to diligently search the Scriptures and history to learn for myself how to tell the difference between Christ and the Antichrist, so that not only I keep myself from falling for these traps of the Antichrist, but they of my own household as well!

I spent years in researching the Bible and comparing the horrible things that happened to the ancient Israelites once they departed from obeying the Word of God. After learning from the Scriptures and history as to what Spiritualism actually is, I discovered that modern Christians have been deceived by these same doctrines which are hidden in a Christian guise. Multitudes of sincere Christian writers, while claiming to be experts about the occult and pointing out the sins of witchcraft in the New Age Movement and the history of cults and who they are, are **often** found, as well, promoting doctrines that do not bear the **credentials of Heaven** but instead are found on the pages of Baal worship!

A diligent study of Deuteronomy, Chapter 18, will prove that this is so. However, before we take a spiritual journey through the Lord's Word in Deuteronomy, Chapter 18, we must know that "without faith it is impossible to please him; for he that cometh to God must believe that he is, and that **he is a rewarder of them that diligently seek him**." Hebrews 11:6.

Prayer, faith in God, and being diligent students of the Scriptures will bring a seeker great rewards!

"And ye shall seek me, and **find me**, when ye shall **search for me** with all your **heart**." Jeremiah 29:13.

"Believe in the Lord **your God**, so shall ye be established; believe his **prophets**, so shall ye prosper." 2 Chronicles 20:20.

Jesus said, "He that **believeth on me**, as the **scripture** hath said, out of his belly shall flow rivers of living water." John 7:38.

"For I will give you a **mouth** and **wisdom**, which all your adversaries shall not be able to gainsay nor resist." Luke 21:15.

The main reason ancient Israel fell victim into the most degrading lifestyle and religious beliefs which led to even sacrificing their own children to heathen gods was always caused by not knowing or obeying the Scriptures.

The NWO and the PROMOTION of METAPHYSICS

The main reason most Jews rejected Jesus of Nazareth as their Messiah was because of their ignorance of the Scriptures. Jesus told them that they did err, not knowing the Scriptures nor the power of God. "Why do ye not understand my speech? even because ye cannot hear my word…. He that is of God heareth God's words: ye therefore hear them not, because ye are not of God." John 8:43, 47.

"But unto you that fear my name shall the **Sun of righteousness** arise with healing in his wings; and ye shall go forth, and grow up as calves of the stall.

"And ye shall tread down the wicked; for they shall be ashes under the soles of your feet in the day that I shall do this, saith the Lord of hosts." Malachi 4:2, 3.

From the death of Joshua until the 70 years of captivity by the Babylonians ended, the ancient Israelites kept falling for the sins of the New Age Movement in their day. The New Age Movement was known back then as Baal worship. In the book of Judges we read:

"And also all that generation were gathered unto their fathers: and there arose another generation after them, which **knew not the Lord**, nor yet the works which he had done for Israel. And the children of Israel did evil in the sight of the Lord, and served Baalim.

"And they forsook the Lord God of their fathers, which brought them out of the land of Egypt, and followed other gods, of the gods of the people that were round about them, and bowed themselves unto them, and provoked the Lord to anger. And they forsook the Lord, and served **Baal** and **Ashtaroth**.

"And the anger of the Lord was hot against Israel, and he delivered them into the hands of spoilers that spoiled them, and he sold them into the hands of their enemies round about, so that they could not any longer stand before their enemies. Nevertheless the Lord raised up judges, which delivered them out of the hand of those that spoiled them." Judges 2:10–14, 16.

The Lord would raise up reformers to expose the deceptions of Spiritualism and cause a revival of primitive godliness to be seen again among the Israelites, but as soon as that reformer died the Israelites fell right back into following after the gods and practices of witchcraft. The ancient Israelites participated in the interfaith and ecumenical efforts to unite all of the world's religions in their day! They adopted and blended

The Real Truth About UFO's and the New World Order

precepts that had originated from ancient Hinduism and Babylonian astrology into the worship of the True God. The Lord removed out of northern Israel ten tribes and punished the two remaining tribes by allowing King Nebuchadnezzar to come and eventually take Judah and Benjamin, the two remaining tribes, to Babylon for seventy years. However, the Lord did this with a promise:

"For thus saith the Lord, That after seventy years be accomplished at Babylon I will visit you, and perform my good word toward you, in causing you to return to this place." Jeremiah 29:10.

If Roman Catholics and mainstream Protestants would become diligent Bible students instead of just surface readers, this Spirit of Antichrist that has them chained to the Dragon would be broken.

Here is the major reason both ancient Israel and mainstream Christians today have fallen for seducing spirits and doctrines of devils.

"The priests said not, Where is the Lord? and they that **handle the law knew me not**: the **pastors** also transgressed against me, and the **prophets prophesied by Baal**, and walked after things that do not profit." Jeremiah 2:8.

"Her priests have violated my law, and have profaned mine holy things: **THEY HAVE PUT NO DIFFERENCE** BETWEEN THE HOLY AND PROFANE, NEITHER HAVE THEY **SHEWED DIFFERENCE** BETWEEN THE UNCLEAN AND THE CLEAN, AND **HAVE HID THEIR EYES FROM MY SABBATHS**, AND **I AM PROFANED AMONG THEM**." Ezekiel 22:26.

The Israelites were warned soon after they came out of Egypt **to never** mingle the customs, fashions, festivals, or religions of the pagans with the holy things of God.

"And the Lord spake unto Moses, saying, Speak unto the children of Israel, and say unto them, I am the Lord your God. After the **doings** of the land of Egypt, wherein ye dwelt, **shall ye not do**: and after the **doings** of the land of Canaan, whither I bring you, shall ye not do: **neither shall ye walk in their ordinances**." Leviticus 18:1-3.

However, when the great leader Joshua died, the Israelites allowed their children to mingle with the pagan children, and the peer pressure to be in fashion, along with the heathen music, led them eventually to forsake the Lord.

The NWO and the PROMOTION of METAPHYSICS

"And the children of Israel dwelt among the Canaanites, Hittites, and Amorites, and Perizzites, and Hivites, and Jebusites: And they took their daughters to be their wives, and gave their daughters to their sons, and served their gods. And the children of Israel did evil in the sight of the Lord, and forgat the Lord their God, and served Baalim and the groves." Judges 3:5–7.

Satan, **little by little**, through his human agents **mingled** the unholy with the holy. The worship of Baal by the ancient Israelites did not come upon them all at once. But, little by little they began to apostatize. The Deceiver would bring in one doctrine of heathenism into the worship of God. Then, when another generation of Israelites rose up, Satan added more until the pure worship of God was eventually transformed into the degrading worship of Baal.

Now, it's time to learn from the Scriptures what New Age metaphysics actually is and how it is condemned by God.

"When thou art come into the land which the Lord thy God giveth thee, thou shalt not learn to do after the abominations of those nations.

"There shall not be found among you any one that maketh his son or his daughter to pass through the fire, or that useth **DIVINATION**, or an **OBSERVER OF TIMES**, or an **ENCHANTER**, or a **WITCH**, Or a **CHARMER**, or a **CONSULTER WITH FAMILIAR SPIRITS**, or a **WIZARD**, or a **NECROMANCER**.

"For all that do these things are an abomination unto the Lord: and because of these abominations the Lord thy God doth drive them out from before thee. Thou shalt be perfect with the Lord thy God. For these nations, which thou shalt possess, hearkened unto observers of times, and unto diviners: but as for thee, the Lord thy God hath not suffered thee so to do." Deuteronomy 18:9–14.

Reader, it is super important that we study from Scripture and history what each one of these sciences and practices were that the ancient Canaanites included in their daily life so we can intelligently see today how Satan is, indeed, making the people of the world follow into the same condemnation.

"There shall not be found among you any one that maketh his son or his daughter to pass through the fire." Deuteronomy 18:10.

The Real Truth About UFO's and the New World Order

Among the ancient and modern pagans today, fire is sacred. Why? It was and is sacred because the chief god of astrology is the sun. The sun being wrapped in fire is believed in pagan thought to be the origin of fire here on earth. Pagans believe everything originated from the sun-god. Therefore, the fire here on earth is sacred because it represents the sun-god's presence. Water is the symbol of the mother goddess to whom the spiritual feminist's movement of Wicca identify.

Just like Christians have baptism as a sacrament that must be observed, so do pagan sun worshippers. Ancient pagans would kindle a fire to baptize their infants and dedicate them to their sun-god. While one parent would stand on one side of the flames, the other would throw the infant across the flames with the opposite spouse catching the child. Older children, as well as adults, to show their zeal and power would walk across the burning flames. Today, Buddhist priests show their approval of their deities by walking across burning coals. To Eastern and Western pagan religions, **fire walking** is usually associated with rituals related to purification or transformation among New Agers.[6]

This has become very popular today as a pastime among some social circles. This passing through the fire was demonstrated right before millions of eyes of onlookers on Geraldo Rivera's talk show. Little did these people know that this is an abomination unto the Lord and could lure them to learn even worse things than the ancient Canaanites practiced.

As brought out before, Satan works little by little on those who are ignorant of the Scriptures. Lower and lower will he bring his victim until he has complete control of him. Solomon, the wisest man of all, did not see his spiritual fall as he descended lower and lower into Spiritualism's grip. Witchcraft, like drugs, will become addicting. Like the addiction of alcohol, smoking, gambling, and the impulsive shopper, they find it hard to stop. People who have been delivered by the power of God from witchcraft will testify that they experience a withdrawal as if they were coming off drugs.

When controlled by a false religious spirit, Satan can lead an individual or a whole nation to commit the most abominable practices known to man. This Israel did over and over again.

---

[6]*The New Age Encyclopedia*, Melton/Gordon, p. 175.

The NWO and the PROMOTION of METAPHYSICS

"He said also unto me, Turn thee yet again, and thou shalt see greater abominations that they do. Then he brought me to the door of the gate of the Lord's house which was toward the north; and, behold, there sat women weeping for **Tammuz**.

"Then said he unto me, Hast thou seen this, O son of man? turn thee yet again, and thou shalt see greater abominations than these. And he brought me into the inner court of the Lord's house, and, behold, at the door of the temple of the Lord, between the porch and the altar, were about five and twenty men, with their backs toward the temple of the Lord, and their faces toward the east; and they worshipped the sun toward the east." Ezekiel 8:13–16.

Tammuz is the god of fire to the people of the occult. He is worshipped as the god of vegetation and the bright and morning star, Venus. Tammuz, the messiah to ancient heathenism, is also known in modern heathenism as Krishna, Pan, Bacchus, Horus, or as we saw among some occultists today, Quetzalcoatl.

The apostate Israelites were deceived into believing that if they sacrificed their **first-born child** to Baal, Ashtoreth, and Tammuz, this would cause their crops to grow or ensure fertility. Placing wood on the ground in the shape of a "T" to represent Tammuz, the Israelites then burned up the wood with their first-born on it. Then, after the child was consumed, they would take the ashes of the infant and throw its ashes on their gardens to ensure fertility!

You say, how could people do such a thing? As brought out before, they were led to do this **little by little** by getting more and more involved into the degrading practices of occultism. Their minds became conditioned to be able to commit such atrocities. Such is the case of some of our citizens today! In *The Evansville Courier and Press*, Indiana, April 8, 1990, the following appeared: "**Officials in Western Kentucky** won't discuss how many residents they believe to be involved in Satanic worship. 'I can't give you exact figures because **it could cause the public to panic**,' said Charles Prichard of the Kentucky State Police. 'It's best to just say it's here and seems to be growing.' "

This article found in *The Evansville Courier and Press* of April 8, 1990, written by Kim Husk seven years before the terrible tragedy at the Paducah, Kentucky, High School, warns:

"The right to practice nonconventional religions – including

The Real Truth About UFO's and the New World Order

Satanism – is protected by the First Amendment, police say. However, the nature of the religion and the rituals associated with it raise concern among law enforcement agencies across the nation.

" 'There has been an increase in the number interested in cults and the occult here in this area,' Prichard said. What we have as a problem in our area are 'the dabblers.' They get interested in the occult and form smaller cults of 10–15. They get a copy of the Satanic Bible, which can be picked up in a number of bookstores in Kentucky. They read it and then interpret it for themselves. They make up their own rules. That's what makes it so dangerous.

"A person may **gain interest in the occult** through involvement in **fantasy games** and **music** and **clothing that glorifies Satan** or the darker side of life, such as suicide, Rice said. Police generally define self-styled worshippers or 'dabblers' as possibly having an interest in **occult books, animal mutilation**, and **self-mutilation.** They also may incorporate **sexual acts** and the use of **hallucinogenic drugs** into their rituals, police say."

In *The Tampa Tribune*, October 31, 1988, it is stated, "*Satanism – More Than One Million People Involved.*" The article, compiled and written by Karen Haymon, warns that the 1987 issue of *National Sheriff*, a law enforcement magazine, said back in 1985 it was estimated that there were 1.4 million people involved in Satanism.

In the above article, it goes on to say: "Police investigators say the world of hard-core Satanism can involve drugs, sex rituals, animal sacrifices and **even human sacrifices**. Some sensational crimes have Satanic links. Convicted mass-murderers Charles Manson and Richard Ramirez, accused of being the Night Stalker killer, for example, are self-styled Satanists. Ramirez was charged with burglary, rape and the murder of 13 people in southern California. He reportedly was obsessed with a heavy metal song called *Night Prowler* **from** ***AC/DC's*** *Highway to Hell* **album. He has a tattoo of a pentagram, a five-pointed star that symbolizes the devil, on his left hand."**

The Church of Satan is the best-known Satanist group in the United States. It was founded in 1966 by former San Francisco police photographer, Anton LaVey, who claims 10,000 to 20,000 members, according to *The Tampa Tribune's* article of October 31, 1988.

Later, a split generated by Anton LaVey's hypocrisy caused other

The NWO and the PROMOTION of METAPHYSICS

Satanists to start their own church, according to *Cape Cod Times*, November 16, 1991. Michael Aquino, who retired as an officer from the U.S. Army, left the Church of Satan and founded another Satanist church called the Temple of Set. They claim 3,000 members.

Reader, as you should know by now, the newspapers are full of horrible stories of human sacrifices and mass murders almost daily. I really do not want to dwell on the actual details of some of these crimes, but I do want to point out how much we need to call on God for His protecting care.

Thomas W. Wedge, former Deputy Sheriff from Logan County, Ohio, was interviewed by Marjorie Hyer, a reporter from *The Washington Post*, about how bad modern-day Spiritualism has become. Wedge has written two books about cults and the occult and has toured the country holding seminars for law enforcement officers to learn how to deal with the ever-rising interest in the occult. According to *The Buffalo News*, April 19, 1989, where Marjorie Hyer's column was seen, during his seminars Wedge demonstrated how to distinguish between Satanists and what he termed pagans. A portion of this article is listed below:

" Pagans are fascinating people. You can learn so much from them. But, he added, Don't misunderstand me, they're still pagans.

"He passed around a little green pouch, a Satanist 'mojo bag,' he said. Don't you ever grab this, he warned. It's worn on the belt or around the neck for spiritual protection.... You can ask them to remove it, but don't you grab it. They'll fight you for it.... You might even instruct your jailers about this. It can save a lot of people from getting hurt.

"He taught the officers how to decode symbols used by Satanists and other occult groups such as the one on the Mexican border that is believed to have led to the deaths of at least 15 people.

"Wedge said Satanists shun 'everything that deals with the right hand' because Christ sits at God's right hand. Wedge goes on to point out – those who become involved with non-traditionalists (Satanism) tend to be 'white males, extremely intelligent, from upper-class homes, with very little self-esteem.' There's a void in their lives, and they're looking to fill that void."

The Real Truth About UFO's and the New World Order

There will be a void in every life until he learns to abide under the shadow of the Almighty and make Him his fortress and refuge, instead of trusting in a mojo bag, a good luck charm, or even a cross.

It is a baffling thing to try to imagine any who would actually trust in Satan for protection instead of God. However, this is what is going on today. The same abominations the Israelites were led to practice when they turned from worshipping God are being repeated today in an alarming manner. Human sacrificing is with us, and the anger of the Lord shall be seen in the last wicked days of this earth's history.

"Come, my people, enter thou into thy chambers, and shut thy doors about thee: hide thyself as it were for a little moment, until the indignation be overpast.

"For, behold, the Lord cometh out of his place to punish the inhabitants of the earth for their iniquity: the earth also shall disclose her blood, and shall no more cover her slain." Isaiah 26:20, 21.

The next science of astrology which is an abomination unto the Lord found in Deuteronomy 18:10 is:

"OR THAT USETH DIVINATION."

What is divination? Divination is foretelling the future by the use of crystal balls, palm reading, tarot cards, playing cards, tea leaf reading, the Ouija board, automatic writing, and phrenology. It also includes using a string with something tied on the end, reading the liver of calves, using a forked stick to find water (divining rod), or by the spirit of the glass.

In the Bible, the people who practiced these things were known as diviners, soothsayers, or simply called witches. Today, they are known as psychics. Billions of dollars have been made by these modern-day diviners. Instead of inquiring of the Lord through His Word for advice, the worldly-minded and Christians, as well, think it is but a light thing to inquire advice from these modern-day witches of Endor. Even the police use the services of psychics in trying to solve crimes. These diviners have now come out of their closets and are boldly advertising their witchcraft a.k.a. metaphysics for a price.

Television talk show hosts seek their presence on their shows as often as well-known movie stars or politicians. They are socially accepted by the general American public as heros of the day. But the Lord says:

The NWO and the PROMOTION of METAPHYSICS

"For all that do these things are an abomination unto the Lord: and because of these abominations the Lord thy God doth drive them out from before thee." Deuteronomy 18:12.

All down through Israel's history, the prophets of God had to contend with the **psychics** or **diviners** in their day. When a messenger of God gave the Israelites a warning from the Lord, there were always psychics (diviners) in the midst of Israel preaching to the same people the **opposite thing** would come to pass.

"For thus saith the Lord of hosts, the God of Israel: Let not your **prophets** and your **diviners**, that be in the midst of you, deceive you, neither hearken to your dreams which ye cause to be dreamed. For they prophesy falsely unto you **IN MY NAME**: I have not sent them, saith the Lord." Jeremiah 29:8, 9.

Here, we see the combining of the holy with the profane. These diviners among Israel were also claiming to be God's people, while at the same time using divination to foretell the future. The apostle Paul ran head on with a Shirley MacLaine in his day. This psychic was very famous also among the people of the city of Thyatira in Greece.

"And it came to pass, as we went to prayer, a certain damsel **POSSESSED** with a **SPIRIT OF DIVINATION** met us, which brought her masters much gain by **soothsaying**.

"The same followed Paul and us, and cried saying, These men are the servants of the most high God, which shew unto us the way of salvation.

"And this did she many days. But Paul, being grieved, turned and said to the **spirit**, I command **thee** in the **name** of **Jesus Christ** to come out of her. And **he came out** the same hour." Acts 16:16–18.

Notice verse 16 again. This soothsayer has a spirit (demon) of divination. Verse 16 in the original Greek says, "*Or, of Python*." (See the marginal reference in the Bible.) Again, what is a python? It is a snake. What did Satan use to deceive Eve? As pointed out earlier, the priests of the Temple at Delphi were called **Pythians** which derived from the word "*Pytho*."

It is interesting to note what *Funk and Wagnall's New Standard Dictionary of the English Language* on page 2021 says about the word "*python*."

The Real Truth About UFO's and the New World Order

"**py´thon**[2], n. A soothsayer or soothsaying spirit: from the tradition that the Python delivered oracles at Delphi; also, a ventriloquist. [< L. *Pytho(n-)*, spirit of divination, < Gr. *Python*; see Python[1].] – **py´tho-ness,** n. The priestess of the Delphic oracle; hence, any woman supposed to be possessed of the spirit of prophecy; a witch. **py´´tho-nis´sa** [Rare]. – **py-thon´ic**[2], a. Foretelling future events; inspired; prophetic; pretending to prophesy. **py-thon´i-cal** [Rare]. – **py´tho-nism,** n. The art of predicting future events by divination. – **py´tho-nist†,** n."

What about **ventriloquism**? You see it in the entertainment field numerous times. You have seen ventriloquists and how they have the power to change their voice and **throw their voice to a puppet** to make it sound like it is speaking. So did Satan, the author of ventriloquism, **channel his voice through the serpent** to speak to Eve causing her to disobey the Lord and eventually die because of it. Reader, ventriloquism is also a condemned science of the occult.

This diviner (psychic) that the apostle Paul met face to face with was possessed with a demon named divination. Demons take the names of the problems that they cause in people. "My name is Legion: for we are many," said the captain of the 3,000 – 6,000 demons that possessed the body of the man from the country of the Gadarenes. (See Mark 5:1–9.)

The apostle Paul was facing a similar situation. Look again at verse 17 at the words recorded coming from the mouth of this pythonist.

"The same followed Paul and us, and cried, saying, These men are the servants of the most high God, which shew unto us the way of salvation." Acts 16:17.

Why did this witch exalt Paul and his Christian companions? The soothsayer wanted the people to think that she too was a Christian so she would not lose her popularity among the people or the huge sums of money she was bringing in for her services.

"And **this did she many days**. But Paul, being grieved, turned and said to the **spirit**, I command thee in the name of Jesus Christ to come out of her. And he came out the same hour." Acts 16:18.

When Paul cast the **demon of divination** out of this ancient psychic, she could not foretell certain events any longer.

She lost not only her confidence of the people, but also the money she was making for the political leaders of that city. As a

The NWO and the PROMOTION of METAPHYSICS

result, Paul and his brethren were thrown in jail and their feet were made fast in the stocks. (See Acts 16:24.) However, later the Lord miraculously delivered Paul and his brethren out of jail, and even the jailer who witnessed all these things said, "**Sirs, what must I do to be saved? And they said, Believe on the Lord Jesus Christ, and thou shalt be saved, and thy house.**" Acts 16:30, 31.

It is almost considered blasphemy to speak against psychics today in certain religious interfaith circles. All psychics today claim to have **spirit guides** which they say give them knowledge and understanding about future events. These spirit guides (**familiar spirits**) are not **ascended masters** from the Great White Brotherhood, as they claim, but are demons personating dead ancient heros, kings, relatives, etc.

Those who seek their advice better take heed for those who communicate with fortune tellers are not only talking to a mere human being, but actually a demon hiding under the exterior of that individual.

There are always fakes found among the occultists who claim to have the power of divination but have proven themselves to be pretenders, even among their own brethren. Christians that think that all occultists are fakes also are deceived when their real power is demonstrated. They think it must be the power of God.

Reader, there is ***wonder-working power*** from the Evil One.

"For they are the spirits of devils, working miracles." Revelation 16:14.

"Ye are of God, little children, and have overcome them: because greater is he that is in you, than he that is in the world." I John 4:4.

"And as ye go, preach, saying, The kingdom of heaven is at hand. Heal the sick, cleanse the lepers, raise the dead, cast out devils: freely ye have received, freely give." Matthew 10:7, 8.

The next abomination that the Canaanites practiced which is actually the foundation to all of the metaphysical sciences today is:

"AN OBSERVER OF TIMES." Deuteronomy 18:10.

What is an observer of times? **It is an astrologer.** A witch cannot cast her spells, a magician cannot work his illusions, and a fortune teller or diviner cannot foretell the future without the **aid of astrology. It is the basic foundation to all of the doctrines of the occult.**

"Hear ye the word which the Lord speaketh unto you, O house of Israel: Thus saith the Lord, **Learn not the way of the heathen**, and

The Real Truth About UFO's and the New World Order

be not dismayed at the signs of heaven (the horoscope): for the heathen are dismayed at them." Jeremiah 10:1, 2.

Reader, how many people have you seen today that will not as much step out their front door without consulting their daily horoscope from their local newspaper? We will be studying more about the deceptions of astrology and its most famous promoters from the past and present in the next chapter.

The next abomination that the ancient Canaanites led ancient Israel into doing was the practice of voodoo, which is known as **ENCHANTMENT**. This includes **casting spells** on people and practicing magic of which enchantment is a brother to the sorcerers.

"Therefore hearken not ye to…your **enchanters,** nor to your **sorcerers**…. For they **prophesy a lie unto you**, to remove you far from your land." Jeremiah 27:9, 10.

"And I will come near to you to judgment, and I will be a swift witness against the sorcerers." Malachi 3:5.

"OR A CHARMER." Deuteronomy 18:11.

What is a **charmer**? A charmer is a hypnotist and includes other mind-controlling sciences which we will investigate in our continued study.

"OR A CONSULTER WITH FAMILIAR SPIRITS." Deuteronomy 18:11.

As pointed out before, **familiar spirits** are known to the people of the occult as **spirit guides**. Those who consult with familiar spirits or spirit guides today are known as **mediums, channelers,** or **parapsychologists**.

"A man also or woman that hath a familiar spirit, or that is a wizard, shall surely be put to death." Leviticus 20:27.

In verse 11 of Deuteronomy, Chapter 18, it warns not to have any **WIZARDS** among us. What is a wizard? It is a **male witch**.

"OR A NECROMANCER." Deuteronomy 18:11.

A necromancer is a person who through various ways makes claims like the channeler today. He or she claims to speak to the dead.

"For all that do these things are an **abomination** unto the Lord: and because of these abominations the Lord thy God doth drive them out from before thee." Deuteronomy 18:12.

The NWO and the PROMOTION of METAPHYSICS

This is why God destroyed the people of Canaan. This is why He will destroy most today. However, our God does not want to destroy any of the people of the world for the abominations which they are committing. He wants everybody to choose to walk in His ways and keep His commandments and do the things that please Him by taking hold of His covenant. As we can clearly see, there has been a **great departure** from the living God by both pagans and Christians. Before that great and dreadful day of Jesus' Second Coming, the Lord is giving **everyone** an opportunity to turn from their abominations and obey the Gospel of our Lord Jesus Christ.

"Fear God, and give glory to him; for the hour of his judgment is come: and **WORSHIP HIM** that made heaven, and earth, and the sea, and the fountains of waters." Revelation 14:7.

This present world is a curse today to both man and beast, but one day the curse of this earth shall be removed. In that day, God himself will cleanse this world of its filth and wickedness by his purifying agent. The earth shall be **cleansed by fire**. (See Malachi 4:1 and 2 Peter 3:2–14.) The wicked who have refused the offer from God to return to him by confession of sin and repentance and have refused the saving grace of Jesus' sacrifice for mankind shall God's people "tread down." "For they shall be ashes under the soles of your feet in the day that I shall do this, saith the Lord of hosts." Malachi 4:3.

Satan, who knows the Scriptures better than we do, **counteracts** every plan and purpose of God. Just like Christians are preparing for translation (See 1 Corinthians 15:51–55), "For this corruptible must put on incorruption, and this mortal must put on immortality," (1 Corinthians 15:53), so have the New Agers this doctrine within their beliefs. They teach that these UFO's are coming to teach man the secrets of immortality. In order to receive immortality, New Agers have been taught by their most learned doctors of divination that they **must become vegetarian** before the year 2000. Occultists teach their newly converted proselytes that nobody will enter into the coming Golden Age or Age of Aquarius unless they clean up the earth and become vegetarian. New Agers are quick to point out the truth about how it is not safe to eat meat today. They use scientific evidence to prove that the diseases mankind is subject to are the same diseases the animals are victims to. Cattle get

The Real Truth About UFO's and the New World Order

cancer, tuberculosis, etc. like people do. When the flesh of a dead carcass of an animal is consumed, so are its diseases. Mother Earth today is full of pollution and the animals are full of diseases because of it, says Spiritualists.

Back on February 9, 1993, on *Dateline* of *NBC News*, Jane Pauley tried to warn the American public about **meat eating**. *Dateline* exposed that as many as 400,000 *Jack in the Box* hamburgers were contaminated with a deadly strain of bacteria known as **E. Coli 0157H7**. This deadly **bacteria** has killed and hospitalized many. Investigators of this tragic illness pointed out that they found animal **feces** in those hamburgers. Lea Thompson, who investigated this serious illness, said on this same program the following to Jane Pauley: "This 14-bed intensive care unit and others in the Seattle area have been overwhelmed with children whose **kidneys** are shutting down, whose **livers** and **pancreases** are failing, who are off and on dialysis and cannot eat; who, if they survive, face a lifetime of kidney problems – all because they ate **hamburgers** that were federally inspected and assumed to be safe."[7]

Actually one year later, Dan Rather of *CBS News* exposed on his program *48 Hours* not only how **red meat is dangerous** to our health, but **fish** and **chicken** as well. During this same program, Dan Rather exposed the danger of fruits and vegetables imported from other countries. **Pesticides** that the government of the United States will not allow to be used in this country because they are unsafe and may cause cancer still get in. They are on the fruits and vegetables from foreign farmers whose governments are **ignorant** about health or **do not care**. On this same program, Rather showed footage taken from meat and fish processing plants. Decades ago, this writer worked briefly in a meat processing and packing plant. After seeing what went on day by day, I became a vegetarian! If the reader cannot see the value of coming back to the original vegetarian diet that Christ gave Adam and Eve, just spend some time at a slaughter house. The reader may also be surprised to know how many butchers and those who handle meat are vegetarians. I saw with my own eyes, while working at a meat packing plant, hamburger that was accidentally dropped on the filthy floor and bagged for someone to put in their mouth and eat.

---

[7]*Dateline Transcript, NBC News*, **February 9, 1993, p. 26.**

The NWO and the PROMOTION of METAPHYSICS

The reader may question if the meat is contaminated, then why do federal meat inspectors allow this? Dan Rather answered this question during *48 Hours'* investigation of meat processing plants. When cattle are slaughtered, they know ahead of time that they are about to be killed. They try desperately to climb out of their corrals. At the same time the cruel process of killing the animals is going on, the animals are in a state of terror. They defecate and urinate all over each other. I saw this myself while I worked at this kind of place. It turned my stomach. To watch this process of killing defenseless animals was appalling to me.

During the *48 Hours* television broadcast, February 9, 1994, Dan Rather had Joe Heubner, a meat inspector, on his program. Heubner explained that it is the job of meat inspectors to check for disease and contamination of animals. They are to make sure that there are no hairs or fecal material left on the meat once the hides of the animals are removed, but he was asked if you can check for E. Coli. Mr Heubner admitted, **"No. It's a bacteria. You can't see it, you can't smell it, you can't detect it."**[8]

It was also brought out by Dr. Dale Hancock of Washington State University that this dangerous bacteria is found in the animal's gastrointestinal tract, particularly in the lower bowel. Furthermore, not all cattle have E. Coli. When meat is ground up into hamburger, **it is not from just one cow**. Hamburger comes from the less desirable parts of several cows. These are some of the reasons why **E. Coli is hard to detect**. Not only is this very disturbing news for the meat eater, but *48 Hours* exposed an even darker side to why meat eating is not safe.

A former employee of Federal Beef Processors at Rapid City, South Dakota, admitted while he worked there that he saw hair and feces on the meat which was allowed to come through to be shipped to go into the mouths of meat eaters. *48 Hours* had taken footage from a hidden camera showing the same man while working there and how unclean the plant was. Federal Beef Processors at Rapid City, South Dakota, upon learning about the footage taken at their plant, went to court to try to stop *48 Hours* from showing the video tape.

---

[8]*48 Hours Transcript, CBS News,* **February 9, 1994, p. 9.**

The Real Truth About UFO's and the New World Order

The case went as high as it could go, but the United States Supreme Court ruled in favor of *48 Hours*.

Another man from this same Federal Beef Processors who actually took the footage of the above meat processing plant for *48 Hours* also showed on the tape another employee **scraping his knife on the contaminated floor of this plant to get a dull edge off his blade**. Reader, just a **single hair** of a cow could **harbor millions of E. Coli bacteria**. Could it be that other meat processing plants are also in violation of federal standards? Could the love of money turn away the eyes of those who process meat to look the other way?

In *The Wall Street Journal*, Friday, May 31, 1991, it pointed out how government researchers say a viral cousin of the human **AIDS** virus is *"widely distributed"* in U.S. cattle herds, but they and other scientists insist this poses no threat to human health.

Another bacteria caused by fecal matter is found in chicken. The illness is called **Salmonella**. The bacteria poisons an estimated 800,000 to four million poultry eaters every year, according to Howard Dow who was also interviewed on the February 9, 1994, program of *48 Hours*. A test to determine how safe chickens are to eat was conducted on kosher, national brand chickens, free range, and no brands. There were thirty chickens tested and Richard Schlesinger of *48 Hours* said, "Eight of the chickens had Salmonella, 12 had Listeria and 21 had another kind of bacteria called Campylobacter that every year makes up to four million Americans sick. In fact, out of the **thirty** chickens we **tested**, only **five** got a clean bill of health. So which kind of chicken was best? **The answer: none.** Free range, national brands, no brands, kosher all proved as likely to carry bacteria. In our tests, in the eyes of bacteria, all chicken was created equal."[9]

In *Time* magazine, it warned that Salmonella bacteria can be found in eggs as well. "This toxic raw-egg bacteria caused more than 2,000 cases of food poisoning in the U.S. last year."[10]

If the reader wants to continue to eat eggs, the best way is to **boil them or make sure they have been thoroughly cooked not runny.**

When Moses was told by the Lord that it would be lawful to eat

---

[9]*48 Hours Transcript, CBS News*, **February 9, 1994, p. 26, 27.**
[10]*Time*, **May 13, 1991, p. 50.**

The NWO and the PROMOTION of METAPHYSICS

clean animals, our Lord spoke these words about 4,000 years ago when the world was free of pollution and chemical contaminants. However, today this present world is waxing old. The animals today are not safe to eat. The fish in the oceans, rivers, and lakes are contaminated as well. According to the *The Environmental Magazine*, it says, "Since 1964, **liver cancer** has been found in **15 species of fish** from about 50 polluted sites, from Washington's Puget Sound to Boston Harbor, and numerous inland waterways in between. Chemical contaminants and pesticides are suspected of causing the cancers."[11]

Many non-Christians, but environment-conscious and health conscious people, are turning away from meat eating to a vegetarian diet. The vegetarian diet is becoming very socially fashionable and meat eating is beginning to be looked down upon by society, like smoking cigarettes. However, it is not the Christians as a whole who are proclaiming this loud message about meat eating. It is the New Agers. Very few are there in the mainstream Christian churches who know these things. They generally eat anything that moves and do not want to change their eating habits, **"whose God is their belly."** Philippians 3:19. Both Catholics and Protestants are ignoring the warning in 2 Corinthians 3:16, 17: "Know ye not that ye are the temple of God, and that the Spirit of God dwelleth in you? If any man defile the temple of God, him shall God destroy; for the temple of God is holy, which temple ye are."

While condemning the drug dealers and abortionists from the pulpit, some Catholic priests and some Protestant pastors pronounce condemnations while their words come forth from a mouth whose odor is that of tobacco or alcohol. What the pastor is generally so is the congregation. People who say they are followers of the Sinless One are to reflect His sterling appearance and character. Can the reader imagine Jesus with a cigarette in his mouth or drinking from a beer bottle? Not hardly. Jesus explained how we can tell a real Christian. He said, "Ye shall know them by their fruits." Matthew 7:16.

In New Age circles, health reform is a very important doctrine. They are teaching their disciples to stop smoking, drinking, and eating harmful foods. They promote the truth about the wonderful

---

[11]*The Environmental Magazine*, Jan./Feb. 1993, p. 37.

The Real Truth About UFO's and the New World Order

healing powers of certain herbs and the dangers that drugs have on the body. New Agers point out how people who have had cancer, diabetes, arthritis, eye trouble, heart trouble, etc. have been cured by herbal medicine and by changing to a vegetarian diet.

The Bible itself promotes healing by using natural remedies. King Hezekiah who was dying from an infected boil was told by the prophet Isaiah to put a **poultice made of figs on the affected area** and he would recover. "For Isaiah had said, Let them take a lump of figs, and lay it for a plaster upon the boil, and he shall recover." Isaiah 38:21. Jesus removed an obstruction that was blocking the vision of a blind man by **spitting into clay and rubbing it on the eyes** of the man. Afterwards, he washed out the clay, and the blind man could see. "When he had thus spoken, he spat on the ground, and made clay of the spittle, and he anointed the eyes of the blind man with the clay, And said unto him, Go, wash in the pool of Siloam, (which is by interpretation, Sent.) He went his way therefore, and washed, and came seeing." John 9:6, 7.

While holding a series of meetings in Orlando, Florida, a little girl was brought to my wife and I by her father. On her face, there was a terrible sore that was infected. I recommended that she should use **activated charcoal** on it by making a paste with it by using some water and **Vitamin E ointment** I just happened to have with me. This was done. The very next day we saw that this terrible sore began to heal. By the time my meetings were over, the little girl's infection was gone. However, it did leave a discolorment on her skin where the sore once was.

So does sin leave spiritual scars, but Jesus shall heal us all soon. For "there shall be no more death,… neither shall there be any more pain." Revelation 21:4.

Healing through natural remedies was given to us from the Father. The herbs of the field were created by the Lord, not Satan; but, some Christians are afraid of learning how to heal themselves or others by using natural remedies because of the fear of being led into witchcraft for New Agers also use natural remedies to heal people. While Christians are becoming more aware of just how large this New World Order conspiracy really is and how they have penetrated just about into every area of human existence, especially man's environment and his health, the truth about vegetarianism and healing by natural

The NWO and the PROMOTION of METAPHYSICS

remedies is looked upon by many Christians as a New Age trap. Some Christians who observe other Christians using herbs as a natural remedy to heal sickness and/or are turning to a vegetarian diet often brand them as New Agers.

However, New Agers often call themselves Christian when the purpose is needed to win unsuspecting Christians to their cause. Indeed, New Agers have made the environmental crisis and the truth about healing through natural remedies and vegetarianism their recruiting station to usher multitudes into their Aquarian conspiracy. However, when the sincere Christian humbles himself before God and prays for **spiritual discernment** so he may see the difference between the Spirit of Christ and the Spirit of Antichrist, the promise is, "And ye shall know the truth, and the truth shall make you free." John 8:32. But the spiritually proud Christian, who thinks he is rich and in need of nothing, as in Revelation 3:17, will receive nothing.

Again, there is no other passage of Scripture that will help a sincere Christian find the root of the deceptions from the tree of knowledge of good and evil, which today have blended themselves with Christianity, than Deuteronomy, Chapter 18. It is here where a disciple of Christ may find a spiritual ax to uproot any philosophies from Spiritualism that may have rooted unwittingly into the reader's life. It is understanding these ancient warnings from God that will give us wisdom in how to tell the difference between the holy and the unholy, and God's natural remedies from New Age holistic medicine, which has entangled multitudes.

As we have seen, God warned through Moses that the ancient Israelites were not to have among them anyone who practiced "divination." Deuteronomy 18:10. Not only is **divination** used in foretelling the future by occultists, but they also use divination in **diagnosing illnesses as well**. These sciences of metaphysics in the medical field of New Age practitioners are part of what New Agers sell today as **holistic medicine**. Holistic is purely a New Age word invented by them to let others of their persuasion know who they are.

Two of the most popular sciences of which multitudes, even Christian pastors, are entangled in are **iridology** and **reflexology**! This is shocking, but true. Iridology and reflexology are both rooted in the philosophies of **Spiritualism** which derived its philosophies

The Real Truth About UFO's and the New World Order

from astrology. No? Well, let's investigate this by using documented proof from these practitioner's own words.

Many people once they are enlightened about these deceptions find it hard to give them up because reflexology and iridology brings them much money; but in the eyes of the Lord, they are modern Balaams **who have the rewards of divination in their hands**. Those Christian pastors who teach and practice these sciences to their members are also guilty of laying a foundation of Spiritualism in the church in which other deceptions of Spiritualism akin to them can enter in.

The basic belief in all forms of Spiritualism is centered around Satan's first lie, "**Ye shall not surely die**." Genesis 3:4. The false doctrines of **immortality of the soul** and **pantheism** can be found not only among New Agers, but also among Jews, mainstream Christians, and Muslims as well. The ancient Scriptures reveal that the inhabitants of this planet in the past, present, and in the remaining future worshipped the Dragon because they both received and obeyed his precepts from astrology of which the Dragon was a symbol in ancient Babylon. Ironically enough, in modern Asian countries the Dragon is still today at the center of their cultures. It is very common indeed to see buildings, lamp shades, furniture, and folk dancing displaying the symbol of the **great red Dragon** which deceiveth the whole world. The great red Dragon is freely used to symbolize China, Japan, and other southeastern Asian nations.

In Oriental or Eastern religions, there is also found the doctrine of "**THE FORCE**." To the Chinese, it is known as the **CHI**; and to the Korean, it is known as the **YIN YANG**. To the Indian Swami, the force is the **CHAKRAS**. According to the *Encyclopedic Psychic Dictionary* on page 240, we read: "**FORCE** – (capitalized) pertains to the highest power there is; encompasses 'all' as a whole; an energy field generated within all living things; infinite intelligence that penetrates all life and holds the galaxies together; neutral in character but can be switched to have good or bad characteristics when utilized by the human mind. **Syn. GOD. [cf.DIVINE ENERGY, COSMIC GOD, GUIDING PRINCIPLE]**"[12]

Reader, notice here it said the **FORCE** is an energy field generated within all living things. Again, from the same *Encyclopedic Psychic*

---

[12]*Encyclopedic Psychic Dictionary*, Bletzer, p. 240.

The NWO and the PROMOTION of METAPHYSICS

Dictionary on page 103, we read: "**CH'I** – (China) an immutable principle in the air needed for life, taken in by breathing; circulates throughout the entire body making up the twelve meridian lines in the body; this vital force is found in the ethers divided into opposite but complimentary halves and appears in the body as positive and negative areas; see **VITAL LIFE FORCE. Syn. TCH'I, QI, PRANA, L-FIELDS, BIOCOSMIC ENERGY. [cf. YIN AND YANG, BREATHING]**"[13]

This knowledge about the Force or the Chi or the Yin Yang is promoted as cosmic consciousness. Reader, here is how to tell the difference between New Age witchcraft and healing through natural remedies in which God intended.

Generally, most psychics today claim to be healers too. They have relieved many of their hard-earned money by practicing on them or teaching them their crafts for a price. Psychic healers attribute their ability to heal the body and the mind to the **Force**, or **electricity**, or an **electromagnetic energy field**. In the past, psychic healers were also known as **electric physicians** or **phrenologists**. Today, they can be known also as **Jungian psychotherapists**, **reflexologists**, or **acupuncturists**. New Agers incorporated **mind-control sciences** such as **hypnosis**, **imagery**, **transcendental meditation**, **biofeedback**, and **self-realization therapies** into their philosophies because they teach their patients how closely related the human mind plays in human sickness. **Pantheism**, which all these therapies are based in, teaches that the universe is one big **microcosm** and that **everything** is connected. It teaches that God is in the trees, flowers, grass, animals, birds, rivers, mountains, and man. Therefore, since the **Force**, which according to Spiritualists is **divine energy** which encompasses all things, then man is a **miniature microcosm** or **a god**, but must be awakened to this fact.

Again, here is where the UFO's come in or connect with this Spirit of Antichrist. The most learned doctors of occult circles teach that UFO's have aboard gods who were once men here on earth but have already reached this cosmic consciousness and are communicating to a select few that man has hidden latent powers within him and that he too is a god but must be awakened to this fact. This same voice

---

[13] *Encyclopedic Psychic Dictionary*, Bletzer, p. 103.

The Real Truth About UFO's and the New World Order

spoke to Eve almost 6,000 years ago. It said, "Ye shall not surely die: For God doth know that in the day ye eat thereof, then **your eyes shall be opened, and ye shall be as gods, knowing good and evil.**" Genesis 3:4, 5.

This so-called guiding principle that flows through every living thing that controls even the universe, according to Buddhists, is the Yin Yang. Its symbol can be seen everywhere. Occultists teach that illnesses are caused by an imbalance of the mind and the body. Psychic healers tell their clients that their **Yin Yang is unbalanced**. They have too much yin or too much yang or too much good or evil electromagnetic energy.

Hence, occultists attribute their healing powers to **rearranging the electrical energy or current of the body which they say flows from the Force**. This healing technique is used also in the Chinese therapeutic **touch** and forms the basis for **acupuncture**. Students of these occult healing techniques are taught that they must balance their yin yang before they can generate a strong energy field so they can help unclog others and in doing so will promote good health. This is especially taught in the **holistic massage** techniques in which they claim to be able to find and release clogged pressure points in the body. Rearranging the vital energy of the force is also claimed among occultists by simply passing their hand slightly above the body and slowly moving their hand from the top of the patient's head to the bottom of his feet without touching the body. This is known as "**balancing the energies**."

Now, here lies the **foundation** of the ever popular healing technique called **reflexology**. Its roots are indeed **rooted** and **grounded** in this same pagan philosophy. It was brought from the Orient to the United States by Eunice Ingram. Reflexology is plainly taught by its practitioners to be based in the belief of the Chi (force) which occultists say flows through **ten energy zones of the body**. In the book, *Feet First: A Guide to Foot Reflexology*, on page 22 we can read the following: "Each zone can be considered a **channel** for the intangible life energy, called *chi* or *qi* **in oriental medicine and martial arts.**"[14] (Emphasis mine.)

---

[14]*Feet First: A Guide to Foot Reflexology*, **Norman, p. 22.**

The NWO and the PROMOTION of METAPHYSICS

Again, from the *Encyclopedic Psychic Dictionary*, **under REFLEXOLOGY**, we can find this statement: "compression on various parts of the foot, by the **THREE PSYCHIC FINGERS** of the practitioner's hand; **RELEASES A FLOW OF ELECTRICAL ENERGY TO THE BLOCKED NERVE ENDINGS**, which show in the feet when parts of the body are congested." (Emphasis mine.)

Just as the pythonist (palm reader) **divides the palm** into different sections to be able to diagnose his/her client's future, so does the reflexologist **divide the feet** into different sections to diagnose his/her client's illness. This is divination of which our Lord warned Israel they had better not have those who practice these things among them.

There are many fakes among occultists who claim to have healing powers who can only relieve their clients of their money. However, there are those who do have power from the *prince of the power of the air* who can perform miracles as it was warned of over and over again in the Bible. Like ancient prophets of Baal, these modern sorcerers claim to have or are **channels** to receive electrical energy from their deity. In reality, it is Lucifer who is worshipped as the god of forces.

One 19th and 20th-century messenger of God warned about electric physicians in her day. "His (Satan's) agents still claim to cure disease. They attribute their power to **ELECTRICITY, MAGNETISM,** or the so-called 'sympathetic remedies.' In truth, they are but **CHANNELS FOR SATAN'S ELECTRIC CURRENTS**. By this means **he casts his spell** over the bodies and souls of men."[15]

When the Christian hears "**balancing of the energies**," watch out! All New Age health approaches are based in this deception. **Iridology** is also. Its basic belief is also entangled with astrology's doctrine of the Force, and there are variations. As we have read from their own beliefs, the universe, according to occultists, is governed by the Force. It holds the galaxies together. Doctors of occultism divide the Force into 96 rooms and our galaxy into 36 rooms which is the zodiac band. The zodiac band is the origin of the common clock we use today. In numerology, **if you add the numbers from one to 36 they will add to 666**. This number of doom is sacred to occultists. It is looked upon as having good luck.

---

[15]*Testimonies to the Church,* Vol. 4, White, pp. 192–193.

The Real Truth About UFO's and the New World Order

The twelve numbers on the clock represent the twelve signs (horoscope) of the zodiac. There are lesser gods under the twelve signs. All these gods on the zodiac band are known as house gods and room gods. They are **divided ten degrees** apart around the 360 degree circle of the zodiac which totals to 36 house and room gods. However, the Force, according to occultists, holds together all the galaxies and is divided into **96 rooms**.

It is not by chance that the **iridologist divides the iris of the eye into 96 rooms** claiming each room is like a window to peek into the body to see what is wrong, or each room is like a television monitor which will flash on the screen of each room a damaged or sick organ. All psychic healers claim to have ever present with them their "**spirit guides**." They **help tell them** what is wrong with their client's health. These "spirit guides" who approach the learned student of Spiritualism are not **ancient gods**, **ascended masters**, or from dead loved ones or heros. These **voices** are coming from the fallen angels of Lucifer who have **fooled occultists** into following them for millenniums and have **fooled billions** in posing as ghosts. This is how **water witching is done**. This popular way of finding water is nothing less than divination. This is how humans are uniting with demons just as the Bible foretold. We will see more and more of this as we continue to study the rise and the evolution of this Atlantean Plan for a New World Order.

Nevertheless, unto you who can recognize the **voice of the Good Shepherd**, "Beloved, I wish above all things that thou mayest prosper and be in **health**, even as thy soul prospereth." III John 2. Good health comes **not** from the knowledge of the Yin Yang or the Force. The Christian's **secret** to restoring good health will come by learning how to **cleanse the bloodstream and the bowel canal and following the eight natural laws our Creator has fixed in the natural world**. These eight natural laws need to be studied individually, and they are God's way of restoring health. Good nutrition, exercise, the use of pure water, the healing powers of sunshine, temperance in all things, pure air, rest, and most importantly, trusting and obeying God are, indeed, the right paths to follow in restoring good health. I can testify to this personally. I grew up in a home where practically anything was to be eaten save a horse, dog, cat, monkey, or rodent.

The NWO and the PROMOTION of METAPHYSICS

Alcohol flowing like a river, cigarettes smoked like a coal furnace, and eating fat and blood together in the meat helped put my mother and father into early graves. From my youth up, I ignorantly abused my body by eating, drinking, and smoking. I damaged my liver and developed arthritis, gout, and psoriasis. I had gout so bad that my fingers were beginning to twist, my left hand was not able to make a tight fist because of pain, and I ended up on crutches. I suffered the torture of gout for many years, even when I became a vegetarian. My first contact with gout was in 1977. This first attack put me on crutches for about two weeks, and then the pain would go away enough where I could walk limping without them. This I suffered off and on until 1991! Today, I am happy to say that I have found out what was causing gout and what to do about it. First, I bought two books that opened my ignorant mind about the diet and its effect on the mind and the body. The titles of these wonderful books are: 1) *Back to Eden*, Jethro Kloss, Review and Herald Publishing Association, 1949, and 2) *Make Your Juicer Your Drug Store*, Laura Newman, Benedict Lust Publications, 1970.

Both of the above books showed me the cause of gout and how to treat this terrible illness which attacks millions today. Another book that especially helped me put my crutches into storage is, of course, the Bible. The Bible taught me something about eating that most Protestant pastors and Catholic priests are completely in the dark about.

When our Lord told Noah he could eat clean animals, this was to be temporary. This was allowed because the Flood had destroyed all plant life and there was not much to eat.

However, God plainly told Noah that he may eat of clean animals, "but flesh with the life thereof, which is the **BLOOD** thereof, shall ye not eat." Genesis 9:4. Later, this same warning was told again to Moses, "It shall be a perpetual statute for your generations throughout all your dwellings, that ye eat neither **FAT** nor **BLOOD**." Leviticus 3:17. "For the life of the flesh is in the blood: and I have given it to you upon the altar to make an atonement for your souls: for it is the blood that maketh an atonement for the soul…For it is the life of all flesh; the blood of it is for the life thereof: therefore I said unto the children of Israel, Ye shall eat the **BLOOD** of no manner of flesh: for

The Real Truth About UFO's anf the New World Order

the life of all flesh is the **BLOOD** thereof: whosoever eateth it **SHALL BE CUT OFF**." Leviticus 17:11, 14. It was also preached by the apostle Paul as he went holding crusades for the Gentiles, "But that we write unto them, that they abstain from pollutions of idols, and from fornication, and from things strangled, and from **BLOOD**." Acts 15:20. Again in Acts 21:25, we can read where Paul continued to warn people about the eating of flesh with the blood. This was one of the sins King Saul was guilty of, like most religious and political leaders are today. "And the people flew upon the spoil, and took sheep, and oxen, and calves, and slew them on the ground: and the **PEOPLE DID EAT THEM WITH THE BLOOD.** Then they told Saul, saying, **BEHOLD, THE PEOPLE SIN AGAINST THE LORD, IN THAT THEY EAT WITH THE BLOOD.** And he said, Ye have transgressed: roll a great stone unto me this day. And Saul said, Disperse yourselves among the people, and say unto them, Bring me hither every man his ox, and every man his sheep, and slay them here, and eat; and **SIN NOT AGAINST THE LORD IN EATING WITH THE BLOOD**. And all the people brought every man his ox with him that night, and slew them there." 1 Samuel 14:32–34.

The **blood** of animals is **sacred** to God. It was used in the old sanctuary service as a symbol of **Christ shedding His blood for us**, and it is still used by Christ today as a reminder that His **blood** saves us from the penalty of death. "And I have given it to you upon the altar to make an atonement for your souls." Leviticus 17:11. "For if the blood of bulls and of goats, and the ashes of an heifer sprinkling the unclean, sanctifieth to the purifying of the flesh: How much more shall the **BLOOD** of Christ, who through the eternal Spirit offered himself without spot to God, **PURGE YOUR CONSCIENCE FROM DEAD WORKS** to serve the living God? And for this cause he is the mediator of the new testament, that by means of death, for the redemption of the transgressions that were under the first testament, they which are called might receive the promise of eternal inheritance." Hebrews 9:13–15.

The ancient Israelites soaked the meat in **salt water** to bring out the blood. They restored flavor to the meat by using spices. Having worked at a meat packing company, I know that they do not drain the carcass of the blood thoroughly. What is that red juice which is coming

The NWO and the PROMOTION of METAPHYSICS

from your steak as you cut it? What comes to the top of a hamburger and forms a little pool while they are frying on the barbecue grill?

As pointed out earlier, the poor animals know they are going to be slaughtered before they are, and they try desperately to climb out of their corrals. While they are trying to save their lives, they are in a state of terror. They defecate and urinate on themselves and other cows. Some of this fecal matter gets on the meat and can give its consumer E. Coli, but what *Dateline* and *48 Hours* did not bring out is this. Some of the urine from the animal is also reabsorbed into the meat. When you eat the blood which God has most strikingly told us not to do, not only are you eating **blood**, but **urine** as well. This mixture of blood and urine is **one** of the best ways to produce a poison in the body known as **uric acid**, which is a major cause for **arthritis and gout**, bright's disease, kidney stones, and gallstones. Another way of bringing uric acid into the body via the mouth is by drinking coffee, tea, and soft drinks that have caffeine in them. Most do. Very few know that even chocolate has caffeine, as well. For years, I ignorantly filled my body with the above. For years, I suffered for it as well.

It was by learning about how important the diet plays in promoting good health or bad health that my sleepy eyes began to open. I read from testimonies written in the book, *Make Your Juicer Your Drug Store*, how many became wise about how to get rid of these dreadful diseases and how to rejuvenate the body. I met and talked with people who have had cancer, diabetes, arthritis, and gout and how they were healed. My wife and I saw a woman who was healed of borderline diabetes within one week by going on a strict vegetarian diet, exercising, and by using hydrotherapy while we visited a self-supporting clinic that taught these things.

I learned how to cleanse my own body of uric acid and, as a result, the arthritis and gout also left. However, not without a struggle. The first time I cleansed my body was in 1984. For 14 days, I went on a pure raw vegetable and fruit juice fast. I ate nothing. The highest form of nutrition is from raw fresh vegetable juices. Fruits are a wonderful cleanser. For 14 days, I drank fresh raw carrot, cucumber, celery, and beet juice for supper and a broth from brewed vegetables

The Real Truth About UFO's and the New World Order

for lunch. For breakfast, I took the advice from Jethro Kloss' book, *Back to Eden*, and combined fresh grape juice with almond milk. Slowly but surely, my arthritis and gout left me for about four years. It is also very important to learn how to cleanse the colon and restore friendly bacteria.

Then, again in 1989, I had an even worse case of gout than I had in the past! I could not understand this. I was a vegetarian. Why am I having gout again, but, here I am again walking on crutches. I suffered for about three years more until I finally found out what my problem was. It was my diet! Even though I was a vegetarian, my body was producing high levels of uric acid which crystallized around the big toe and ankles of my feet and spread inflammation that becomes absolutely torture to those who have felt the pains of gout.

What was producing the uric acid? It wasn't from coffee, tea, or from soft drinks that have caffeine because I quit drinking them for years. It was coming from eating fried foods and eating too many beans and bean products, like soybean meats. I learned the hard way that fried foods and too much protein will also produce uric acid.

As long as I eat steamed vegetables and stay away from fried foods, gout and arthritis will not come to visit my temple. Since Jesus gave me the victory over appetite, I am hiking up mountains again!

CHAPTER IV

SOCIALISM, COMMUNISM, AND THE AQUARIAN CONSPIRACY ARE BROTHERS AND SISTERS

"For rebellion is as the sin of witchcraft, and stubbornness is as iniquity and idolatry."
1 Samuel 15:23.

The Real Truth About UFO's and the New World Order

As pointed out, I have been investigating the history of this New World Order conspiracy for over a quarter of a century now. Except for a period of three years between 1975 and 1978, I have tried to sort out and bring together evidence that there is truly a worldwide conspiracy, and how this was, indeed, foretold in the Scriptures.

If the reader truly wants to know what will bring about "a time of trouble, such as never was since there was a nation," as the mighty prophet Daniel foretold, study what caused the French Revolution! From here, the New Age Movement and the New World Order began. Here can be traced the origin of Marxism and Leninism and Lucifer's last stand to overthrow the power and influence of Jesus Christ and His people. The voices of Socialism heard around the world are calling for world revolution.

As pointed out, the voices calling for a Utopian world federation can be traced back to Nimrod, the great rebel against the Lord. After our God confused the plans of the Babel builders, then again in the fourth century B.C. another rebel named Plato, an apostle of Spiritualism, began to design another plan for a world federation. Plato's plan was based in the myth about Atlantis having once enjoyed a Golden Age. Plato wrote that Atlantis in the myth was divided into ten kingdoms and that there was no such thing as private property for **the Atlanteans held all goods and property in common**. Everything was socially owned. Plato's Atlantean Plan was accelerated, as we saw, later by humanist European philosophers during the revival of arts and letters which became known as the **Renaissance**.

A champion of **re-establishing** the Atlantean Plan of Plato's during the Renaissance Era was the English statesman and author, Thomas More (1478-1535), who wrote *Utopia* of which got him beheaded. Most of Plato's ideas were continued mainly by English, German and French humanist rebels who by pen and voice called for a world revolution. The first time the word *"Communism"* was heard was from humanist French rebels hiding in secret societies in France.[1]

During the **Reign of Terror** in France, the religion of Jesus was forbidden by law. The Bibles were publicly burned in their streets. At the same time, not only were the Ten Commandments thrown out

---

[1]*Encyclopedia Americana*, **Vol. 7, 1994, p. 435.**

Socialism, Communism, and the Aquarian Conspiracy

by the Enlightenment, but all human laws which protected the French citizens were abolished as well. While the secret society of the Illuminati caused the people of France to ignore the First Commandment, "Thou shalt have no other gods before me" (Exodus 20:3), so did Illuminism cause the citizens of France at that time to reject, "Thou shalt not kill, Thou shalt not commit adultery, and Thou shalt not steal," along with the other commandments. This spiritual fall of France brought national ruin!

Can you imagine what the great cities of the United States would be like if all the laws of God and the laws of man were removed? What would protect the citizens? Are not multitudes ignoring, "Thou shalt not kill, Thou shalt not commit adultery, and Thou shalt not steal?"

When my wife and I went to New York City to hold lectures in the burrows of the Bronx, Brooklyn, Queens, Yonkers, and Manhattan areas, it became commonplace to hear gunshots ring out above the noise of this evil city. While we were there, a newsbroadcaster reported that within one month 40 children were shot by stray bullets while in or around their homes. Will America **repeat** the horrors of the French Revolution?

France reached an era during the 18th century known as the Reign of Terror. The citizens had to fend for themselves for three and one-half years! Neighbor was against neighbor! Police killed police! Politicians killed politicians! No one was safe for there were no laws of God or human laws to protect the citizens from murder, rape, and robbery during the Reign of Terror. Total anarchy broke out.

This is what Satan shall cause to happen again to those who again throw out God's Law and who obey not the Gospel of our Lord Jesus Christ. This time **anarchy** shall break out worldwide, but not only in France.

However, Daniel the prophet says, "And at that time thy people shall be delivered, every one that shall be found written in the book." Daniel 12:1. The horror of the French Revolution and of its Reign of Terror did not come suddenly.

For over 10 years around the closing of the 18th century, Satan conditioned the minds of the citizens of France for anarchy by using France's government officials to promote atheism or humanism among its student population. To **combat** Christianity,

The Real Truth About UFO's and the New World Order

the **entertainment field** of that day was used to degrade their morals. This same attack that Satan used in the 18th century to overthrow Christianity, humanists and Spiritualists are doing today in these closing years of the 20th century!

However, before we can discern what role the Entertainment Industry is playing today in this conspiracy of universalism, we must explore the political side of this conspiracy. Let us again look at the beginning of the Illuminati conspiracy and what its primary goal was. The whole focus of the Illuminati conspiracy was to **condition** the citizens of the world to establish a universal government here on earth which would unite all religions as well. Does not mainstream Christianity today teach that Christ will establish His kingdom here on this earth during the thousand-year millennium?

However, says Jesus, "My kingdom **IS NOT OF THIS WORLD**: if my kingdom were of this world, then would my servants fight, that I should not be delivered to the Jews: but now is my kingdom not from hence." John 18:36.

Reader, this is very important to keep this in mind!

The first-century Jews **misinterpreted** the Scriptures about the prophecies of the Messiah. They **misapplied** Christ's prophecies of **His Second Coming with that of His first**. The religious leaders took the Scriptures that warned about how the Messiah was to overthrow all the nations at His Second Coming, and taught that Christ would overthrow the Roman Empire and place the Jews as rulers of the other nations. Even the disciples of Christ were ignorant of Jesus' **First Advent**. They, too, had to be taught by Jesus that "**My kingdom is not of this world**."

Just what did Jesus mean when He prayed, "Thy kingdom come. Thy will be done in earth, as it is in heaven." Matthew 6:10. The Scriptures are very clear that one day this evil world we live in will become the **capital of the universe**. Believe it or not, reader, the Scriptures predict that the Godhead will make His home on this planet! However, this is to come after the 1,000-year reign of Christ in Heaven. Here, more than most are confused. **Satan, again**, has even Christians today believing that what the world needs now is a one-world government established to save the planet. Even Christians have been conditioned to believe the prophet Plato that our society

Socialism, Communism, and the Aquarian Conspiracy

will one day reach a Utopian society in this present world. However, the Scriptures say plainly that God shall **destroy** this present world. Let us look at this from Scripture.

"And I saw a **NEW** heaven and a **NEW** earth: for the **FIRST** heaven and the **FIRST** earth were passed away; and there was no more sea.

"And I John saw the holy city, new Jerusalem, coming down from God out of heaven, prepared as a bride adorned for her husband. And I heard a great voice out of heaven saying, **Behold, the tabernacle of God is with men, and he will dwell with them, and they shall be his people, and God himself shall be with them, and be their God.**

"And God shall wipe away all tears from their eyes; and there shall be no more death, neither sorrow, nor crying, neither shall there be any more pain: for the former things are passed away." Revelation 21:1–4.

Notice verse one. John, the penman of Revelation, saw in vision that there would be a **NEW HEAVEN AND A NEW EARTH**. Jesus said, "Heaven and earth shall pass away: but my words shall not pass away." Luke 21:33.

Can you imagine the Holy God of Israel, who is without sin, living in such a place like New York City, Calcutta, Paris, Moscow, London, Manila, or any place on this polluted earth, including Jerusalem? The polluted creeks and streams of Israel are one of its shameful sore spots.

"For, behold, I create **NEW HEAVENS** and a **NEW EARTH**: and the former shall not be remembered, nor come into mind." Isaiah 65:17.

Old Jerusalem is only a **shadow** of the one that is coming.

"But now they desire a **BETTER COUNTRY**, that is, an **HEAVENLY**: wherefore God is not ashamed to be called their God: for he hath **prepared for them a city**." Hebrews 11:16.

"And I John saw the holy city, **NEW JERUSALEM**, coming down from God out of heaven, prepared as a bride adorned for her husband." Revelation 21:2.

Over and over again, Jesus and His disciples taught that this present world in which we live in today **will be destroyed**, but a new heaven and a new earth shall take its place.

"The Lord is not slack concerning his promise, as some men count slackness; but is longsuffering to us-ward, not willing that any should perish, but that all should come to repentance.

The Real Truth About UFO's and the New World Order

"But the day of the Lord will come as a thief in the night; in which **the heavens shall pass away with a great noise, and the elements shall melt with fervent heat, the earth also and the works that are therein shall be burned up**.

"Seeing then that all these things shall be dissolved, what manner of persons ought ye to be in all holy conversation and godliness, Looking for and hasting unto the coming of the day of God, wherein the **heavens being on fire shall be dissolved**, and the elements shall melt with fervent heat?

"**Nevertheless we, according to his promise, look for new heavens and a new earth, wherein dwelleth righteousness.**" 2 Peter 3:9–13.

Jesus warned over and over again not to get involved with the cares of this world.

"And take heed to yourselves, lest at any time your hearts be overcharged with surfeiting, and drunkenness, and cares of this life, and so that day come upon you unawares. For as a snare shall it come on all them that dwell on the face of the whole earth.

"**Watch** ye therefore, and pray always, that ye may be accounted **worthy** to **escape** all these things that shall come to pass, and to **stand** before the **Son of man**." Luke 21:34–36.

Jesus' Second Coming will **not** be to **usher** in any **new era** or a thousand-year reign of peace here on earth as mainstream Christianity teaches and which both Socialist humanists and New Age Socialists are determined to establish. Nevertheless, "**Alas for the day! for the day of the Lord is at hand, and as a destruction from the Almighty shall it come.**" Joel 1:15.

There will **never** be peace in this world until Satan, his angels, and those who have placed themselves on the side of the Evil One by rejecting the Gospel of Christ are destroyed. The apostle Paul foretold that shortly before Christ's Second Coming there would be in our present time a promotion of peace and safety in the world. That is just what is going on today through the United Nations. The world is looking to the United Nations as the great hope of our planet. After the reader studies more about the history of the United Nations and who actually founded it, you will understand what Daniel the prophet of God meant when he prophesied,

Socialism, Communism, and the Aquarian Conspiracy

"**BY PEACE SHALL DESTROY MANY.**" Daniel 8:25. The Great Destroyer of human lives in the past has many times come in the name of peace.

The apostle Paul warned, "For yourselves know perfectly that the day of the Lord so cometh as a thief in the night. For when they shall say, **Peace and safety; then sudden destruction cometh upon them**, as travail upon a woman with child; and they shall not escape." 1 Thessalonians 5:2, 3. We will see how the United Nations is, indeed, connected today with this prophecy shortly.

As there were apostles and prophets promoting the Gospel of Jesus of Nazareth, so have there been apostles and prophets promoting the Gospel of Spiritualism. The great prophet of Spiritualism, Plato, taught just the opposite of what Jesus taught would happen to the present world. Plato, of whom both pagans and humanists draw their beliefs, prophesied of a coming **Golden Age of Atlantis reappearing in this world**. New Agers call this coming 21st century the Utopian Age a.k.a. the Age of Aquarius. Hitler saw himself as the messiah of this Golden Age. Communists, also trained in this thought, made it their goal to achieve this Utopian Age by using force.

However, the prophet of God, Daniel, prophesied that antichrists "shall divide the land for gain." Daniel 11:39. The main ecumenical theme that shall gather the people of the world into the fold of the Evil One (Revelation 16:13–19) is what Daniel the prophet of God prophesied, "divide the land for gain." What does this mean?

This means that these religious and political ecumenical movements which were prophesied to come (See 1 John 4:3) would not only be preaching peace and safety, but also that all the wealth of the world will be divided equally among its inhabitants. This guile that has fooled so many today which is coming forth from the Dragon himself can be summed up into one word. It is called **Socialism**.

Did not Karl Marx, Lenin, and Stalin preach this? Do not New Agers preach this? Has not the Pope preached this? Are not American citizens being **conditioned** to accept this New World Order theme today by our presidents? The main theme which can be found today among New Agers and Roman Catholicism is **forced international Socialism** a.k.a. **globalism**!

The Real Truth About UFO's and the New World Order

The propaganda that all the wealth of the world will be distributed equally by the year A.D. 2000 shall become more and more audible from the mouths of the great men of the earth. As I write, free trade is going forth determined to break down all barriers that separate nations. Forced international **Socialistic medicine** is trying to make its way into this country as well. Who will pay for this forced public insurance? Who shall divide the land for gain? You and I. How? This will come about by being forced to pay more taxes. Christians should pay taxes to their governments because Jesus did. (See Matthew 17:24–27; 22:17–21.)

As long as the Christian is protected by the Constitution of the United States to worship God as he pleases, we should help support our country. However, what better way could clever politicians **shift** the **wealth of individuals** to be divided among the inhabitants of a nation or world than by raising **taxes**? What if we sat down one day and calculated all the **hidden taxes** we have paid for goods purchased, plus income tax, along with local taxes, and found out that over 50% of one's income went towards taxes? Could this happen? Ask a resident of Quebec, Canada, about how much of their income goes towards taxes. What if the IRS was not a government institution, and our income tax money collected was given out to other world governments? What happens to those who do not pay their taxes? What would happen if the taxes are raised so high that you cannot pay the taxes on your house? The state takes it. What would happen if the average citizen could not pay the tax on their private property and the state took it? What if the state ended up owning everyone's property? Under what kind of government would the citizens find themselves? It would be Communism!

There is a controversy among the nations today to unite the world again into a one-world religion and a one-world Socialist government as Nimrod did at Babel. Christians must realize that the nations of the world are not on the Lord's side!

"Ye adulterers and adulteresses, know ye not that the friendship of the world is enmity with God? whosoever therefore will be a friend of the world is the enemy of God." James 4:4.

Just as there is a controversy with the nations to unite, leaving Christ out, so does:

Socialism, Communism, and the Aquarian Conspiracy

"The Lord hath a controversy with the nations, he will plead with all flesh; he will give them that are wicked to the sword, saith the Lord. Thus saith the Lord of hosts, Behold, evil shall go forth from nation to nation, and a great whirlwind shall be raised up from the coasts of the earth.

"And the slain of the Lord shall be at that day from one end of the earth even unto the other end of the earth: they shall not be lamented, neither gathered, nor buried; they shall be dung upon the ground." Jeremiah 25:31–33.

However, like the days of old, there will always be those who will be preaching another gospel other than that of Jesus and His apostles.

"And many shall follow their pernicious ways; by reason of whom the way of **truth shall be evil spoken of**." 2 Peter 2:2.

May 1, 1776, launched Lucifer's all-out war and last effort to destroy the Gospel of Christ and His people. Satan planned to use the philosophies of humanism or atheism to **de-Christianize the world**. Once Christianity's morality and its founder would be removed, then he could fuse all of his deceived followers into a **global confederation**.

During the third quarter of the 18th century until 1848, the light of the Gospel of Jesus was especially warred upon by the Dragon. During these 72 years, **Bibles were publicly burned** in the streets of **Paris**. Darwin's theory of evolution gave birth. During this time, Karl Marx began to rewrite the occult's plan for world revolution which was known as Illuminism in the 18th century. In 1848, this same plan was declared by Marx and Engels as *The Communist Manifesto*. In 1848, Spiritualism began its **revival** in New England.

Communism, which began as a nonviolent movement calling itself the **Enlightenment**, later in the 19th century became the **League of the Just**. It changed its name again to the **League of Communists** after *The Communist Manifesto* was published in 1848.[2]

However, it was Communism's elder sister, Socialism (Illuminism or humanism), whose train of thought can be **traced back** to Plato down to the ancient founder of the Tower of Babel, Nimrod.

---

[2]*Cyclopedia of World Authors*, Magill, p. 724.

The Real Truth About UFO's and the New World Order

These seeming great humanitarian Deists of Freemasonry of the 18th century, who were experts in occultism, included Adam Weishaupt, Voltaire, Benjamin Franklin, Thomas Jefferson, and Thomas Paine. These men were promoting a New World Order in their day and were just **setting the stage for Communism** to come later and attack Christianity with guns and bullets. Through his chosen few, Satan attacked the faith of Jesus. All of the above names were French Revolutionists and Freemasons. This is shocking information, however, this as we have seen is a historical fact. The reader cannot read about this history of the French Revolution **without stumbling over** the names of Franklin, Jefferson, and Paine as some of their revolutionary leaders.

"And the serpent **cast out of his mouth** water as a flood after the woman, **that he might cause** her to be carried away of the flood." Revelation 12:15.

What were the weapons of warfare used by these enemies of Christ? It was **hate propaganda**. In the 18th century, this was promoted by well-known politicians and celebrities in Europe. In the 20th century, this same theme is being preached against Christ today using the same tactics.

However, while the attack of secular humanism displayed itself in the pages of *The Communist Manifesto* to the people of the Old World, the Mother of Harlots, first beginning her mission at Babylon, resurrected another daughter in the New World. The very year the Dragon published *The Communist Manifesto*, his daughters, the Fox sisters of Hydesville, New York, begat a **revival of Spiritualism** in America. This revival of the occult begat the infamous Theosophical Society which adopted Marxism. The Theosophical Society was founded for the sole purpose of **contacting ascended masters** or **Mahatmas** who were believed to be **advanced humans** who are guiding their select few into a New Age. Later, this Theosophical Society of the occult also begat other secret societies of witchcraft which produced other prophets of Spiritualism as we shall see. Please keep in mind that **Socialism, Communism, and Spiritualism are brothers and sisters**. They are all *red* revolutionary threats.

The science of witchcraft that Leah, Kate, and Margaret Fox can be credited with reviving here in the United States was **necromancy**. The Fox sisters claimed to communicate with the dead by answering mysterious rapping noises in their home which they said were spirits

Socialism, Communism, and the Aquarian Conspiracy

of the dead. They said they had **devised a code** by which the mysterious rapping could be **answered back** by using the letters of the alphabet. Thousands of Americans were soon attending the Fox sister's seances each year to seek the **spirit's advice** through them. Christians and worldlings, ignorant of what the Scriptures warned of what these **familiar spirits** actually were and what God will do to those who claim to communicate with them (See Deuteronomy 18:11, 12), **communicated with evil spirits**. The Fox sister's seances led to other areas of Spiritualism. Multitudes in the 1800s began to explore into the occult which is **forbidden** by God. Psychics began to spring up everywhere, not only in America, but in Europe as well.

The war on the faith of Jesus, which actually began at the garden of Eden, has **milestones** that **mark** decisive battles down through history. The years **1776** and **1848**, along with some other dates, we will see shortly can be said to be **spiritual D-days** in the history of the Christian people! However, the year **1844** is a very important date in Bible prophecy which shall be diligently studied in Volume Five entitled *Ancient Prophecies About The Dragon, The Beast, and The False Prophet*.

While Spiritualism raised its ugly head in 1848 in America and has almost reached its peak today, Socialism and Communism came forth out of the mouth of the Dragon (Satan) **as a flood** threatening to **drown all voices** who would remain loyal to Jesus and preach the Gospel according to the Scriptures. While *The Communist Manifesto* was published in 1848, the Fox sisters began their mission to revive Spiritualism in the United States.

Names like Voltaire, Weishaupt, and Paine stand out in 18th-century history, as does the name Nimrod, the "mighty hunter *against* the Lord." Names like Karl Marx, Lenin, Trotsky, and Castro certainly stand out in history as some of the **worst enemies** of the cause of Christ in the 19th and 20th centuries. However, Shaw, Besant, Blavatsky, Crowley, Bailey, Wells, and Orwell of the late 19th and early 20th century will equally be responsible at the Day of Judgment for causing multitudes to **worship** "the dragon which gave power unto the beast." Revelation 13:4.

George Bernard Shaw, the author of the famous musical *My Fair Lady* who was born on July 26, 1856, in Dublin and died on November 2, 1950, was a **playwright** for the entertainment field. This Irish

The Real Truth About UFO's and the New World Order

comic, writer, dramatist, literary critic, musician, and artist was determined to do his best in destroying Christian thought by **replacing it with the religion of Reason** as his humanist brethren of the Communist Party did. However, unlike Lenin, Trotsky, and Stalin, this non-violent Socialist would **war** on Christianity with the **pen and with his voice**. Posing as a great humanitarian, he used his influence to promote the cause of Communism in Russia and was determined to make England a Socialist state. To the worldly-minded, he was a brilliant humanist; but, to the Bible believers, he did his best to ridicule those who claimed the name of Jesus. Shaw can be quoted in a poem in a play, *Back to Methuselah*, in which he wrote:

"**He who bears the brand of Cain shall rule the earth.**"[3]

Cain, as any Bible student knows, was the **first murderer** and the first in the antediluvian world to build a city. He called it Enoch. Shaw certainly had the brand of Cain for **he is responsible for helping inspire Leninist Stalinists to murder multitudes of Christians through his hate propaganda.**

Shaw, at the age of 25, became a vegetarian, neither smoked nor drank, and to many in that age of history stood out among thousands as a reformist. Like Voltaire, who was one of his heros, Shaw had some redeeming personality traits. This great prophet of the cause of Socialism and Communism, along with his contribution, was recognized by Stalin. Here from *Collier's Encyclopedia*, Vol. 20, p. 651, we read the following:

"At an age when most people prefer to stay at home, Shaw began to see the world, visiting the United States, the U.S.S.R., South Africa, India, and New Zealand. At Moscow, accompanied by **Lady Astor,** he interviewed **Stalin**. When the Labour Party, **WHICH HE HAD DONE SO MUCH TO CREATE**, came to power, he was offered a knighthood and a peerage, both of which he declined; when asked if he would accept the **Order of Merit**, he replied that he had already **conferred it on himself**." (Emphasis mine.)

George Bernard Shaw's efforts to exalt the cause of Communism/Socialism through **pen and voice** helped place millions of Christians,

---

[3]*The New International Dictionary of Quotations*, **Rawson & Miner, p. 57.**

Socialism, Communism, and the Aquarian Conspiracy

who were against Communism in Russia, Eastern Europe, and China, into **untimely graves**. Much history has been written about the outrageous persecutions of the Ashkenazi Jews by Hitler, but few are the pages written about the millions of Christians, both Roman Catholic and Protestant, who felt the deadly blows of the arm and sickle of Lenin, Stalin, and Chairman Mao. Gullible Americans, as a whole, never saw the connection between Soviet Communism and British Socialism. Both wanted to establish a Utopian government.

While Lenin, Stalin, and Mao used force to overthrow Christian nations, the British novelist George Bernard Shaw was **using the theater** to send out his **propaganda** against Christianity through the plays he wrote. While the actors and actresses poked fun at Christ and His people, Shaw also used actors and actresses to **parrot** his revolutionary plans through the script of the plays he wrote. Shaw **promoted** Socialism by using propaganda tactics.

Shaw's spiritual military headquarters which he helped pioneer was the dangerous secret society in London called the Fabian Society, and England is a Socialist country.

Here from *The New Encyclopaedia Britannica* we read the following:

"Despite his failure as a novelist in the 1880's, Shaw found himself during the decade. He became a vegetarian, a socialist, a spellbinding orator, a polemicist, and tentatively a playwright. He became the force behind the newly founded (1884) Fabian Society, a middle-class Socialist group that aimed at the **transformation** of English society not through revolution but through 'permeation' (in Sidney Webb terms) of the country's intellectual and political life. Shaw involved himself in every aspect of its activities, most visibly as editor of one of the classics of **British Socialism**, *Fabian Essays in Socialism* (1889), to which he also contributed two sections.

"In 1882 Shaw's conversion to socialism began when he heard Henry George, the American author of *Progress and Poverty*, address a London meeting. George's message 'changed the whole current of my life.' "[4]

In that same year, Shaw read the infamous *Das Kapital (The*

---

[4] *The New Encyclopaedia Britannica*, Micropaedia, Vol. 10, pp. 706, 707.

The Real Truth About UFO's and the New World Order

Communist Manifesto) and can be quoted as saying the following statement, "**It made a man out of me**."[5]

Two other British Socialist propagandists, who joined Shaw in promoting this *red* revolution, were H.G. Wells and Eric Blair. They became convinced atheists. It was H.G. Wells, the well-known science fiction author, who not only helped spark the interest in UFO's through his novels such as *The War of the Worlds* (1898) which Hollywood later made into a movie, but Wells used his popular influence as a so-called visionary novelist to promote this Atlantean Socialist conspiracy until his death in 1946. Wells joined the British secret society of Socialism calling itself the Fabian Society in 1903.[6] Four years later, he left the Fabians and began **his own** campaign to establish Plato's Atlantean world federation.

Wells, considered a prophet of the Socialist movement, wrote novels that promoted the tenets of international Socialism such as *Anticipations* (1901), *Mankind in the Making* (1903), and *A Modern Utopia* (1905). He also wrote syndicated articles showing how inevitably a world Socialist federation would eventually be established. Some of his syndicated articles expressing his determination to force a Socialist Utopian world federation on the citizens of this planet were expressed in *The Open Conspiracy: Blue Prints for a World Revolution* (1928).[7]

This other *red* revolutionary, Eric Blair, who wrote under the pen name of George Orwell, was another British novelist and essayist who wrote the infamous novel about international enslavement entitled *Nineteen Eighty-four*. This Fabian Socialist was said to have hated totalitarianism and Communism, yet he was a professed Socialist.[8] Orwell's book, *Nineteen Eighty-four*, is where we get the term "**big brother is watching you**." He was said to have hated intellectuals, yet he helped earn his living by being a literary critic. He was also the author of *Animal Farm*, a political satire which was turned down by several publishers because of its **political innuendoes**. This fantasy relates what happens to animals who free themselves and then are again enslaved through violence and fraud. Orwell (Eric Blair)

---

[5]*The Encyclopedia of World Biography*, Vol. 10, p. 25.
[6]*Ibid.*, Vol. 11, p. 311.
[7]*Ibid.*, Vol. 11, p. 311.
[8]*Nineteen Eighty-four*, Orwell, biographical page.

Socialism, Communism, and the Aquarian Conspiracy

died of tuberculosis in London in 1950 four years after his comrade H.G. Wells died in London in 1946. Shaw, Wells, and George Orwell were all **red** revolutionaries using their pens instead of guns to force international Socialism from the camp of **diehard atheists**. Some historians may argue that Communism and Socialism divided into separate factions from 1917-19, and this is true. However, Communism and Socialism are sisters born in London, England, by father Marx whose great, great, Socialist grandfather (spiritually speaking) was Adam Weishaupt, who was inspired by the writings of Plato. Plato borrowed his Utopian ideas from Greek mythology which originally began with Nimrod, who was **first** to unite the known world into a **world federation leaving God out**. While it is true that totalitarian Communism, which was Leninism/Stalinism, and Socialism seemingly were not in the same camp, they both worked to overthrow the power and influence of Christianity. Both have the same ultimate goals. History shows this to be true. Like the Marxist-based Theosophical Society, they helped Leninism/Stalinism at a distance.

Another comrade of Shaw's who has been recorded in Heaven as another "mighty hunter against the Lord" was Annie Besant. This well-read, personally attractive, Christian girl, who visioned herself as becoming a great religious leader one day preaching a new faith, at the age of 20 married a clergyman named Frank Besant. However, the marriage between this dominating clergyman and this ambitious, self-supporting, independent young woman was doomed from the beginning. Annie Besant craved a new experience in her Christian walk and became very critical about the church she and her husband belonged to. After causing a scandal by refusing to take the sacrament, her husband threw her out of the house. Having this terrible experience, this poor young woman became embittered and depressed.[9]

How many times has the Christian reader been through bad experiences with church members? How many times have we been disappointed by our church leaders? How many times have you wanted to quit the church? Annie Besant, instead of going to the Scriptures and seeking God through prayer for strength and grace to be able to endure her trials and wait on the Lord for direction, blamed Christ for

---

[9]*The Fabians*, Mackenzie, p. 46.

The Real Truth About UFO's and the New World Order

her problems and turned against Christianity. She soon fell victim to secular humanism (freethought) and began writing pamphlets promoting it.[10]

Meanwhile, Besant went to London and found a temporary home with another freethinker named Moncure Conway who was a Unitarian preacher. Many of Moncure Conway's friends were also freethinkers, which is an 18th-century term given to the Enlightenment or Illuminati supporters. Conway's South Place Chapel was a forum for cults in London in the 1870s. It was through Moncure Conway that Annie Besant met Charles Bradlaugh, the leader of the anti-Christian National Secular Society in England, which she just joined. Its leader, Charles Bradlaugh, was 40 years old at the time when he met Annie Besant. Bradlaugh was already making a reputation in England as a **militant atheist** and popular educator. In just a year's time, Annie Besant who had a natural talent for public speaking found herself as the vice president of the National Secular Society. Instead of using her God-given talents for the advancement of the Kingdom of God, **she became a militant foe against Christ**. She also **swapped** the preaching of the coming Kingdom of Christ for establishing a **Utopian society** in this present world.[11] Besant also became a prophetess of this Socialist Atlantean scheme that can be traced to Plato.

Soon, this one-time Christian young woman began to rub elbows with Eleanor Marx, Karl Marx's daughter. Annie was jealous of Eleanor because of a love triangle she was in. Annie soon met George Bernard Shaw. After being introduced to the militant Fabian Society, she became a member in 1885, and after about one year she was elected to the executive committee in 1886. George Bernard Shaw and Annie Besant eventually were running the Fabian Society's efforts to further advance the cause of Communism and Socialism. Sergius Stepniak, who fled from Russia after murdering the head of Tzar Nicholas II's security police and who was hailed as a hero, joined the Fabian Society's efforts to overthrow the Russian government.[12]

---

[10]*The Fabians*, Mackenzie, p. 46.

[11]*Ibid.*, Mackenzie, p. 47.

[12]*Ibid.*, Mackenzie, p. 55.

Socialism, Communism, and the Aquarian Conspiracy

However, Annie Besant, this ex-Christian woman who converted to atheism (Communism), was to have another conversion in 1889. Herbert Burrows, a disciple of the notorious Russian witch named Helena Blavatsky, introduced Annie to Spiritualism. Still having those early visions stored in the back of her memory as a child of one day becoming a religious leader of a new religion and after reading *The Secret Doctrine* written by Blavatsky and meeting her, Annie **dropped** the Fabian Society and became a **disciple** of Madame Blavatsky.[13]

Socialists use **social issues** as a **cover** or a springboard to advance their cause. Karl Marx used the poor to gain sympathy for his cause against capitalists who, by the way, helped finance his 40-page *The Communist Manifesto*. It was Horace Greeley and Friedrich Engels who helped Marx financially. Greeley **hired** Marx as a European correspondent.[14] Annie Besant used the feminist movement for the emancipation of women along with the birth control gimmick to stir up citizens against their government.

Annie Besant was George Bernard Shaw's right hand partner until she met another Marxist of a different kind. In 1889 Besant, indeed, **fell under the spell** of the Russian **pythonist** Madame Blavatsky.[15] This was the very year that Blavatsky published *The Secret Doctrine* describing Plato's Utopian government of **Atlantis**, which was borrowed from Ignatius Donnelly's book, *Atlantis: The Antediluvian World*. No doubt Annie Besant was **mesmerized** by Blavatsky's own plans for world revolution and how similar Fabian Socialism and New Age Marxism were. Both Communism and Socialism have ideologies that derived from Spiritualism's apostle named Plato. While Lenin and his Bolsheviks were busy in Russia trying to **overthrow** the Tzar, the Marxist Annie Besant was busy with Mahatma (Mohandas) Gandhi in India in an effort to throw out Christianity and its British government. Besant was jailed in 1917 for her Marxist revolutionary propaganda.[16]

---

[13] *The Fabians*, Mackenzie, p. 145.
[14] *Funk & Wagnall's New Encyclopedia*, **Vol. 12, 1988, p. 214.**
[15] *The Encyclopedia of Parapsychology and Psychical Research*, **Berger, p. 33.**
[16] *Ibid.*, **Berger, p. 33.**

The Real Truth About UFO's and the New World Order

American Christians have been **very naive** about Gandhi's whole career. How very few are there who realize that not only was Gandhi a prophet of the New Age Movement, but he was, indeed, a Marxist as well as was his comrade Annie Besant.[17] He was also a member of the Theosophical Society.[18] Using his voice, his pen, and nonviolent protest marches and sit-ins, he overthrew the British government. All this was done under the **auspices** of the Theosophical Society. Besant and Gandhi **threw out** the Church of England and **replaced it** with Blavatsky's compilation of her religious and metaphysical ideas, many of which were based in **Hindu pantheism**. According to the *Encyclopedia Americana*, Vol. 26, 1991, page 641, it says:

"**Theosophical thought** may be found in the speculative writings of the philosophers **PLATO**, Plotinus, Apollonius of Tyana, in such mystics as Jakob Boehme and Paracelsus, as well as in the writings of the medieval mystics." (Emphasis mine.)

This above article was placed in the above encyclopedia by Joy Mills of the Theosophical Society in America.

Spiritualism has a left hand and a right hand. It is both political and religious. The left hand promotes the precepts of Socialism and Communism, while the right hand promotes the sciences of Spiritualism. Many times the left hand does not know what the right hand is doing. Such was the case of the leftist George Bernard Shaw. When Shaw found out that Annie became involved with the New Age religion of Blavatsky, he was overwhelmed with shock for Shaw was a convinced atheist.

While Spiritualism is divided into political and religious sections, **often** the political victims do not **subscribe** to the religious tenets. What is so **mind boggling** about trying to understand why anyone would fall for either of these snares of Satan is that the people who join the ranks of Spiritualism, like Annie Besant, many times were originally from Christian homes and highly intelligent people. However, "**professing themselves to be wise, they became fools**." Romans 1:22. Socialists are divided. There is **atheistic** Socialism and **religious** or ethical Socialism. Marxism actually divided this way in 1848.

---

[17]*Gandhi: Voice of a New Age Revolution*, Green, p. 18.

[18]*Ibid.*, Green, p. 98.

Socialism, Communism, and the Aquarian Conspiracy

Just as humanistic Socialists look to Marx, Lenin, Trotsky, Stalin, Gramsci, Shaw, and others as champions for the Socialist movement, so does its spiritual side, the New Age Movement, look to the Fox sisters, Madame Blavatsky, Annie Besant, Alice Ann Bailey, and Aleister Crowley as among the first to spread Spiritualism after its revival in America in 1848 for the above leaders of Spiritualism also promoted their version of Socialism. Communism and Marxism are words that identify with the same cause. These **reds** are determined to force the entire world into **international Socialism**.

The Marxist Madame Helena Petrovna Blavatsky (1831–1891) came to the United States as a missionary of Spiritualism in 1873. Just two years after Helena P. Blavatsky arrived in America, she co-founded this school of occultism called the Theosophical Society of which she would beget daughters. Here is some more information about this esoteric secret society. According to *The Academic American Encyclopedia*, Vol. 19, p. 159, we will read the following about the Theosophical Society:

"The term *theosophy* is derived from the **Greek** *theos* ("**god**") and *sophia* ("wisdom") and means wisdom of or about God."

Reader, this word *theosophy* may mean wisdom of god, but what god are they referring to? They are absolutely not referring to the God of the Bible.

The Academic American Encyclopedia, Vol. 19, p. 159, goes on to say:

"More specifically, the **term refers** to the Theosophical Society, its offshoots, and the doctrines held by its members. The most important early figure in the movement was Helena Petrovna Blavatsky, who, along with H.S. Olcott (1832–1907) and W.Q. Judge (1851–96), founded the society in 1875. In numerous works, including *Isis Unveiled* (2 vols., 1877) and *The Secret Doctrine* (2 vols., 1888), Blavatsky elaborated an amalgamation of previous theories that were claimed to be derived from the **mahatmas** of ancient India. The Theosophical Society grew rapidly in Europe and the United States, its two most influential adherents being Annie Besant and Rudolf Steiner."

Another well-known member was Thomas Edison and Edgar Cayce!

The Theosophical Society claims it is not a religion for it has no dogma, creed, or ritual. However, they are a huge secret society of

The Real Truth About UFO's and the New World Order

Spiritualism which today has at least **151 branches** in major cities of the United States with its headquarters in Wheaton, Illinois.[19]

Blavatsky, the Russian **pythonist**, upon arriving here in the United States began to roam the circles of Spiritualism where she met Colonel Henry Olcott (1832–1907). Col. Olcott, who converted to Buddhism, became the Theosophical Society's first president. Olcott had a lot of influence in New England in the mid 1800s. In his middle 20s, he worked for Horace Greeley's *New York Tribune* as its associate agricultural editor. He later served in the Civil War and eventually became a special commissioner with the rank of colonel. He was also a lawyer and was commissioned by the President of the United States to report on trade relations between the United States and India. Having to travel extensively, this **missionary** of **Spiritualism** found himself in an excellent position to promote the school of the occult which he, H.P. Blavatsky, and William Q. Judge, a New York attorney, would begin in New England.[20]

It should also be brought out that Horace Greeley, the founder of *The New York Tribune* at which Olcott worked as a young man, was not only a promoter of Spiritualism[21] that was spreading like wild fire in New England in the mid and late 19th century, but Horace Greeley, the well-known newspaper editor, was also using his newspaper as his personal mouthpiece to promote not only his beliefs in Spiritualism but those of Karl Marx as well.[22] Greeley used his *New York Tribune* to not only promote Marxism, but Spiritualism as well! He personally involved himself with the Fox sisters and promoted their efforts to revive the dangerous powers of Spiritualism here in the United States. Ironically enough, this same Horace Greeley was exalted to be a **presidential contender** against Grant, but lost by a landslide.

Because of the great revival of Spiritualism brought about by the Fox sisters in 1848, the founding of the Theosophical Society in New York in 1875 was quickly accepted and became the center in America

---

[19]*Encyclopedia Americana*, Vol. 26, 1991, p. 642.
[20]*Encyclopedia of Occultism and Parapsychology*, Vol. M-Z, 3rd ed., pp. 1214-1215.
[21]*Collier's Encyclopedia*, Vol. 2, p. 430.
[22]*Encyclopedia of World Biography*, Vol. 4, p. 525.

Socialism, Communism, and the Aquarian Conspiracy

to learn the sciences of occultism. What the Word of God warned in Deuteronomy 18:10–11 which the ancient pagan Canaanites practiced of which caused their destruction, the Theosophical Society **boldly** advertised! The Theosophical Society did not claim to be any particular religion, but an educational institute. Because there was a **great falling away** from the Word of God by Christians as the apostle Paul foretold in 2 Thessalonians 2:3 and because the Papacy locked out the knowledge of God in the Middle Ages by putting the Scriptures into an unknown Latin language, Spiritualism was able to go forth from New England **sweeping multitudes into its web**. This happened not only in the United States, but in Christian countries in Europe as well. While Russians and Europeans were feeling the power of forced Marxism, Americans were **being corralled** into this Atlantean scheme through New Age Socialism.

Both rich and poor, free and bond, fell for the deceptions of Spiritualism in the mid and late 1800s. However, it is not generally known by mainstream Christians today of how great the bewitching power of Spiritualism's influence was felt in New England. When the reader finds out how many of our well-known political and spiritual leaders were involved with it back in the 19th century, it may open the eyes of sleeping Christian pastors who are preaching to **sleeping** Christians what we will soon have to face here in America shortly!

Because most Christians of the 18th and 19th centuries had only a limited knowledge of the Scriptures, like most Christians today, they could not **distinguish between** the prophets of Baal and the prophets of God. Mainstream Christians **do not diligently study the Bible**. When approached by the sophistry of Spiritualism which the Bible exposes, the ignorant of the Gospel of Christ become easy victims.

"Therefore my people are gone into captivity, **because they have no knowledge**: and their honourable men are famished, and their multitude dried up with thirst." Isaiah 5:13.

One of the greatest and honorable men our country has ever known was Abraham Lincoln. However, this brilliant statesman and hero of the American people was not versed in the Scriptures. Although he professed to believe in the Bible, his knowledge of it was apparently very limited. Spiritualism walked right into the White House in his day with an invitation from his wife.

The Real Truth About UFO's and the New World Order

Sadly enough, Mary Todd Lincoln was heavy into Spiritualism. According to *People Weekly*, May 23, 1988, on page 112, not only did Mary Lincoln **hold seances** at home, but Teddy Roosevelt is said to have kept an astrological chart pasted to the bottom of his chessboard for handy reference. The wives of President Harding, Wilson, Roosevelt, Ford, Reagan, and Clinton, like King Saul of Israel, **sought advice from spirit mediums or astrologers about how to run the affairs of the nation**.

While claiming to be Christians and attending their favorite church, multitudes today think it is but a light thing to seek palm readers, fortunetellers, psychics, and astrologers for advice. However, those who fear God had better take heed to these warnings from the Creator.

"Thou art wearied in the multitude of thy counsels. Let now the **ASTROLOGERS**, the **STARGAZERS**, the monthly **PROGNOSTICATORS**, stand up, and save thee from these things that shall come upon thee.

"Behold, they shall be as **STUBBLE**; the **FIRE** shall **BURN** them; they **shall not** deliver themselves from the power of the flame." Isaiah 47:13, 14.

Certain it is that there has been a great departure from the living God. Multitudes have forsaken the commandments of the Lord and have followed Baalim.

However, as Noah found grace in the eyes of the Lord before God destroyed the antediluvian people of old, so can we find forgiveness if we repent and turn away from idolatry and sin. Those who have been deceived into believing that the wonder-working power of the sciences of metaphysics is of God may find forgiveness when they turn from it.

"And the times of this ignorance God winked at; but now commandeth all men everywhere to repent." Acts 17:30

None will be deceived into following the rulers of the darkness of this world, the spiritual wickedness which governs the affairs of this world behind the scenes, if they will diligently seek God for understanding.

"And that from a child thou hast known the holy scriptures, which are able to make thee wise unto salvation through faith which is in Christ Jesus." 2 Timothy 3:15.

Socialism, Communism, and the Aquarian Conspiracy

The Scriptures warn over and over again that the Devil has captured the whole world.

"He that committeth sin is of the devil; for the devil sinneth from the beginning. **For this purpose the Son of God was manifested, that he might destroy the works of the devil.**" 1 John 3:8.

The Sinless One was born to be our sinbearer and to save us from receiving the same just reward Satan will receive for what he has done in this world.

"For all have sinned, and come short of the glory of God." Romans 3:23.

Jesus never committed one sin. It is hard to imagine someone never sinning in this present world, but Christ never sinned even in His thoughts. Jesus lived in Nazareth which was as evil as south Bronx or south Brooklyn. Jesus prayed constantly for grace and strength to withstand the attacks of the Evil One. Jesus completely depended on our Father's help as we should.

Jesus did not try to escape the sinful influences around him by running to the forest to become a hermit. The worst temptations that came to Him from the Evil One were while He was in the wilderness for 40 days. (See Matthew 4:1–11.)

"And when the tempter came to him, he said, If thou be the son of God, command that these stones be made bread." Matthew 4:3.

Something can be brought out in this verse that we must realize. As pointed out before, Satan will manifest himself as an angel of light or he can **change himself to appear** as a dead relative or famous hero or an ancient god. Satan did not come to Jesus in the wilderness as Pan or a scary demon, but as an angel of God. Satan and his angels today can personate Jesus, the Virgin Mary, the twelve apostles, or famous prophets of God of ancient times, such as Samuel who was the first to start the school of the prophets for God. To see how dangerous Spiritualism is, let's take a look again at what happened to King Saul of Israel.

"Now Samuel was dead, and all Israel had lamented him, and buried him in Ramah, even in his own city. And Saul had put away those that had **familiar spirits** (psychics), and the **wizards** (male witches), out of the land." 1 Samuel 28:3. (Emphasis mine.)

The Real Truth About UFO's and the New World Order

Because King Saul and the people of Israel constantly disobeyed God, the enemies of Israel were gaining in their struggles to destroy them. Double-minded Saul, seeing his shortcomings, sought to try to rid Israel of the influences of Spiritualism which became popular. Saul commanded that all the psychics and wizards be destroyed if found among the people of Israel. Those who escaped fled to the neighboring towns or forests to hide.

As today, among the ancient Israelites there were psychics and wizards communicating with evil angels who were posing as sun-gods, mother goddesses, ascended masters, or prophets for them. However, Saul in his earlier days as king was privileged to communicate personally with God by way of dreams and visions which the Lord communicated through his prophets.

"And he said, Hear now my words: If there be a **PROPHET** among you, **I THE LORD WILL MAKE MYSELF KNOWN UNTO HIM IN A VISION, AND I WILL SPEAK UNTO HIM IN A DREAM**." Numbers 12:6.

As we have seen, God does not communicate with His people through psychics who claim to be messengers of God which use crystal balls, palm readings, Ouija boards, tarot cards, horoscopes, etc. Neither does God communicate through those who claim to communicate with so-called ascended masters of the Great White Brotherhood.

"But, **THE DEAD KNOW NOT ANY THING**.... Also their **LOVE**, and their **HATRED**, and their **ENVY**, is now **PERISHED**." Ecclesiastes 9:5, 6.

"**THE DEAD PRAISE NOT THE LORD, NEITHER ANY THAT GO DOWN INTO SILENCE**." Psalm 115:17.

"And when they shall say unto you, Seek unto them that have **familiar spirits, and unto wizards that peep, and that mutter: should not a people seek unto their God? for the living to the dead**?" Isaiah 8:19.

Because Saul did not wholly repent of the sins he committed and seek God for forgiveness by prayer, fasting, confession, and repentance, the advantages he had over his enemies by communicating with God through the **Urim and Thummim** by the priests and by the visions and dreams given to the prophets were cut off. We will investigate some more things King Saul did against the Lord as we continue.

Socialism, Communism, and the Aquarian Conspiracy

"Surely the Lord God will do nothing, but he revealeth his secret unto his servants the prophets." Amos 3:7.

"Knowing this first, that **NO PROPHECY** of the scripture is of any private interpretation. For the prophecy came not in old time by the will of man: but holy men of God spake as they were moved by the Holy Ghost." 2 Peter 1:20, 21.

"God, who at sundry times and in divers manners spake in time past unto the fathers by the prophets, Hath in these last days spoken unto us by his Son, whom he hath appointed heir of all things, by whom he also made the worlds." Hebrews 1:1, 2.

However, the rebellious king forfeited these gifts. God in the past used prophets to communicate His instructions to His people. Then, when the fullness of time had come, Jesus Himself came to show us the way of salvation.

"Then spake Jesus again unto them, saying, **I am the light of the world**: he that followeth me **shall not** walk in darkness, but shall have the light of life." John 8:12.

Sadly enough, "This is the condemnation, that light is come into the world, and **men loved darkness rather than light**, because their deeds were evil. For **every one that doeth evil hateth the light**, neither cometh to the light, lest his deeds should be reproved.

"But he that doeth truth cometh to the light, that his deeds may be made manifest, that they are wrought in God." John 3:19–21.

"Thy word is a lamp unto my feet, and a light unto my path." Psalm 119:105. The Scriptures were given to us as a guide for life that will lead those who believe and obey through the Heavenly gates of New Jerusalem! Yet, to the worldly-minded person, the Gospel of Christ is as a rock blocking the road.

"For the preaching of the cross is to them that perish foolishness; but unto us which are saved it is the power of God." 1 Corinthians 1:18.

King Saul could have saved himself from not only the armies of his enemies, but also from losing his salvation. There is only one sin that God will not forgive.

"Wherefore I say unto you, All manner of sin and **blasphemy** shall be forgiven unto men: but the **blasphemy against the Holy Ghost shall not be forgiven unto men**." Matthew 12:31.

The Real Truth About UFO's and the New World Order

King Saul did not reach that sin that is beyond God's forbearance. Saul still could have sought God as Manasseh later did and was forgiven; but, instead of humbling himself before God, **he went to find the witch of Endor**. The witch was living in fear for her life because of Saul's earlier decrees to destroy all those who practiced witchcraft.

"And Saul disguised himself, and put on other raiment, and he went, and two men with him, and they came to the woman by night: and he said, I pray thee, divine unto me by the familiar spirit, and bring me him up, whom I shall name unto thee." 1 Samuel 28:8.

Here is some of the saddest recorded history found in Scripture. It should be noted that King Saul, the first king of Israel, in the beginning of his reign was a **brilliant and brave leader of Israel**. However, his military victories and his position over God's people began to produce that pride so often seen in military dictators in the past and present. The king started taking the glory which came from the victories of war on himself instead of giving the glory to God. He became more and more proud, and less and less dependent upon God. He developed into a cruel tyrant, full of jealousy and envy.

Saul in his insane pride cut himself off from the protective care of the Almighty. The channels of communication with God Saul had stopped himself. Samuel who loved Saul dearly was forced to turn his back on him because of his rebellion and disobedience to God. Because of Saul's rebellion against God, Samuel was told by the Lord to anoint David as king. Becoming outrageous over this, Saul not only tried to kill David, but his own son as well. Later, in his blind rage, he put to death 85 of the priests of the Lord which silenced the Urim and Thummim. (See 1 Samuel 22:18, 19.)

Separating himself from the prophet of God by his own actions and cutting himself off from receiving approval or not from the Urim and Thummim of the priest, Saul was left to himself to wander into certain folly. Even though Saul committed terrible sins against God, the Lord did not completely give Saul up.

"Say unto them, As I live, saith the Lord God, I have no pleasure in the death of the wicked; but that the wicked turn from his way and live: turn ye, turn ye from your evil ways; for why will ye die, O house of Israel?" Ezekiel 33:11.

Socialism, Communism, and the Aquarian Conspiracy

However, King Saul refused to humble himself before the Lord. His self-will and pride would not allow himself to go to the Lord with a contrite spirit and ask God's forgiveness by the conditions the Lord demands. Only by genuine sorrow for sinning against the Lord, confession, and repentance will a sinner be brought back in favor with the Lord. However, when the proud king approached God he did not come because of sorrow for sinning, but for fear of his enemies. Even though Saul seemed to honor the Lord by banishing witchcraft which crept into the camp of the Israelites, the Lord would not accept Saul's service until he met the conditions the Lord requires. However, even though the haughty monarch would not repent, he was not left entirely to himself. The prophet that Saul so many times rejected was sent once more to deliver a message to him. The Lord commanded Saul to destroy the Amalekites who were bent on the destruction of Israel. Here once more the Lord showed Saul that he had a chance to make his peace with God. If this was not so, the Lord would not have sent Samuel again. However, the proud king, impatient with Samuel's delay, offered up a sacrifice to the Lord which only the priests and prophets were allowed to do. Saul, again, showed his continual independence and rebellion against God. After the Lord gave Saul's armies victory over the Amalekites, Saul disobeyed the Lord's commands to destroy everything of the Amalekites. Instead, Saul and his men selfishly took the best animals left by the Amalekites to use as sacrificial offerings, so they would not have to use their own. Also, Saul did not kill the king of the Amalekites as the Lord commanded, but brought him back alive into the camp of the Israelites. The proud king of Israel upon meeting Samuel the prophet later said:

"Blessed be thou of the Lord: I have performed the commandment of the Lord. And Samuel said, What meaneth then this bleating of the sheep in mine ears, and the lowing of the oxen which I hear?" 1 Samuel 15:13, 14.

The prophet was not fooled by Saul's lie that he performed the commandment of the Lord. Here was the evidence that he did not. The animals Saul took and the Amalekite king he had with him were witnesses that the stubborn king did not completely obey God's

The Real Truth About UFO's and the New World Order

commands. The king tried to reason away his disobedience to God by saying the animals were to be used as a sacrifice.

However, the prophet said: "Hath the Lord as great delight in burnt offerings and sacrifices, as in obeying the voice of the Lord? Behold, to obey is better than sacrifice, and to hearken than the fat of rams. **For rebellion is as the sin of witchcraft, and stubbornness is as iniquity and idolatry."** 1 Samuel 15:22, 23.

Shortly afterwards, "Then said Samuel, Bring ye hither to me Agag the king of the Amalekites. And Agag came unto him delicately. And Agag said, Surely the bitterness of death is past.

"And Samuel said, As thy sword hath made women childless, so shall thy mother be childless among women. And Samuel hewed Agag in pieces before the Lord in Gilgal.

"Then Samuel went to Ramah; and Saul went up to his house to Gibeah of Saul." 1 Samuel 15:32–34.

After the prophet accomplished for the Lord what Saul did not do, the prophet came no more to see Saul until his death by suicide. However, that great prophet of the Lord still mourned for Saul while he was alive.

Before Saul died, Samuel told the disobedient king that rebellion against the Lord is as bad as practicing witchcraft. The king of Israel made an all out effort to rid Israel of idolatry and all forms of Spiritualism found among them. However, at the same time he had ignored the commands of God through His prophet. When the prophet pointed out his errors, Saul added stubbornness to his rebellious nature. **Even though Saul seemed to help the cause in one area, he was causing confusion in another.**

We who are called and chosen, we who claim to be followers of Christ had also better take heed! We are quick to point out the idolatry of the New Age Movement, but are we today also rebellious and stubborn to other requirements of God? Are we walking in the same footsteps as Saul did?

The apostle Paul exhorted, "Thou therefore which teachest another, teachest thou not thyself? thou that preachest a man should not steal, dost thou steal? Thou that sayest a man should not commit adultery, dost thou commit adultery? thou that abhorrest idols, dost thou commit sacrilege?

Socialism, Communism, and the Aquarian Conspiracy

"Thou that makest thy boast of the law, through breaking the law dishonourest thou God?" Romans 2:21–23.

Reader, have you been guilty of rebuking sin, but at the same time sin lieth at your door? I know I have been guilty of this; what about you?

"For not the hearers of the law are just before God, but the doers of the law shall be justified." Romans 2:13.

There are pastors who teach their congregations that they do not have to obey the Ten Commandments any longer. They say we are saved by grace, not by the works of the Law. **Some even go as far to say that to obey is legalism.**

"Know ye not that the **unrighteous shall not** inherit the kingdom of God? **Be not deceived**: neither fornicators, nor idolaters, nor adulterers, nor effeminate, nor abusers of themselves with mankind,

"Nor thieves, nor covetous, nor drunkards, nor revilers, nor extortioners, shall inherit the kingdom of God." 1 Corinthians 6:9, 10.

We can excuse or blame our sins on somebody else or some bad circumstance, but the truth is that Susie doesn't sin because she is sinful. **Susie sins because she wants to.** "The Devil made me do it" is false. We sin because **we choose to** and stand guilty before God as the Amalekites if we do not humble ourselves before our God. Putting all pride aside, along with all excuses, we must admit our wrongs to the Lord **instead of covering them up**. This is our first step in being **restored** to divine favor. Perhaps, the reader has been a witch, a Marxist, a fornicator, an idolator, or a gay. I have seen the power of Christ's Word deliver people from all these things and have through the grace of Christ been **restored as sons and daughters of God**.

"Go and proclaim these words toward the north, and say, Return, thou backsliding Israel, saith the Lord; and I will not cause mine anger to fall upon you: **for I am merciful**, saith the Lord, and I will not keep anger for ever.

"**Only acknowledge thine iniquity**, that thou hast transgressed against the Lord thy God, and hast scattered thy ways to the strangers under every green tree, and ye have not obeyed my voice, said the Lord.

"Turn, O backsliding children, saith the Lord; for I am married unto you: and I will take you one of a city, and two of a family, and I will bring you to Zion." Jeremiah 3:12–14.

The Real Truth About UFO's and the New World Order

All through the Bible, we can read of grievous sins committed by God's people. We can also read where many were forgiven and shall walk through the gates of the Heavenly Zion. They **repented and humbled themselves before God**. This Saul and Judas never did, and both ended up destroying themselves by committing self-murder. It has been foretold that most of the inhabitants of this world will not repent.

"And the rest of the men which were not killed by these plagues yet repented not of the works of their hands, that they should not worship devils, and idols of gold, and silver, and brass, and stone, and of wood: which neither can see, nor hear, nor walk: **"Neither repented they of their murders, nor of their sorceries, nor of their fornication, nor of their thefts."** Revelation 9:20, 21.

When Saul cut himself off from receiving counsel of the Lord and was brought into a desperate situation, instead of humbling himself to the Lord and sorrowing for his great sins which he committed, he chose to go to the Arch Enemy of God to inquire what to do. Here, instead of letting God control his will, the king in his blind desperation chose to walk on Satan's ground. Saul still had an opportunity for repentance until he went to inquire of the witch of Endor. Although Saul disguised himself, the witch knew it was King Saul. After Saul's true identity was discovered by the ancient psychic, he assured her no harm would come to her if she would cause the spirit of Samuel to appear. The first thing the demon **channeled** through this ancient psychic was:

"Why hast thou deceived me? for thou art Saul. And the king said unto her, Be not afraid: for what sawest thou? And the woman said unto Saul, **I saw gods ascending out of the earth**." 1 Samuel 28:12, 13.

The ancient worshipper of the forces of nature instead of nature's God said she saw these gods of nature ascend out of the earth along with an old man dressed in a mantle.

"And Saul perceived that it was Samuel, and he stooped with his face to the ground, and bowed himself." 1 Samuel 28:14.

Again, this was not Samuel, but a strong delusion. Today, demons are also **pretending** to be these so-called spirit guides or ascended masters.

Socialism, Communism, and the Aquarian Conspiracy

Reader, do not be surprised one day if Buddha, Krishna, Muhammad, Isis, or another pagan god makes his debut publicly in our day; but an even worse delusion shall come. **Satan himself shall personate Christ in these last days.** We will look into this warning from Scripture as we continue.

When Samuel was living, Saul hated his counsel; now this poor man hungered for it. The Christian today has Bibles in his reach everywhere for "reproof, for correction, for instruction in righteousness." 2 Timothy 3:16. However, most do not study it. Like in Saul's day as it was during the French Revolution when the counsel of the Lord was silenced, so shall it be in the near future.

"Behold, the days come, saith the Lord God, that I will send a famine in the land, not a famine of bread, nor a thirst for water, but of hearing the words of the Lord:

"And they shall wander from sea to sea, and from the north even to the east, they shall run to and fro to seek the Lord, and shall not find it." Amos 8:11, 12.

It had been whispers from Satan that had supplied the temptations which encouraged Saul to rebel against God; but it was Samuel, the Lord's Heavenly messenger, who caused Saul to hear the voice of God. However, Saul chose to disobey the voice of Samuel the prophet while he lived. Now, instead of listening to the voice of God which came from the mouth of Samuel, Saul again chose to listen to the **voice** of the Devil speaking through the mouth of this witch.

It was Satan who was bent on Saul's destruction that helped Saul to try to kill not only David but his own son as well. It was Satan that Saul yielded to when he took it upon himself to exterminate 85 of the Lord's priests. It was Satan that led Saul to not destroy God's bitter enemy, Agag the Amalekite. The very deeds Satan so successfully tempted Saul in committing, he later used against him to make Saul lose all hope so he would self-destruct. While personating Samuel the prophet, **the voice** of the tempter said to Saul:

"Then said Samuel, Wherefore then dost thou ask of me, seeing the Lord is departed from thee, and is become thine enemy? And the Lord hath done to him, as he spake by me: for the Lord hath rent the kingdom out of thine hand, and given it to thy neighbour, even to David:

The Real Truth About UFO's and the New World Order

"Because thou obeyedst not the **voice of the Lord**, nor executedst his fierce wrath upon Amalek, therefore hath the Lord done this thing unto thee this day. Moreover the Lord will also deliver Israel with thee into the hand of the Philistines: and tomorrow shalt thou and thy sons be with me: the Lord also shall deliver the host of Israel into the hand of the Philistines.

"Then Saul fell straightway all along on the earth, and was sore afraid, because of the words of Samuel: and there was no strength in him; for he had eaten no bread all the day, nor all the night." 1 Samuel 28:16–20.

During the rage of the battle with the Philistine army, Saul's sons were killed and Saul himself was struck by arrows.

"Then said Saul unto his armour-bearer, Draw thy sword, and thrust me through therewith; lest these uncircumcised come and thrust me through, and abuse me. But his armour-bearer would not; for he was sore afraid. Therefore Saul took a sword, and fell upon it." 1 Samuel 31:4.

The king of Israel died with the guilt of **self-murder** on the books of Heaven, and so did Marshall Applewhite and his disciples who were led by demons to commit suicide so that they could meet a UFO. **They believed a lie.**

However, "If we **confess** our sins, he is faithful and just to forgive us our sins, and to **cleanse us** from all unrighteousness." 1 John 1:9.

If we do not confess our wrongs to God, we will have to answer for them on Judgment Day. The grave is not the end of the road.

"Marvel not at this: for the hour is coming, in the which **all that are in the graves shall hear his voice**,

"And shall come forth; they that have done good, unto the resurrection of life; and they that have done evil, unto the resurrection of damnation." John 5:28, 29.

"And as it is appointed unto men once to die, but after this the judgment." Hebrews 9:27.

However, as we have seen, God does not have any pleasure in seeing any of His creation lose eternal life.

"The Lord is not slack concerning his promise, as some men count slackness; but is longsuffering to us-ward, not willing that any should perish, **but that all should come to repentance**." 2 Peter 3:9.

Socialism, Communism, and the Aquarian Conspiracy

"If my people, which are called by my name, shall humble themselves, and pray, and seek my face, and turn from their wicked ways; then will I hear from heaven, and will forgive their sin, and will heal their land." 2 Chronicles 7:14.

Those who have been deceived by the curious arts of Spiritualism also have this promise. However, those who refuse to hear or obey God's Word, like Saul, are placing themselves willingly into the hands of the worst enemy of man. The Arch Enemy **will prosper some** so he can use them as an example to bring others to him. Devil possession does not always appear in a hideous, insane, and violent character as the demoniac of Gergesenes in Matthew 8:28–34. Often times people possessed with devils may appear highly educated, with an air of class and sophistication. Such was the case of the Pharisees who held the position in Israel as the Supreme Court judges do in our country.

Jesus told them, "Ye are of your father the devil, and the lusts of your father ye will do. He was a murderer from the beginning, and abode not in the truth, because there is no truth in him. When he speaketh a lie, he speaketh of his own: for he is a liar, and the father of it. And because I tell you the truth, ye believe me not." John 8:44, 45.

The more intelligent, the more proud, and the more attractive and congenial a person may be, the more Satan wants him. Spiritualism today has lost its evil connotation in our evil society. Spiritualism also has an **air of class and sophistication**. In the ancient days of Israel, Spiritualism appeared as a mortal enemy of God. Today, it expresses both a belief in God and Jesus and even claims to be Christian. Using words such as **metaphysics**, **parapsychology**, **clairvoyance**, or **mysticism**, witchcraft has been accepted under the guise of being scientific. Spiritualism has entered the halls of our colleges so it may ensnare multitudes into its curious arts enabling them too to become its agents.

The worst of all the colleges in this country to be used by Satan to promote his sciences after the revival of Spiritualism which took place in 1848 was the Theosophical Society. This school was specifically set up to train the ignorant of God's Word how to communicate with the spirit world of which they claim, like the witch of Endor, are departed souls of the dead. The religion this school promotes is

The Real Truth About UFO's and the New World Order

known as Theosophy, and it has lured multitudes of Christians because it blends Jesus into their beliefs. However, **Theosophy is nothing less than pagan spirituality.**

Men and women of talent, sophistication, and of pleasing addresses such as Eleanor Roosevelt, the hero of the feminist movement, became connected with one of the offshoots of this college.

Founded in New York in 1875 by Madame H.P. Blavatsky, Col. H.S. Olcott, and W.Q. Judge, the Theosophical Society's underlying doctrine was the belief of bringing one self in contact with the **Mahatmas or Adepts of ancient India**.[23] As Moses, Samuel, Elijah, Elisha, Isaiah, Jeremiah, Ezekiel, and Daniel were to the Israelites, so are these so-called ascended masters to theosophists. Blavatsky taught that these ascended masters have been **communicating the secrets of the occult for ages through their select few**.

Madame Blavatsky, like the Fox sisters, claimed to have direct communication with these heavenly teachers. These theosophists teach to those who do not know the Scriptures that these Mahatmas (teachers) are evolved human beings which have reached perfection through the process of the **law of karma and reincarnation**.

"As morning, noon, and night are succeeded by morning again, so birth, youth, adulthood, and death are succeeded by rebirth. Reincarnation is the process of human development in which all growth is governed by the law of justice or Karma."[24]

However, the Bible says: "So man lieth down, and **RISETH NOT**: till the heavens be no more, **THEY SHALL NOT AWAKE, NOR BE RAISED OUT OF THEIR SLEEP.**" Job 14:12.

Another lie found in Theosophy is that God and nature are one. They teach that **everything in the universe is connected** and flows or emanates from God. In other words, they teach that the universe is a microcosm and that man is a **miniature microcosm**. According to occultists, therefore, man is a god but has to be awakened to this fact.

Hence, they say, this is the mission of the Mahatmas of India: to show man that he is god. You see, according to Theosophy,

---

[23]*Academic American Encyclopedia*, **Vol. 19, p. 159.**
[24]*Ibid.*, **Vol. 19, p. 160.**

Socialism, Communism, and the Aquarian Conspiracy

Mahatmas are those who have reached **perfection**, have died, and were resurrected or reincarnated or have conquered death itself like Jesus did. They are considered to be advanced human beings or what New Agers term as **ascended masters**. However, other people if they lived a bad life are reincarnated into an animal until they have learned to become Christ conscious and godlike like the Mahatmas. This is what Hindus call **karma**.

The Theosophical Society's concepts of a spiritual hierarchy (the Great White Brotherhood), which they have claimed to communicate with **by telepathy** with these Mahatmas, has attracted multitudes. Today, as we have seen, **they are now supposed to be the UFO's**.

Blavatsky claimed also to have received letters from a Mahatma which would appear suddenly dropping out of the air. They are known today as Mahatma letters, which Christian missionaries unmasked as fraudulent with the help of Dr. Richard Hodgson of *The Society for Psychical Research* in Britain.[25]

Nevertheless, when Blavatsky, who was the co-founder of the Theosophical Society, and her Mahatma letters were exposed as being a fraud, Spiritualists just **reasoned away this truth** about Blavatsky. They began to circulate among themselves that the other medium, whom Blavatsky associated with where that scandal broke out, lied. The other medium admitted that the letters were a fraud, but Blavatsky's followers said this **was just a plot to discredit** Madame Blavatsky and the Theosophical Society. So, the society of mediums was able to survive and continue. Through this society, Blavatsky later produced volumes of esoteric teachings based on working miracles through the Mahatmas.

This Russian medium claimed to have written her books, *The Secret Doctrine* and *Isis Unveiled*, because the Solar Deity (god) had chosen her to be the earthly vessel which the **spiritual hierarchy** was to use to bring their knowledge to human beings.

Blavatsky claimed that one of these Mahatmas (teachers) of the spiritual hierarchy who was sent from their Solar Deity (god) to enlighten the world was named Koot Hoomi. Koot Hoomi, this so-called ascended master of the **Great White Brotherhood**, dictated,

---

[25]*Encyclopedia of Occultism and Parapsychology*, Vol. A-L, p. 1693.

The Real Truth About UFO's and the New World Order

according to Blavatsky, the sciences of witchcraft that were contained in her books.[26]

These books are found in most libraries throughout the United States, waiting to **ensnare** the inexperienced and ignorant of Scripture into Theosophy. Just like Christianity has doctors of divinity, so does the occult have their doctors of Spiritualism. Just like Christianity has their missionaries who go forth throughout the world to preach the Gospel of Christ, so does Spiritualism have their missionaries going forth to preach their gospel.

Most citizens of the world have never heard of the Theosophical Society. However, this unknown secret society of witchcraft did more to advance the cause of Spiritualism than any other Spiritualistic group other than its granddaddy, which is the highest order of Freemasonry known as the Illuminati.

After the Theosophical Society suffered a set back when Blavatsky's Mahatma letters were proven to be a fraud, Blavatsky's books, *The Secret Doctrine* and *Isis Unveiled*, were published. However, Blavatsky again was exposed as a fraud. Like the Mahatma letters, she claimed that her books were dictated to her by Koot Hoomi, one of these Indian Mahatmas. However, it was exposed that Blavatsky plagiarized about one hundred books from other occult writers to produce *Isis Unveiled*. Similar charges were leveled against *The Secret Doctrine*, which was also produced by plagiarizing three other books of witchcraft.[27]

Even though its main leader was proven to be a liar and a fake, the Theosophical Society still managed to continue. However, a power struggle emerged between the Society's leaders (Blavatsky, Olcott, who was the president, and W.Q. Judge, the vice president). When Blavatsky died in 1891, **Annie Besant** of the **Fabian Society**, of whom we studied earlier, saw her opportunity to take the place of Blavatsky. Nevertheless, W.Q. Judge, the vice president of the society, had the same thought. By this time, the Theosophical Society had grown into an enormous worldwide threat to those who would preach that Jesus is "the Way, the Truth, and the Life", and "no man cometh unto the Father" but by Him.

[26]*Man, Myth, and Magic*, **Vol. 1, pp. 290–292.**
[27]*The Fringes of Reason, A Whole Earth Catalog*, **Schultz, p. 24.**

Socialism, Communism, and the Aquarian Conspiracy

Shortly before Annie Besant was laid to rest to wait for her reward for warring against Christ on Judgment Day, another Marxist Spiritualist was to emerge to take the place of Annie Besant. Like Annie Besant, Alice Ann Bailey (1880–1949) was raised in a Christian home in England but had bad experiences with name-only Christians and had an unhappy childhood. However, as a teenager, **Alice Bailey** claimed a mysterious stranger wearing a turban walked into her room and sat beside her. She thought it was Jesus, and this mysterious stranger told Bailey that she should prepare herself for an important mission.[28]

Meanwhile, Bailey was brought up in the Church of England and after finishing school, she went to work for the Young Women's Christian Association (Y.W.C.A.) at which she worked later in India. It was here she met her first husband, Walter Evans, who became an Episcopal priest, while Alice and Walter Evans had moved to the United States. Like Annie Besant, Alice Bailey saw herself as becoming a great spiritual leader some day, and her spiritual feminist views clashed with her husband's priesthood. They eventually divorced. Again, like Annie Besant, the bitter experiences with some Christians, her unhappy marriage and the emotional ordeal of marital breakdown, and ignorance of Bible doctrine, all made her ripe for Satan's delusions. While living in California, she was introduced to a lodge of the Theosophical Society in Pacific Grove, California, in which she fell for the theosophical concepts of a spiritual hierarchy, karma, and reincarnation. This mysterious stranger wearing a turban that told Bailey when she was a teenager to prepare herself for an important mission, which she had thought to have been Jesus, turned out to be Koot Hoomi (a supposed ascended master) whom Madame Blavatsky claimed to have dictated her books to her. Bailey saw a picture of this so-called ascended master on the wall of the Theosophical Society.[29] **Christians, Satan does appear in human form to win his disciples.**

Bailey joined the Theosophical Society and in 1919 claimed to have another visitor from the Great White Brotherhood named Djwhal Khul, better known by occultists as *The Tibetan*. Like Koot Hoomi,

---

[28]*Encyclopedia of Occultism and Parapsychology*, 3rd Ed., Vol. A-L, p. 150.
[29]*Ibid.*, pp. 150, 151.

The Real Truth About UFO's and the New World Order

who supposedly appeared to Madame Blavatsky, this ascended master, *The Tibetan*, was going to use Alice Bailey to write books that would guide New Agers in preparing themselves and others for the **Age of Aquarius**.[30] Alice Bailey was chosen by Lucifer to help continue his Atlantean plan to unite this whole world into a world socialist government of which Bible prophecy predicts and **businessmen** of this present world say will be divided into **ten divisions**. Bailey soon learned that the Atlantean gods were really Lucifer and his angels. Alice Bailey became like Adam Weishaupt before her. She became one of Lucifer's most trusted apostles.

Bailey became a high official in the Theosophical Society and became editor of the society's periodical, *The Messenger*. She married the national secretary of the society whose name was Foster Bailey. It was in 1920 when Bailey married her husband, and it was the same year that launched Alice and Foster Bailey into their own effort to advance the religion of Spiritualism throughout the world.

Of all the occult apostles and doctors of metaphysics, four names stand out among multitudes who can be credited in causing the gospel of Christ much suffering. They are Adam Weishaupt who was the first to write the New World Order conspiracy in the 18th century and Karl Marx who updated it for the 19th century. The other two are H.P. Blavatsky and Alice Ann Bailey. Bailey is looked upon by these theosophists or doctors of Spiritualism as the apostle of the 20th century.

Full of wisdom from below and ambition to match, both Annie Besant's and Alice Bailey's personalities soon clashed causing a power struggle within the international headquarters of the Theosophical Society. The Baileys, who had been high officials of the American section of the society, left. They soon started their own occult publishing company calling it *Lucifer's Trust*, which was changed later to Lucis Trust because of the bad connotation it received.

Lucis Trust published volumes after volumes of books which Alice Bailey claimed were dictated to her by her mysterious spiritual master named Djwhal Khul a.k.a. *The Tibetan*. Before the Baileys left the Theosophical Society, Alice had written her first book entitled

---

[30]*Contemporary Authors*, Vol. 116, Chapman/Jorgenson, p. 28.

Socialism, Communism, and the Aquarian Conspiracy

Initiation, Human and Solar in 1920. From here, she began her appointed mission as Djwhal Khul, her spirit guide **which in reality was one of the fallen angels**, assigned her. For the next 30 years, Alice Bailey produced 18 books dealing with how New Agers were to overthrow the influence and power of mainstream Christianity. Along with this goal, they would **usher in the Age of Aquarius** by the return of a christ (**not to be confused with Jesus of Nazareth**).

Alice Ann Bailey's books soon became the talk of the town among occult circles. With the funds which came in from the sale of her books and by the support of her disciples, the Baileys were soon able in 1923 to establish a college of witchcraft which they called the ***Arcane School***. Specializing in the sciences of Deuteronomy 18:10–12 which are an abomination unto our Lord, this college of sorcery is going strong and has missionaries to spread their gospel worldwide. Since 1923 when the Baileys founded their Arcane School, it has grown into an international college branching into special groups. These missionaries for the cause of the gospel of Lucifer are calling themselves ***The New Group of World Servers***. The college's publishing company, Lucis Trust, publishes a magazine called *The Beacon* to ensnare the innocent and inexperienced into its conspiracy and to take this world for Lucifer before the year A.D. 2000.

This Arcane School developed special prayers and meditations, such as the ***Great Invocation*** and ***Full Moon Meditation*** to be used during their efforts to unite Christians with the Eastern religions. This spirit guide of Alice Bailey dictated to her to write that their Arcane School was chosen to promote the reappearance of ***the christ***. Again, this is not to be confused with Jesus Christ. These theosophists have their own christ they are promoting. In occult circles, he is called **Maitreya**.

Alice Bailey died in 1949, and her husband Foster Bailey continued to publish and promote their scheme to take this world for Lucifer using the United Nations up until his death in 1977. By the way, their headquarters up until recently was at the United Nations Plaza, which is directly across the street from this modern Tower of Babel. We will see some other things about what the Baileys contributed towards this New World Order conspiracy later as we study more of the history of the United Nations.

The Real Truth About UFO's and the New World Order

Another offshoot of the Theosophical Society was founded in 1934 by Guy and Edna Ballard. The blasphemous name of this promotion of sorcery was the *I Am* movement which was also centered around contacting these so-called ascended masters from the Great White Brotherhood. Here, another spirit guide was to gain popularity among psychics today. This spirit guide is considered among the *Who's Who* of the psychic circles of channelers today. This great master of the mediums, like Koot Hoomi *The Tibetan*, is an angel of Satan's posing as Saint-Germain!

Guy and Edna Ballard claimed to be able to **channel the voice** of Saint-Germain which brought them much wealth from traveling the country promoting the art of channeling. Donations poured in from those ignorant of the Scriptures, and the Ballards lived a luxurious lifestyle until Guy Ballard's death in 1939. Then, numerous counts of mail fraud hit Edna Ballard, and her son and these psychics were out of business. However, when the Ballard's *I Am* movement fell apart because of mail fraud, a few of their disciples remained hidden away in the hills of California practicing their art.

Another couple in California claiming to communicate with the same ascended masters which Guy and Edna Ballard did arose in the 1950s. Their names are Mark and Elizabeth Clare Prophet. Soon funds came pouring in from their seances which enabled them to start an organization in California called the Summit Lighthouse, which is now called the Church Universal and Triumphant. Mark Prophet died in 1974,[31] but Elizabeth Clare Prophet has continued until recently. **Prophet includes Jesus as an ascended master.**

According to *Time* magazine, March 26, 1990, page 20, Elizabeth Clare Prophet's Church Universal and Triumphant moved their headquarters from Malibu, California, to a 33,000-acre ranch just north of Yellowstone National Park. The reason for it was because Prophet, who **claims to be the voice** of the **ascended masters** of which Jesus and her husband Mark who died in 1973 are included, said there would be Armageddon by April of 1990. Responding to the warnings of Prophet, at least 2,000 of her 30,000 disciples she claims she has fled to the 33,000-acre ranch where she began building 46 steel-and-concrete shelters to be dug deep into the mountain soil. Many of

---

[31]*The Fringes of Reason, A Whole Earth Catalog*, Schultz, p. 27.

Socialism, Communism, and the Aquarian Conspiracy

The above photograph was taken when my wife and I visited the Yellowstone National Park in August 1997. Elizabeth Clare Prophet's 33,000-acre Royal Ranch near Gardiner, Montana, borders the first national park in the world. They have a Church Universal and Triumphant in Livingston, Montana, and a restaurant, gift shop, and store in Corwin Springs, Montana, of which their members use to help recruit new members. We stopped at their Ranch Restaurant in Corwin Springs and interviewed two of their leaders, one of which ran the store adjoining their restaurant who was named Kathleeen and another named Theres who is a writer and spokesperson for their church. We were quickly informed by these very polite members of Prophet's church that they were, indeed, occultists (mystics) who blend Jesus and the worship of the Virgin Mary with the worship of Buddha and Krishna. In their grocery store and gift shop, there are books and tracts which promote ascended masters from the Great White Brotherhood and books written by Elizabeth Clare Prophet promoting New Age philosophy. However, the above church has had a setback. Many of their members have left their church because of internal divisions and because of the recent rumors from the media that the Royal Ranch of Elizabeth Clare Prophet may be the next Waco, Texas. Amazingly, the Church Universal and Triumphant is against the New World Order and knows about the international threat of the Illuminati and the Council on Foreign Relations. However, they failed to see that both the New Age Movement, which they advocate, and the New World Order originally derived out of the Enlightenment Movement of the Illuminati of the 18th century. They have been raided by the government for stockpiling weapons which they intended to use in defense of their compound.

The Real Truth About UFO's and the New World Order

her disciples sold all their possessions, quit their jobs, and emptied their savings accounts to pay fees of up to $10,000 for space in the shelters.

This is not the first time Elizabeth Clare Prophet proved herself a false prophet. Back in 1987, she predicted that California would fall into the sea. However, according to *People Weekly*, June 4, 1990, page 49, when the end of the world did not occur as she had prophesied, she can be quoted as saying:

"**That Jesus, Pope John XXIII, Confucius, the saints, and all the angels in heaven speak to the world through her.**"

She supposedly takes *spiritual dictation* from **Buddha, Shakespeare, Christopher Columbus, and Merlin the Magician, as well as someone named Cosmic Master Ray-o-Light**. She also believes in reincarnation. Again, she can be quoted:

"As a child, I walked and talked with **Jesus**. We've all lived thousands of times," she told *People Weekly*.

It was Mark Prophet who claimed to be the **reincarnation of Sir Lancelot** who actually founded the Summit Lighthouse which later became the Church Universal and Triumphant. When he suddenly died in 1973, Elizabeth Clare found herself the keeper of a sprawling spiritual empire worth about $50 million. It was **Saint-Germain**, one of Prophet's **spirit guides** who was an 18th century male witch and magician, that supposedly told Prophet that nuclear war was imminent. That is why she decided to move to Montana in 1981.

Despite the failed prophecies by Elizabeth Clare Prophet, her disciples became reassured by Prophet when she proclaimed that her prophecy about the end of the world coming by April 1990 was postponed because her disciple's prayers had averted a nuclear first-strike by the Soviets.[32]

Another prophet of the gospel of Spiritualism who claimed to have communion with the **ascended masters** was John Paul Twitchell, founder of **ECKANKAR**. Like Blavatsky, Besant, and Bailey, Twitchell claimed to have had a visit by a spirit guide named ***Rebazar Tarzs*** who first appeared to Twitchell in 1944 while serving on a United States Navy vessel in the Pacific.[33]

---

[32]*Maclean's*, May 7, 1990, p. 33

[33]*Encyclopedia of Occultism and Parapsychology*, Vol. M-Z, 3rd Ed., p. 1739.

Socialism, Communism, and the Aquarian Conspiracy

John Paul Twitchell spent time in India after the war and after his return to the United States, he claimed that his spirit guide *Rebazar Tarzs* **dictated to him secret knowledge** from Hinduism about how to have out-of-the body experiences and t**hat man is a god**.

After joining the Swami Premananda's Self-Revelation Church of Absolute Monism in Washington, D.C., he was later introduced to Scientology[34] of which he became a staff member. From here, he was initiated into the Sikh movement, Ruhani Satsang, until 1963. In 1964, he became interested in starting his own Sikh mysticism. He called it ECKANKAR **which millions**[35] have fallen for today. While they claim not to convert anyone from their religion whether he be Christian, Muslim, Buddhist, Jewish, etc., ECKANKAR promotes its religious and political ambitions through its mail order propaganda. While claiming to be a small religious sect, ECKANKAR is a worldwide network of Spiritualists who are determined to unite all religions under the same roof.

It is interesting to note that ECKANKAR has been under attack by many mainstream Christians as being anti-Christian. However, ECKANKAR claims to believe in Jesus, but blends Eastern thought with some Christian beliefs. Because of this, the inexperienced and those who are ignorant of Deuteronomy, Chapter 18, have been lured into its philosophy. Recently, ECKANKAR ran a huge newspaper article warning Christians to stop the bad public image they have been giving ECKANKAR.

ECKANKAR claimed in its huge advertisement that they were not anti-Christian or involved in psychic phenomena. However, John Paul Twitchell, their founder, claimed all his books were dictated to him by the Tibetan master named *Rebazar Tarzs*. They themselves claim today that their founder who died in 1971 is now **one** of these **ascended masters**! As a result of Christians giving ECKANKAR a bad image to the public by supposedly making false statements about them, their huge warning to Christians seen in their advertisement also included how they have filed lawsuits in Los Angeles and Minneapolis against those who have been shining a different kind of light

---

[34]*Encyclopedia of Occultism and Parapsychology*, Vol. M–Z, p. 1739.
[35]*Ibid.*, Vol. A–L, p. 483.

The Real Truth About UFO's and the New World Order

on their **out-of-body experiences** which, they say, lead to their spiritual path to God.

Like Christianity, modern Spiritualism **is divided** today into multitudes of various denominations and sects which have produced sensationalists and charlatans, along with reformers; but, among occultists, the Theosophical Society is still looked upon today as a place that has preserved the purity of occultism. This occult society has a huge library of books on the curious arts. Other than the Freemasons, no other occult society can be credited in being first to bring Hindu witchcraft into the United States than the Theosophical Society.

However, the western world already had **its own version** of Babylonian Spiritualism centuries before the Fox sisters caused a general revival of it in 1848. My wife and I, having worked among the Navajo Indians in New Mexico one summer and being used by the Lord of the Sabbath to bring some to baptism, learned first-hand of what the ancient American Indian religion actually is. It's the same as Hinduism, only in a different form. It is nature worship which is known in the Old World as **pantheism**.

The North, Central, and South American Indians, like the Hindus, had their own ancient system of witchcraft which is **astrology** and **its many sciences**.

Two of the most controversial authors who can be credited with bringing multitudes into American Indian sorcery were Carlos Castaneda and Lynn Andrews.

Astrology among American Indians is called **shamanism**, and a priest in American Indian culture is a **shaman or a medicine man**. Like the witch doctors of Africa, the shaman is a magical healer of the American Indian culture. By the 50s, Spiritualism had grown immensely, and it was in the 50s that the ancient deadly knowledge of **hallucinogenic drugs** was revived among the British and Americans. The birth of this revival in the United States of putting one self into a **hypnotic state** by the use of **psychedelic drugs** can be first traced to Aleister Crowley and then to Aldous Huxley, who both wrote books promoting its uses. Their books described their own visionary experiences (trips). However, the American Indian medicine man had known about LSD and mescaline long before Aleister Crowley and Aldous Huxley came from Europe. These mind-destroying drugs were

Socialism, Communism, and the Aquarian Conspiracy

sacred to the **Indian medicine man** and were used during their religious rituals. **Mescaline and LSD** are the active agents found in the buttonlike tubercles of the **mescal cactus**. The Indians call these buttonlike tubercles **peyote**. While chewing on peyote, occultists claim to see **devas**; and, like the witch of Endor, they are **fooled** by **demons** into believing that they are the **spirits of the dead or ancient gods**.

The American Indian shaman is what English-speaking people would call a **sorcerer**. A sorcerer is not only one who deals in the supernatural powers of witchcraft, but also a person who deals in drugs. It is very interesting to note that, according to *Strong's Exhaustive Concordance of the Bible* on page 75 in its Greek dictionary of the New Testament, it states that the Greek word *"pharmakos" means "sorcerer."* The word *"pharmakon"* means *one who gives spell-giving potion* or *a druggist* or *poisoner* or *a magician*. The word *pharmakeia* in Greek is where we today have derived our word, *pharmacy*!

Another pharmakon was Carlos Castaneda who is an anthropologist and created a huge interest in American Indian shamanism (sorcery) in the late 60s and 70s. He authored a fictional book which he pawned off to his readers as being fact about his experiences in learning the curious arts of sorcery from a mysterious Indian sorcerer named Juan Matus. The book is named *The Teachings of Don Juan: A Yaqui Way of Knowledge* which can be credited for causing multitudes to explore into not only shamanism, but also drugs like peyote and other hallucinogenic drugs. It was almost an overnight best seller. However, critics have proven that his book about his journey to Sonora, Mexico, to learn from the pharmakon is a hoax. Even though occultists later found out that their hero of occultism hoodwinked them, there are still those in strong delusion who say, "**Castaneda wasn't a common con man: he lied to bring us the truth**."[36]

Psychedelic drugs have not only induced hallucinations, but have caused some to believe that they could fly while under its hypnotic spell. Because of this, some have hurled themselves off bridges or out of windows to meet their deaths. Still others, while under a drug-induced **altered state** of consciousness, have seen out-of-body experiences or apparitions of the dead.

---

[36]*The Teachings of Don Juan: A Yaqui Way of Knowledge*, Castaneda, pp. 21-26.

The Real Truth About UFO's and the New World Order

Before the 50s, psychiatrists and doctors began to experiment with psychedelic drugs to see if they could help those who suffer from schizophrenia; but, it was Aleister Crowley's and Aldous Huxley's books that began the use of these **drugs to escape reality** in the U.S.A. However, it was a Harvard psychologist named Timothy Leary, a rock group known as the Beatles, and the media that followed them which helped to spread the concept of instant **chemical mysticism** which has led to chemical dependency that the general masses of Americans have experienced or are experiencing.

The degradation which drugs have induced, especially in the large cities, needs no introduction. The promotion of psychedelic drugs in the 60s and 70s by Leary, the Beatles, and other celebrities from the entertainment field has also led to the **promotion of rebellion** against all authority, sexual permissiveness, and hideous crimes, like mass murders, human sacrifices, rape, and robbery. These crimes are common place in the news. The combination of drugs and witchcraft has led multitudes into insanity. Drug addiction has become so socially accepted in our evil world that some hippie families think it is but a light thing to lace their children's drinks with LSD. What is also amazing is how a holy God who created man in His image, who is watching all this, has still refrained himself from destroying mankind.

I have discovered that the use of hallucinogenic drugs to **produce visions and dreams** among modern-day **shamans** and **occultists** is a very common practice. Here in the West, it was especially made popular by H.P. Blavatsky and Aleister Crowley, who was the pope of Satanism in his day. A lot of the Beatles' songs they sang were **drug-related**. The Beatles were not only followers of the late Aleister Crowley, but they were deeply involved in the New World Order conspiracy to overthrow Christianity and replace it with a Utopian Socialist society in the 21st century. In Volume Four of this series of reference books on Time of the End events, I show the rise and evolution of Marxism and Socialism. With documented proof, the reader will see how Marxism split into many different factions, like Christianity did, and how the Beatles became Marxists and how there are, indeed, Hindu Marxists, Jewish Marxists, Catholic Marxists, and, believe it or not, Protestant Marxists!

Socialism, Communism, and the Aquarian Conspiracy

In Revelation, Chapter 16, Jesus through his apostle John warned us that Satan would use **three general movements**, symbolized as the **Dragon**, the **Beast**, and **the False Prophet**, to gather the people of this world **who do not obey the Gospel of Christ** into that last great battle of God Almighty. These three powers were foretold to unite into an **unholy alliance** in these last days against the Biblical Jesus and His people. The **untempered mortar** that is currently being used to unite this three-fold union is a **mixture** of Spiritualism and Marxism as well. There are Christian Marxist fronts that have been at work for decades now in an effort to bring about not only the overthrow of Biblical Christianity, but also the United States government. This will be completely studied in Volume Five entitled *Ancient Prophecies About The Dragon, The Beast, and The False Prophet*.

This volume, as pointed out, is focusing primarily on the religious side of this Atlantean Plan for a New World Order. We started our journey to see the origin of the rise and evolution of the Atlantean plan from Nimrod to Plato down to our day.

It is a historical fact that the religion of astrology, which the red Dragon is symbolizing, began at Babylon and from there the worship of the stars as the home of the gods spread everywhere. The Dragon's most hideous deceptions to lead the inhabitants of this world away from the true Christ of the Bible came when the religion of astrology slowly blended into Christianity through the Roman Catholic leaders, and then was handed down to those who call themselves Protestants. Babylon the Great is the whole world today being corralled into one stall by the Devil.

The Dragon is symbolizing the general worldwide movement of the people of Spiritualism who are determined today to overthrow Christianity by using the United Nations which their prophets of the Wainwright House founded in the year 1941. These nonviolent revolutionaries of this religious side of the New World Order are continuing to reach their goal of complete globalism by the beginning of the 21st century leaving the God of Abraham, Isaac, and Jacob out. This event was first launched at the founding of the secret society of the Illuminati in the 18th century.

Now, we need to see how modern-day Jews today have also become victims of Spiritualism and Socialism and who was actually

The Real Truth About UFO's and the New World Order

behind the founding of modern Israel in 1948. Reader, these shocking facts are very important to understand today for the Scriptures foretold that **Satan will use Israel** to bring the inhabitants under his banner in these last days. Not only this, but the Bible prophecies foretold that Satan's headquarters has long been established in the city that is surrounded by seven mountains (See Revelaton 17:9), and that Satan **will move his "tabernacles of his palace *between* the seas in the glorious holy mountain; yet he shall come to his end, and none shall help him**." Daniel 11:45.

We will continue to investigate this Atlantean Plan of Plato's for a Utopian world government and how the Jews were drawn into this same conspiracy in the next chapter.

CHAPTER V

HOW THEOSOPHY DECEIVED THE WORLD IN ANCIENT DAYS AND HOW IT WILL BRING ITS HEADQUARTERS TO ISRAEL

"And he shall plant the tabernacles of his palace between the seas in the glorious holy mountain; yet he shall come to his end, and none shall help him."
Daniel 11:45

The Real Truth About UFO's and the New World Order

The cosmic seven-headed red dragon symbolizing Lucifer and his great divisions of Spiritualism is surely uniting all his forces in preparation for that last great battle against God Almighty. This last chapter is about the **evolution of the Jewish people**, what the Jewish prophets foretold about them, and what Satan's plans for Israel are today. We will investigate how some Jews did connect themselves with this Atlantean Plan to bring about a world federation. We will investigate the history of the development of a non-Hebrew people who adopted Jewish Theosophy found written in the Kabbalah in the sixth century and how they eclipsed the original Hebrew population and became the actual founders of modern Israel today. We shall also investigate the **Rothschild family** and their connection with the establishment of modern Israel as a national homeland for modern Jews.

As we study on, we will see, indeed, that there are just **two** ecumenical movements. The origin of these two ecumenical movements of both Christ and Satan actually can be traced back on this side of the Flood to Noah and his family. All the people of the antediluvian world who were living at the time of the Deluge were destroyed except Noah and his family, totaling **eight** people. This does not mean that only eight people were saved on the other side of the Flood. They that be Christ's shall be resurrected at Christ Jesus ' Second Coming. Multitudes chose God instead of Satan before the Flood. They were laid to rest before Noah finished his ark.

"The Lord knoweth how to deliver the godly out of temptations, and to reserve the unjust unto the day of judgment to be punished." 2 Peter 2:9. What were the people like before the Flood?

"And it came to pass, when men began to multiply on the face of the earth, and daughters were born unto them, That the sons of God saw the daughters of men that they were fair; and they took them wives of all which they chose.

"And the Lord said, My spirit shall not always strive with man, for that he also is flesh: yet his days shall be an hundred and twenty years. There were giants in the earth in those days; and also after that, when the sons of God came in unto the daughters of men, and they bare children to them, the same became mighty men which were of old, men of renown.

How THEOSOPHY DECEIVED the WORLD

"And God saw that the wickedness of man was great in the earth, and that every imagination of the thoughts of his heart was only evil continually. And it repented the Lord that he had made man on the earth, and it grieved him at his heart.

"And the Lord said, I will destroy man whom I have created from the face of the earth; both man, and beast, and the creeping thing, and the fowls of the air; for it repenteth me that I have made them.

"But Noah found grace in the eyes of the Lord." Genesis 6:1–8.

Verse two says, "That the sons of God saw the daughters of men that they were fair; and they took them wives of all which they chose." New Agers who mix portions of Scripture with science fiction of astrology teach that extraterrestrial beings who were once humans revisited the earth and had intercourse with the females of Noah's day after the Flood. These beings begot a super race of **giants**. These giants, they claim, settled originally on the continent of Atlantis where they developed a Utopian society which Plato promoted among the Greeks. When the continent of Atlantis began to sink, the people who survived fled to Europe, Persia, and Mexico. The people who fled to Europe were known as Aryans. The people who fled to Mexico were known as Toltecs and Mayans who are believed to have built the pyramids in central Mexico. These giants in mythology were also known to the Greeks as **Titans**, of which the word "*Titan*" in our vocabulary today means "*of colossal size*." This is history mixed with myth.

Much of the Hitler madness, as well as other White Supremacist groups here in the United States and abroad, have their roots in this legend. As the reader may know from history, Hitler saw himself as the **messiah** of the **Utopian Age** in which there would live a master race of people. In Nazi ideology, which the KKK, skinheads, and some Christian churches have adopted, it is taught that these superhumans of prehistoric times were the Caucasian (Aryan) people who spoke in an Indo-European language.

First, let us go back to Genesis 6:2 and look at this verse again. It says that the sons of God saw the daughters of men that they were fair. Those antediluvian people were divided in their beliefs as the people today are. Those who remained worshippers of the God of Abraham the Lord called the sons of God. Those who apostatized

The Real Truth About UFO's and the New World Order

from Adam's time were called by God *the sons of men*. These sons of men were the descendants of Cain who murdered Abel his brother.

"And Cain went out from the presence of the Lord, and dwelt in the land of Nod, on the east of Eden. And Cain knew his wife; and she conceived, and bare Enoch: and he builded a city, and called the name of the city, after the name of his son, Enoch." Genesis 4:16, 17.

Two different ethnic groups of people developed here. Cain begat sons and daughters.

"And Adam knew his wife again; and she bare a son, and called his name Seth: For God, said she, hath appointed me another seed instead of Abel, whom Cain slew.

"And to Seth, to him also there was born a son; and he called his name Enos: then began men to call upon the name of the Lord." Genesis 4:25, 26.

Sadly, these sons of Seth who called upon the name of the Lord began to take wives of the sons of Cain who did not call upon the name of the Lord, and their hearts were turned away from following God, like Solomon when he married unbelieving women.

Genesis 6:4 plainly states that there were already "**GIANTS** in the earth **IN THOSE DAYS**; and **ALSO AFTER THAT**, when the sons of God came in unto the daughters of men, and they bare children to them, the same became mighty men which were of old, men of renown." Genesis 6:4.

Moses, who was under the inspiration of God, wrote this. These giants originally derived from our first parents on earth, not from extraterrestrial beings who are believed to have once been men. Our first parents, Adam and Eve, and their children were giants compared to us. The Lord created Adam and Eve of huge stature, and they would have lived forever if they had not eaten of the tree of knowledge of good and evil of which multitudes do today when they seek and practice forbidden knowledge of the occult.

When Adam and Eve sinned against the Lord, they began to die.

"And all the days that Adam lived were nine hundred and thirty years: and he died." Genesis 5:5. These *mighty men which were of old* turned their backs on the Lord and followed the ways of Cain. What did these giant human beings develop into when they chose not to obey the Lord?

How THEOSOPHY DECEIVED the WORLD

"And God saw that the wickedness of man was great in the earth, and that every imagination of the thoughts of his heart was only evil continually." Genesis 6:5.

These antediluvian giants with their giant intellects were not backward cavemen as often promoted. They lived hundreds of years. They had many times over the strength and ability to accumulate knowledge over the centuries than us today. They did not live a mere 70 or 80 years, but centuries. "And Noah was six hundred years old when the flood of waters was upon the earth." Genesis 7:6.

The mighty men of old used their abilities for evil instead of for good, and all they thought about was doing evil. Man today has headed in the same direction. Have they not used their intellect for evil? Mankind has invented weapons of war that could destroy the whole earth. The entire world is filled with violence today. Children are taking the lives of their parents. Parents are taking the lives of their children. Murder, rape, and robbery are common place in the cities. Drugs have made the cities war zones.

Nation has risen against nation and kingdom against kingdom. We have been witnessing famines, pestilences, and earthquakes in divers places as Jesus foretold in Matthew 24:7.

"But as the days of Noe (Noah) were, so shall also the coming of the Son of man be." Matthew 24:37.

"This know also, that in the last days perilous times shall come. For men shall be lovers of their own selves, covetous, boasters, proud, blasphemers, disobedient to parents, unthankful, unholy,

"Without natural affection, trucebreakers, false accusers, incontinent, fierce, despisers of those that are good, Traitors, heady, highminded, lovers of pleasures more than lovers of God." 2 Timothy 3:1–4.

Have not most become like this today? This is what the Lord saw upon the earth before the Flood.

"And God looked upon the earth, and, behold, it was corrupt; for all flesh had corrupted his way upon the earth. And God said unto Noah, The end of all flesh is come before me; for the earth is filled with violence through them; and, behold, I will destroy them with the earth." Genesis 6:12, 13.

"But Noah found grace in the eyes of the Lord." Genesis 6:8. So can we follow the example of Noah.

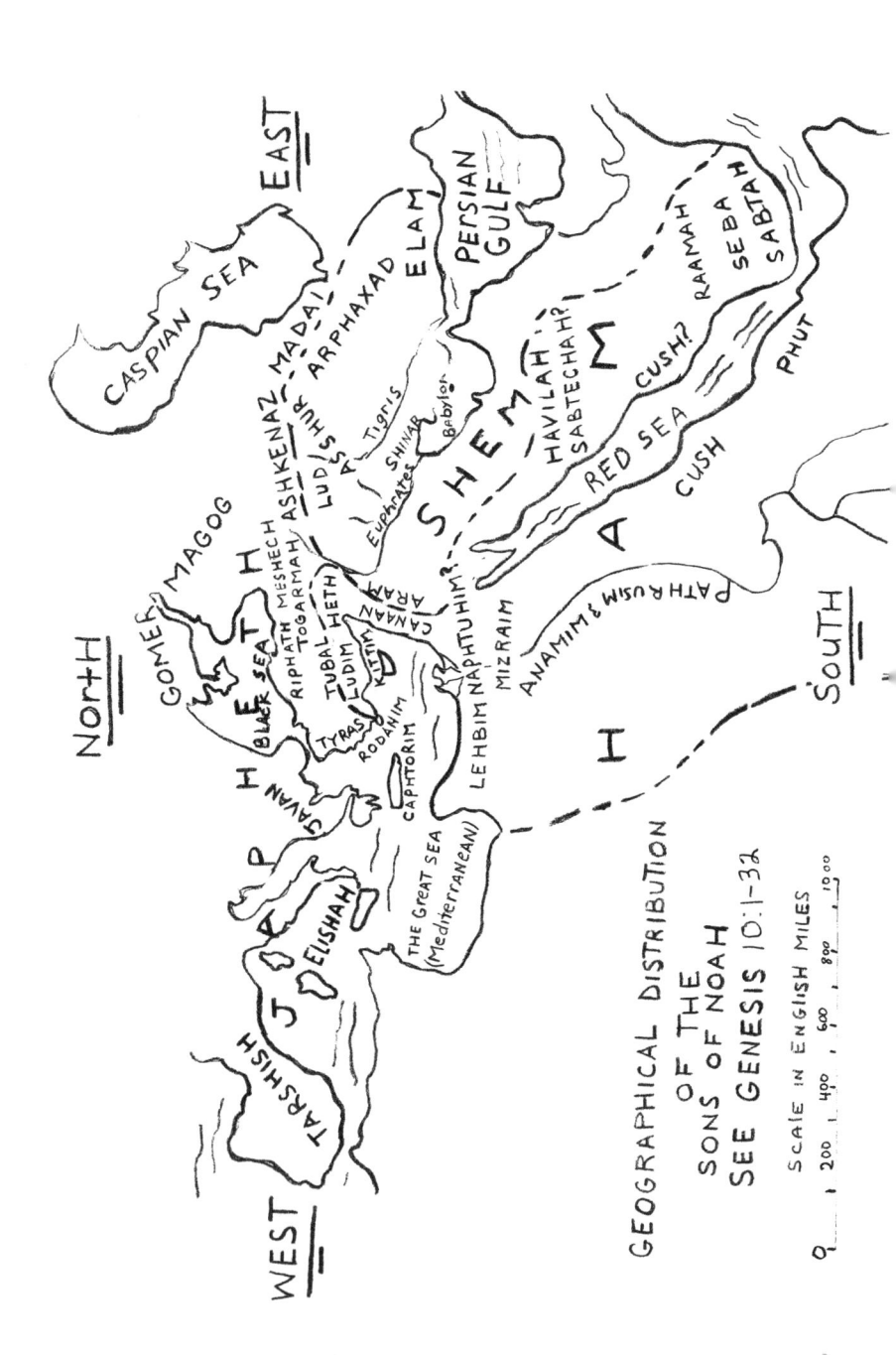

The Real Truth About UFO's and the New World Order

How THEOSOPHY DECEIVED the WORLD

"Submit yourselves therefore to God. Resist the devil, and he will flee from you. Draw nigh to God, and he will draw nigh to you. Cleanse your hands, ye sinners; and purify your hearts, ye double-minded. Be afflicted, and mourn, and weep: let your laughter be turned to mourning, and your joy to heaviness. Humble yourselves in the sight of the Lord, and he shall lift you up." James 4:7–10.

Jesus predicted that the people in these closing days of history would eventually, as time goes on, reach the same condition of the people shortly before the Flood. On this side of the Flood, Cush, Nimrod, and Semiramis can be credited for starting the **first rebellion** against the Lord. These principles of thought have been passed down through the centuries and handed down to us today.

Going back in history, the descendants of Noah, Shem, Ham, and Japheth began to have sons and daughters. Has the reader ever wondered where all these different religions come from? If we have one God, why do we have so many different religions? Where can we find the origin of this religious confusion? These are the questions I needed answers to back in 1970.

After studying Bible history, the science of anthropology, mythology, and Biblical archaeology from books found in college and public libraries and from Bible-related books, a seeker of truth can prove the credibility of the record of the Flood and what happened to Noah's descendants through the natural sciences.

Here also can be found the answer to the question: Where did all of these different religions and ethnic groups come from? It took me about a total of five years to compile this information and write a book on this interesting subject. I entitled it *Beware It's Coming – The Antichrist 666*.

This volume cannot go into detail of where a seeker of truth may go to prove how the **gods of mythology are the gods of astrology**, and how these false gods were, indeed, believed by pagans to **have once been humans**. However, we will study a brief history of this account for it is necessary to do so to be able to show the origin of the occult and that of the New Age Movement we see today. If the reader would like to study more in-depthly into how these pagan gods evolved, please obtain a copy of *Beware It's Coming – The Antichrist 666*.

The Real Truth About UFO's and the New World Order

Again, to find the origin of the original Jews and some very astonishing facts about modern Israel today and what Bible prophecy predicted that Satan shall do in the Holy Land in these last days, we again need to go back in history to the builders of the Babel society for the Scriptures surely foretold that Satan will move his headquarters *between* the seas in the glorious holy mountain.

"And **Cush** begat **Nimrod**: he began to be a mighty one in the earth. He was a mighty hunter before the Lord: wherefore it is said, Even as Nimrod the mighty hunter before the Lord.

"And the beginning of his kingdom was Babel, and Erech, and Accad, and Calneh, in the land of Shinar. Out of that land went forth Asshur, and builded Nineveh, and the city of Rehoboth, and Calah, And Resen between Nineveh and Calah: the same is a great city." Genesis 10:8–12.

As we have seen, Nimrod on this side of the Flood became the first king and built the **first city** called Babel. The word "*Babel*" itself means "*confusion*."

"And the whole earth was of one language, and of one speech. And it came to pass, as **they journeyed from the east**, that they found a plain in the land of Shinar; and they dwelt there.

"And they said one to another, Go to, let us make brick, and burn them throughly. And they had brick for stone, and slime had they for mortar. And they said, Go to, let us build us a city and a tower, whose top may reach unto heaven; and let us make us a name, lest we be scattered abroad upon the face of the whole earth.

"And the Lord came down to see the city and the tower, which the children of men builded. And the Lord said, Behold, the people is one, and they have all one language; and this they begin to do: and now nothing will be restrained from them, which they have imagined to do.

"Go to, let us go down, and there confound their language, that they may not understand one another's speech. So the Lord scattered them abroad from thence upon the face of all the earth: and they left off to build the city.

"Therefore is the name of it called Babel; because the Lord did there confound the language of all the earth: and from thence did the Lord scatter them abroad upon the face of all the earth." Genesis 11:1–9.

How THEOSOPHY DECEIVED the WORLD

It was around 2200 B.C. when Nimrod attempted to unite the whole world back then into a one-world Socialist government, a one-world religion, with a one-world marketing system leaving God out. This was nothing less than a repeat of what Lucifer tried to do in Heaven. Lucifer tried to take Christ's place in the Heavenly courts by trying to get the angels of God to leave the Lord and rally to join his cause. Only one third of the angelic host chose Lucifer's side.

"And there was war in heaven: Michael and his angels fought against the dragon; and the dragon fought and his angels, And prevailed not; neither was their place found any more in heaven." Revelation 12:7, 8.

After Satan (the Dragon) lost the war with Christ, he was confined to this earth. What Lucifer tried to do with the angels, he would now try to do with humans. Nimrod, whose name means *rebel* became a type of Lucifer. This ancient pagan hero became *a mighty hunter before the Lord*. (See Genesis 10:9.) This text, in the original Hebrew, says the mighty hunter *against* the Lord.

Many of the ancient cities that Nimrod built in Mesopotamia, which in Micah 5:6 the Lord called *the land of Nimrod*, were found. The land of Nimrod was divided into two distinct areas which today are known as Iraq and Iran. Anciently, they were known as Babylonia and Assyria.

The capital of Babylonia was Babylon, and the capital of Assyria was Nineveh. Both of these ancient cities that the mighty rebel against the Lord built were uncovered by archaeologists. Austen Henry Layard, a British archaeologist, found Nineveh, the capital of the Assyrian Empire. Between 1845 and 1847, Austen Layard uncovered a wealth of valuable information that would help prove the credibility of Bible history.

Alexander Hislop, later in the same century, began to compile the archaeological findings that Layard uncovered at Nineveh with texts written by ancient historians. Alexander Hislop compiled astonishing information in how the pagan religions of Mesopotamia, the cradle of humankind today, can be traced back into history to be the original worship of Nimrod, Semiramis, and Tammuz.

Ancient historians and pagan philosophers such as Plato and Homer derived their ancient account of history from the legend of

The Real Truth About UFO's and the New World Order

this unholy trio, which they and their countrymen worshipped ignorantly as Zeus, Athena, Adonis, and a host of other names as they progressed down through the centuries.

When Nimrod died, he was still in his prime. He was not only the first Mason, a builder of cities, but also the first king who taught the arts of war. Those who opposed his plans for a one-world government were warred upon. This mighty hunter against the Lord was killed by his uncle Shem who remained loyal to God.

The legend of Nimrod said that Nimrod, who was Ninus to the early Ninevites and Baal or Belus[1] to the early Babylonians, was cut up in 14 pieces and when he died, his spirit or soul went up to the sun and took possession of it. Nimrod then became the **first sun-god** after the Flood, according to the myth.

According to the ancient Babylonian myth, Nimrod's soul took possession of the sun. Two years after his death, his soul came back and entered into the womb of his surviving wife, Semiramis. As a result, Nimrod's wife begot a god-son named Tammuz who was born December 25. To the ancient Israelites, this pagan trio was worshipped as Baal, Ashtaroth, and Tammuz. This trio was Isis, Horus, and Osiris to the Egyptians.

"And they forsook the Lord, and served Baal and Ashtaroth." Judges 2:13.

"Then he brought me to the door of the gate of the Lord's house which was toward the north; and, behold, there sat women weeping for Tammuz." Ezekiel 8:14.

Nimrod as the sun, Ashtaroth as the moon, and Tammuz as Venus were and are today worshipped as the chief gods of astrology. The Toltec Quetzalcoatl and the Maya Kulkulcán is **just a twisted version** of the gods of Babylonia and Assyria which spread throughout the world after the world federation at Babel was broken up by the God of Abraham.

As I discussed earlier**, astrology** was symbolized by the ancient Chaldeans who invented this nonsense as a huge, **red, seven-headed dragon**. Here, again, are their own words found in the book, *Origins of Astrology*, as follows:

---

[1]*The Two Babylons*, Hislop, pp. 25, 26.

How THEOSOPHY DECEIVED the WORLD

"The **serpen**t was a **symbol** of the planetary system in **astrology**. The **six spheres or six heads** stand for the **six planets** with the **serpent itself as the sun**."[2]

"The seven planets: Saturn, Sun, Moon, Mars, Mercury, Jupiter, and Venus."[3]

Keeping this in mind, the reader may understand Revelation 12:9 more clearly. "And the great dragon was cast out, that old serpent, called the Devil, and Satan, **WHICH DECEIVETH THE WHOLE WORLD**: he was cast out into the earth, and his angels were cast out with him."

Here we find the reason why the apostle John, who was the penman of Revelation, was given this great red Dragon in vision as a symbol for Satan attacking Christ's bride symbolically displayed in Revelation, Chapter 12, as being pregnant.

"And there appeared a great wonder in heaven; a woman clothed with the sun, and the moon under her feet, and upon her head a crown of twelve stars: And she being with child cried, travailing in birth, and pained to be delivered.

"And there appeared another wonder in heaven; and behold a great red dragon, having seven heads and ten horns, and seven crowns upon his heads. And his tail drew the third part of the stars of heaven, and did cast them to the earth: and the dragon stood before the woman which was ready to be delivered, for to devour her child as soon as it was born.

"And she brought forth a man child, who was to rule all nations with a rod of iron: and her child was caught up unto God, and to his throne." Revelation 12:1–5.

It has been the religion of astrology along with its crafts that Satan, its inventor, has used down through the centuries by those who have been deceived by it to war against God and His people.

"And the dragon was wroth with the woman, and went to make war with the remnant of her seed, which keep the commandments of God, and have the testimony of Jesus Christ." Revelation 12:17.

As pointed out, modern New Age Spiritualism, like their ancient brethren, is rooted and grounded in the religion of astrology which started at Babylon.

---

[2]*Origins of Astrology*, Lindsay, p. 375.

[3]*Ibid.*, Lindsay, p. 233.

The Real Truth About UFO's and the New World Order

It is mind-boggling to see how people will not step out of their doors unless they consult their horoscope. The whole system of astrology involves a 360° circle, with its **36 room** and house gods in fixed positions along with its seven chief gods which are the seven planets. Something even more baffling is to know that since the time of the Greeks, this astrological system has shifted one full sign backwards all around the zodiac!

So, a person who is born under the sign of Aries, says *The Buffalo News,* May 19, 1982, is actually born under the stars of the constellation Pisces, the fish. Bill Machmer, who wrote this article for *The Buffalo News* says, "Astrologers say that they make adjustments for this, and no two lots of these soothsayers seem to be able to come up with the same adjustments.

"When we consider the vast scale of this wonderful universe, we can realize just how ridiculous belief in casting horoscopes can be. **Sirius, the dog star**, is claimed by astrologers to directly influence the **fortunes** of individuals. This bright dog star is 51 trillion miles away! Light emitted by this star, traveling at 186,000 miles a second, would need 8.7 years to reach our planet. With some 250 billion stars in our Milky Way galaxy and a possible 100 billion galaxies to influence us, the number of stars that enter our fortunes is indeed endless.

"Our modern astrologers have conveniently forgotten about all this. They pay little attention to all the planets, moons, asteroids, quasars, and pulsars that have been discovered since Ptolemy's time. Unfortunately, the Babylonian fad is still with us. Whatever its function, astrology is an irrationality that serves mankind poorly."

By the way, astrologers use mathematics to foretell the future. If the reader has not read my last book, *The New Age Movement and The Illuminati 666*, I show a chart that astrologers use to work out their divination. The chart has 36 numbers which represent the 36 gods in fixed positions around the zodiac (horoscope) band. If you add the numbers from one to 36, they will add to 666.

In the whole world from Babel (Babylon), Egypt, Persia, India, Russia, China, Greece, Europe, North America, Central America, to South America, there can be found the influences of "that old serpent, called the Devil, and Satan, which deceiveth the whole world." Revelation 12:9. This is why John was given a vision of

How THEOSOPHY DECEIVED the WORLD

Satan symbolically pictured as a seven-headed red Dragon attacking Christ's bride in Revelation, Chapter 12, for all of the attacks on the religion of God and His people have derived from astrology.

Nearly all nations were swallowed up into the darkness of the occult. Only a small remnant of people from the lineage of Shem chose to obey the Lord and kept themselves from worshipping idols, and so will it be today!

By the year 2000 B.C., the descendants of Ham and Japheth who came from Noah spread idolatry everywhere they migrated.

To turn the people of the world from astrology and to cause them to worship Him who created the sun, moon, and five visible planets instead of the created things, the Lord would have raised Himself a whole nation of priests. A Semitic, living in Babylonia in a city called Ur, which archaeologists have found, was called and chosen and faithful to God. We read:

"Now the Lord had said unto Abram, Get thee out of thy country, and from thy kindred, and from thy father's house, unto a land that I will shew thee:

"And I will make of thee a great nation, and I will bless thee, and make thy name great; and thou shalt be a blessing:

"And I will bless them that bless thee, and curse him that curseth thee: and **IN THEE SHALL ALL FAMILIES OF THE EARTH BE BLESSED.**" Genesis 12:1–3.

The word *Semitic* means *from the descendants of Shem*. The descendants of Shem are where all the Oriental people, including the American Indians from North to South America, can be traced. I have traveled much of Guatemala, Costa Rica, Panama, and Mexico and lived almost five years in Hawaii where I began to write my first book. You do not have to be an anthropologist to see that the American Indian is Oriental. The Mayans, Incas, Toltecs, Mexicans, and Aztecs did not originally come from Atlantis, as occultists promote, but came from Mesopotamia.

It appears again from the Scriptures that two ethnic groups developed on this side of the Flood from the lineage of Shem.

"And unto Eber were born two sons: the name of one was Peleg; for in his days was the earth divided; and his brother's name was Joktan." Genesis 10:25.

The Real Truth About UFO's and the New World Order

In the Hebrew language, the word "*Eber*" is pronounced Heber. The word **Heber** or **Eber** is where we get the word **Hebrew** today. The word "*Hebrew*" means "*belonging to Eber*."[4]

The race of the Hebrew people began with Eber. Abram, who lived in the city of Ur, was from the lineage of Eber, who came from the lineage of Shem, not Japheth as Aryanism tries to claim. Racists like the KKK and other White Supremacists try to twist the Scriptures to show that the true Israelites were once White people. Nothing could be further from the truth. However, there are those who are Jews that are White who also claim to be the original chosen people. Therefore, these sons of Japheth, not sons of Shem, claim the Land of Israel is given to them as an inheritance.

However, when the original house of Israel rejected Jesus as their Messiah, Jesus pronounced this warning, "**Behold, your house is left unto you desolate**." Matthew 23:38.

Hence, in A.D. 34 after the stoning of Stephen (See Acts 7:57–60), God's covenant with the original Israelites as a chosen nation ended. The year A.D. 34 **marked the very year** that the Gospel was given to the Gentiles. Shortly afterwards, Saul became Paul. The great Hebrew persecutor of Christianity became converted and became Christianity's greatest evangelist. The Scriptures are very clear. When Israel rejected its Messiah, God rejected them as his chosen nation. All of the promises and blessings from God in the Old Testament were conditional. When they rejected Christ Jesus, they rejected their fount from which every blessing and promise flowed. The reader may question: If God rejected the original Hebrew Jewish nation as His chosen people in A.D. 34, then who are these modern Jews who have established modern Israel today? Let us look into this confusion and see if the Lord's Word will help us untangle this mystery today. This is important to know because the Father of Lies is working today to establish his kingdom at Jerusalem! Speaking about the last days, Daniel the prophet of God foretold:

"And he shall plant the tabernacles of his palace **between the seas in the glorious holy mountain**; yet he shall come to his end, and none shall help him." Daniel 11:45.

---

[4]*Young's Analytical Concordance to the Bible*, **p. 473.**

How THEOSOPHY DECEIVED the WORLD

We will study into Daniel, Chapter 11, later on in this closing chapter. First, it is very important for us to know just who the Lord says are His chosen people.

Abram was called out of Babylonia of the city of Ur to establish a nation. This nation was to become the center of the world where the knowledge of the true God was to go out to the deceived world.

"Now the Lord had said unto Abram, Get thee out of thy country, and from thy kindred, and from thy father's house, unto a land that I will shew thee: And I will make of thee a great nation, and I will bless thee, and make thy name great; and thou shalt be a blessing: And I will bless them that bless thee, and curse him that curseth thee: and in thee shall all the families of the earth be blessed." Genesis 12:1–3.

The name of Abram was changed to Abraham which in Hebrew means "*father of a great multitude*."

"Neither shall thy name any more be called Abram, but thy name shall be Abraham; for a father of many nations have I made thee." Genesis 17:5.

"And Abraham was an hundred years old, when his son Isaac was born unto him." Genesis 21:5. According to Hebrew chronology, Sarah gave birth to Isaac about 1896 B.C. Reader, was Abraham an Israelite or a Jew? Abraham was a Hebrew, not an Israelite or a Jew, because they were not in history at this time. Abraham had Isaac, Isaac then begat Jacob, and then Jacob begat his twelve sons which became the twelve tribes of Israel.

The Lord said to Abraham who was not an Israelite or a Jew at this time, "And I will bless them that bless thee, and curse him that curseth thee: and in thee shall **ALL families** of the earth be blessed." Genesis 12:3.

Notice here the covenant that God made with Abraham, "shall **ALL families** of the earth be blessed." This promise was not just for the Israelites that were to come later, but to **ALL** the families of the earth. Reader, it is most important to understand what modern Judaism has evolved into to understand Satan's plan for Israel.

"**FOR MINE HOUSE SHALL BE CALLED AN HOUSE OF PRAYER FOR ALL PEOPLE**." (Not just for Jews) Isaiah 56:7.

However, Israel was chosen by God to be a nation of priests, which

The Real Truth About UFO's and the New World Order

the Lord would use to teach all nations about how they could receive forgiveness and be restored once again as the sons of God.

As we have seen, the Israelites did not keep God's covenant, so the Lord chose the tribe of Levi only to be His priests. Only the tribe of the Levites was allowed to handle the sacred things of the temple. (See Numbers 1:47–53; Numbers 18:6, 23–30.)

Hence, the original Israelites were Semitic coming from the lineage of Eber out of which the name Hebrew derived. So this means that the chosen people of God were from the Hebrew race, not from the various races who call themselves Jews today. It is astonishing to know that at least 84% of the Jewish population today **are not Hebrew, but are known as Ashkenazim**. What is Ashkenazim?

The Encyclopedia Americana says the Ashkenazim people "are the Jews whose ancestors lived in **German lands**. The name derives from *Ashk'naz*, the traditional Hebrew name for **Germany**. During and after the Middle Ages, Ashkenazi Jews spread all over Europe (except the Mediterranean countries). From there they migrated overseas, retaining their **Yiddish** language. They produced a rich religious and secular literature in Yiddish, a medieval German dialect with an **admixture** of Hebrew."[5]

The Encyclopedia Americana goes on to say: "It was among Ashkenazi Jews that the idea of political **Zionism emerged**, leading ultimately to the establishment of the state of Israel."[6]

Just as the Christians are divided into two mainstreams, the Protestants and the Catholics, so are the Jews divided into two mainstreams. Just as the Protestants and Catholics have argued over doctrine, so do the Jews.

The other small 16% of the Jewish population are the original Hebrew Jews known in Jewish circles as Sephardim. Hence, Judaism is divided into Ashkenazim and Sephardim. The word "*Sephardim*" is a Hebrew word that means *Spanish Jews*.

This writer is not anti-Semitic for I know that the **first Christians were Jews. Jesus was a Hebrew Jew** from the tribe of Judah. However, the Scriptures warn in Daniel 11:45 that this world federation against the God of Abraham will reach its climax when it establishes

---

[5] *The Encyclopedia Americana*, Vol. 2, Grolier Inc., p. 436.
[6] *Ibid.*, Vol. 2, p. 436.

How THEOSOPHY DECEIVED the WORLD

its headquarters (tabernacles) *"between the seas in the glorious holy mountain."* The seas are the Great Sea which is called the Mediterranean Sea, the Sea of Galilee, and the Dead Sea. The glorious holy mountain is Jerusalem. This area between the seas is called **Megiddo Valley**. It has been foretold from Scripture by a Jewish prophet named Daniel in Daniel 11:45 and from a Jewish apostle of Christ named John in Revelation 16:13–16 that this great conflict between Christ and Lucifer **will come to its end in Israel**. To understand how these astonishing events are being set up right before our very eyes, the reader must understand how the modern Jews from the time of the European Renaissance adopted this Atlantean Plan of Plato as well! Not only this, but **Ashkenazi Jews are not Hebrew**, they are of Aryan descent. It was through the branch of the Ashkenazi Jews that not only was Deism accepted among them, but they also adopted early in their history the **Cabala (Kabbalah)**, which is nothing less than ancient **pagan Theosophy** which we have seen has both New Agers and many Christians standing under its banner.

This chapter will focus on how the Jews are also caught up in this New World Order scheme. However, this writer has discovered years ago that this conspiracy **is not solely a Jewish conspiracy** to enslave the world as Hitler preached. We need to understand this for, as the reader knows, today we have a lot of little Hitlers who would enjoy having another holocaust. This Atlantean Plan promoted by Utopists is being promoted out of the mouths of people from every race, kindred, and tongue. This New Age and New World Order scheme is actually a Luciferian conspiracy sometimes hiding under a Christian camouflage and sometimes clothed in Jewish garments.

To begin to show what I just pointed out is true, let's take a look from the Old Testament Scriptures, history, and from Jewish encyclopedias to see how the **original Hebrew Jew has all but disappeared** and how **White European Jews called Ashkenazis have taken their place**.

As pointed out, the Hebrew race can be traced to **Eber** who was a descendant of Shem. (See Genesis 11:10–17.) However, the Ashkenazi Jew can be traced in the Scriptures and in Jewish encyclopedias to the son of Gomer, who was the son of Japheth. (See Genesis 10:2.) **Gomer** had a son named **Ashkenaz**. (See Genesis 10:3.) Gomer was

The Real Truth About UFO's and the New World Order

the **progenitor** of the **Celtic peoples**.[7] These Celtic peoples first settled north of the Black Sea and then spread themselves southward and westward to the extremities of Europe.[8] Gomer's son Ashkenaz and his descendants **originally settled near the mountains of Ararat** which was in the neighborhood of **Armenia**.[9] It was very eye-opening for me to discover while tracing the origin of the Ashkenazi Jews when I read in *The Encyclopaedia Judaica*, Volume 3, 1972, on pages 475, 721, and 722 that the **Ashkenazi Jews developed** at about the sixth century A.D. and were known as the "**Caspian Jews**" who were to be "**THE FUTURE GOG AND MAGOG**." These are the spiritual rulers that will unite this present world into a world confederacy against Christ. It was from this same branch of Judaism that Jewish Theosophy (Kabbalah) spread after the rise of the Muslims who drove these Caspian or Armenian Jews out of their original homeland.

Like the Druids to the Celtic peoples, the Ashkenazi Jews have a branch of their divisions known as **Hasidism** who are deep in magic and sorcery. The **founder** of Hasidism among Ashkenazi Jewry was **Eliezer Ba'al Shem-Tob**.[10] In Deuteronomy, Chapter 18, the sciences of the occult are strikingly forbidden, as also in the Talmud and the Mishnah, which **equates magic with idolatry**.[11] However, the Hasidei Ashkenazi Jews **ignore the Bible's warnings** about witchcraft and magic and continue to openly practice it like New Agers and some Christians.

Because of the idolatry of the ancient Hebrew Israelites, the original Semitic chosen people's population diminished. First, when the kings of **Assyria took ten tribes out of northern Israel**, this left only the tribes of Benjamin and Judah. Again, their numbers were lessened at the destruction of the first temple in Jerusalem by King Nebuchadnezzar. After the 70 years of captivity in Babylon, the Hebrew Jews were allowed by the Lord to return to Jerusalem and rebuild the temple and city. However, only about 50,000 of these original Hebrew Israelites went with Nehemiah to restore the temple and

---

[7] *Young's Analytical Concordance to the Bible*, Young, p. 426.
[8] *Ibid.*, Young, p. 426.
[9] *Ibid.*, Young, p. 57.
[10] *The Jewish Encyclopedia*, 1925, p. 252.
[11] *The Encyclopaedia Judaica*, Vol. 11, p. 706.

How THEOSOPHY DECEIVED the WORLD

the city. Most wanted to stay in Babylonia where they were enjoying prosperity at this time for they got along with the Persians who conquered the Babylonians. The original people of Persia derived from Elam. **Elam was the son of Shem.** (See Genesis 10:22.) So, the Hebrews and Persians spoke the same Semitic language of Aramaic.

A little later, about 2,000 more Hebrew Jews joined their brethren in rebuilding the city of Jerusalem and the temple. However, most of the original Jews remaining from the tribes of Judah and Benjamin mingled with the idolatrous Persians who also had their version of the religion of astrology as the official religion of their country. Here again, we can see in history the mingling of truth with error and the profane with the holy. The Jews that remained in Babylonia began to adopt into Judaism the sciences and philosophies of astrology. This was to grow into Jewish tradition as the **Kabbalah (Cabala)**, the Jewish book of magic. The Kabbalah is a **blend** of Babylonian and Persian witchcraft which was blended with **Judaism** during the time of the rebuilding of the first temple.[12] This is where we find one of the **major sources** of **occultism** from which **secret societies** like Freemasonry and Rosicrucianism **derive** their crafts, as do the Ashkenazi Jews today. Just like the Hindus, Buddhists, and other New Agers have been deceived by the pantheistic doctrine that God and nature are one, so have the Ashkenazi Jews.

However, the **Sephardi Jews**, as a whole, reject the teachings of the Kabbalah (Cabala). The differences of doctrine and ritual between Ashkenazi Jews and Sephardi Jews led to the creation of **separate congregations**.[13]

When the temple of Jerusalem was destroyed the second time in 70 A.D., the **original Hebrews** who survived the destruction of the city **fled to Spain** to join other Hebrews that had already established a colony there. There, these original Hebrew Jews began to enjoy prosperity and became very powerful in Spain. However, Roman Catholicism began to persecute the Sephardim Jews in the Middle Ages almost to the point of extinction. The poor Jews were asked to become Catholic or suffer death during the time of Queen Isabella. Isabella, who financed Christopher Columbus, was bent on making

---

[12]*Encyclopaedia Judaica*, Vol. 10, p. 495.
[13]*Ibid.*, Vol. 3, pp. 721, 722.

The Real Truth About UFO's and the New World Order

the whole world Catholic. Her fiery zeal for her church, amounting at times to **fanatical cruelty**, has made her known in history as Isabella, "the Catholic."[14] The **Spanish Inquisition**s not only slaughtered the remnant of the Hebrew Jews, but also the poor American Indians in the North, Central, and South Americas as well. This is why **the original Hebrew Jew** only makes up 16% of the Jewish population today.[15] **It may be even a smaller figure.**

In the early history of the Ashkenaz people, they did not as a whole adopt any particular religion as the official religion of their nation until the wars between the Roman Catholics and the Muslims were hot. The Ashkenaz people, wishing to remain neutral and caught geographically between Catholicism and the Islamic nations, became Jews but adopted the Kabbalah as their source of doctrine.

According to the *Academic American Encyclopedia*, Vol. K–L, page 3, it says: "*Kabbalah*, the Hebrew word for **tradition**, originally designated the legal **tradition of Judaism**, but it was later applied to the Jewish mystical tradition, especially the system of **esoteric mystical speculation** and practice that developed during the 12th and 13th centuries."

This same encyclopedia goes on to say on the same page: "Kabbalistic interest, **AT FIRST CONFINED TO A SELECT FEW**, became the preoccupation of large numbers of Jews following their expulsion from Spain (1492) and Portugal (1495). The teachings of Kabbalah, as developed by the visionary Isaac ben Solomon Luria, are credited with giving rise to the Sabbatean movement led by Sabbatai Zevi…. Kabbalah was a **major influence** in the development of **Hasidism** and still has adherents among **Hasidic Jews**."

Jesus told the Jews of His day, "I am come in my Father's name, and ye receive me not: if another shall come in his own name, **him ye will receive**." John 5:43.

After Jesus died, resurrected, and ascended into heaven, the Jews had other messiahs claiming to be the deliverer of Israel's problems. One of the worst of these pretenders which embarrasses Jews today was the Jewish occultist **Sabbatai Zevi**. This self-proclaimed messiah caused multitudes of Jews to sell their houses, land, and goods

---

[14]*Harper's Encyclopaedia of the United States*, Vol. 5, 1905, p. 82.

[15]*Encyclopedia Americana*, Vol. 2, 1978, p. 436.

How THEOSOPHY DECEIVED the WORLD

to prepare for the deliverance of the Jewish people worldwide. He convinced them also to regain the city of Jerusalem from the Muslims. Sabbatai Zevi was raised in the city of Smyrna, Turkey. In 1648, Zevi began his mission to take Jerusalem from the Muslims and settle the Jews in their place. The sultan of Turkey heard of Sabbatai Zevi's revolutionary movement against Muslims and captured Zevi. The sultan, not wanting to kill Zevi on the spot to make a martyr out of him, threatened him with death if he did not become a Muslim. Hence, Sabbatai Zevi became a member of Islam on the 15th day of September in **1666**![16]

There are several ways the Cabala is spelled today, but the word *Kabbalah* (Cabala) literally means in Hebrew "*tradition*." Another popular way of describing witchcraft or occultism is using the word "*mysticism*." Those who practice witchcraft are often referred to as mystics, instead of witches, because it has a better ring to it today.

The Encyclopedia of Philosophy, Vol. 1 & 2, page 1, defines the "Cabala is used both as a general name for **Jewish mysticism** and as the specific designation for its major medieval variety. Mystical awareness is to be found in the Biblical and Rabbinic tradition and had literary expression in some of the prophetic writings, Psalms, and Apocalypses. More characteristically, however, what is referred to as Cabala is a type of occult **THEOSOPHICAL FORMULATION** of the doctrines of the Jewish religion, particularly those concerned with creation, revelation, and redemption." (Emphasis mine.)

The above statement is saying that cabalists claim that the miracles of the Bible were done by mysticism (magic), rather than by the power of God. Cabalists also teach "because all substance is thus ultimately an overflowing of God's substance, **Cabala is a pantheistic doctrine**."[17]

I know these statements that some Jews believe that the miracles of the Old Testament were done by magic and that the Ashkenazi Jews believe in the pantheistic doctrine that God and nature are one are hard to believe for some Christians. Nevertheless, this is true. When the reader understands this, he will not have too much of a problem in seeing how Jews are uniting with Buddhists, Hindus, Muslims, and even Catholics today. They are all uniting into a one-world religion

---
[16]*Encyclopaedia Judaica*, Vol. 14, p. 1238.
[17]*The Encyclopedia of Philosophy*, Vol. 1 & 2, p. 1.

The Real Truth About UFO's and the New World Order

being orchestrated by the United Nations. We will investigate this shortly. We will also investigate how modern Ashkenazi Jews, like Catholics and Protestants, have indeed been infiltrated with doctrines of **pantheism** and also **Marxism** as we study on. Karl Marx was born into an Ashkenazi Jewish family, but converted to Lutheranism, then to Satanism, and then died as an atheist in 1883. Marx ended up hating Jews and their national symbol.

The reader needs to know that witches not only draw the **pentagram** ☆ (five-pointed star) on the ground when casting spells or to work magic, but they also draw the **hexagram** (✡ – six-pointed star) as well. After they get in the middle of the pentagram, whose center is called the pentagon, a spirit guide (demon) appears in the center of the hexagram. Unfortunately, this star has been adopted by modern Jews.

What is the hexagram? One pyramid pointing up represents the male aspect of the sun-god; and another pyramid on top pointing down represents the female aspect of the sun-god. These two pyramids or triangles combined form the **evilest sign in astrology**. It is called the hexagram to witches; it is called the Star of David (Magen David) to the Jews. The truth is this six-pointed star which symbolizes Judaism today **was never worn by King David** or by the ancient Israelites. However, the hexagram may be traced to King Solomon of Israel during his apostasy from the Lord. Solomon for a time became a victim of Spiritualism but later returned unto the Lord. The hexagram is sometimes referred to as Solomon's seal.[18] It is the **most powerful sign** in witchcraft. Witches use it to put a **hex** on people or to cast spells. The Jews did not begin to display this sign until sometime during the Middle Ages! This evil symbol has its origin in the Kabbalah. Freemasonry also uses this star. Albert Pike, one of the most recognized scholars of Freemasonry, said:

"All truly dogmatic religions have issued from the Kabalah and return to it. Everything scientific and grand in the religious dreams of all the **ILLUMINATI**, Jacob Boeheme, Swedenborg, Saint Martin, and others is borrowed from the **KABALAH; all MASONIC** associations **OWE IT THEIR SECRETS AND THEIR SYMBOLS.**"[19] (Emphasis added.)

---
[18]*Dictionary of Symbolism*, Biedermann, p. 173.
[19]*Morals and Dogma*, Pike, p. 744.

How THEOSOPHY DECEIVED the WORLD

Albert Pike, one of the most recognized scholars of Freemasonry, freely admits that his order is based in **Jewish Theosophy**!

What the Lord warns is an abomination in Deuteronomy, Chapter 18, the Kabbalah teaches. *The Encyclopedia of Religions*, Vol. 2, page 350, says: "The oldest Kabbalists appear to have taught (as in the Talmud) the doctrine of **metempsychosis**, or **transmigration** of the soul, **WHICH MOHAMMED ALSO ADOPTED FROM THE RABBIS**." Here we see the Muslim connection with Spiritualism. As the Druids are to the Celtic peoples and the cabalists are to the Jews, it is the Muslim sect of the **Sufis** who have preserved their version of the sciences of Theosophy. In December, the Sufi mystics whirl themselves in their spinning dances to open themselves to their divine being.[20]

Transmigration of the soul means when a body dies, the soul of that body can take possession of another living body. Hindus, Buddhists, Muslims, Chinese religions, and some Christians today believe that the soul or spirit does not die, but has immortality. The immortality of the soul is the basic foundation to all of the doctrines of witchcraft with its mother being astrology, and it is the doctrine that is bringing Eastern and Western religions together.

As we have seen, the people of the occult believe that the body is a temporary house in which the spirit or soul is trapped. Once the body dies, the soul becomes stronger. Billions, both Christian and pagan, believe in life after death. Some Christians pay big money to priests to get their poor deceased relative's soul out of purgatory in order that their loved one can continue their journey to the Heavenly courts above. Others pay big money to mediums (channelers) to hear a dead relative or an ancient hero give them information. Still others, who have been psychotic killers, claim to justify their actions by hearing voices from the dead telling them how evil women are or that the President must be killed or that his wife and children are possessed by evil spirits and should die so their souls might be saved. We have seen others kill themselves believing that their soul will have a better hereafter. When controversy arises some strap themselves with bombs in believing their god will bring them (their soul) to Heaven.

---

[20]*The Mystical Year,* **Time-Life Books,** p. 115.

The Real Truth About UFO's and the New World Order

As Albert Pike and the encyclopedias explain, all occult sciences are based in the Kabbalah which is Jewish Theosophy.

The occult practice of claiming to communicate with the dead is **necromancy**. This practice, as we have learned from Deuteronomy 18:11, **is an abomination unto the Lord**. The occult's claim of being able to communicate with dead souls **is a lie from Satan himself**. Other beliefs of the occult, which are also lies from Satan, are the beliefs of **transmigration of the soul** and that the **soul is cast into hell or goes immediately to Heaven at death. Mainstream Christianity, as well, teaches these doctrines.**

Where did mainstream Christianity receive the doctrine of the immortality of the soul? Many use the Scriptures out of context.

"As also in all his epistles, speaking in them of these things; in which are some things hard to be understood, which they that are unlearned and **unstable wrest,** as they do also the **other scriptures, unto their own destruction.**" 2 Peter 3:16.

"Ye shall NOT surely die" was Satan's first lie to Eve in Genesis 3:4. This **lie** has been **repeated** through the mouths of Babylonian high priests, Persian prophets like Zoroaster and Buddha; Greek philosophers such as Plato and Homer; the high priests of Ra, Osiris, Isis, and Horus of Egypt; the high priests of the Temple of Diana in Ephesus; the high priests of the pagan gods of Rome; and the priests of Kulkulcán of the Mayans and Quetzalcoatl of the Toltecs and Aztecs. This lie was also heard from the mouth of Muhammad, American Indian medicine men, the pope, and also from the mouths of most Protestant pastors.

However, the ancient prophet Moses spoke the words of God, "Thou shalt surely die." Genesis 2:17. The hope of Christianity is the resurrection of those who found grace in the eyes of the Lord by believing the Gospel of Jesus Christ. The doctrine of life immediately after death cannot be found on the pages of the Bible, but is found on the pages of the occult.

Today, multitudes of psychics claim they can put you in touch with a dead loved one or even bring you messages from the Virgin Mary or one of Jesus' disciples or even channel a message to the world from Jesus himself.

While living in Hawaii, I quickly learned that the official religion there was not Christianity, but Buddhism. It is common place

How THEOSOPHY DECEIVED the WORLD

to see food left on graves by Buddhists in the belief that they are feeding the souls of their departed loved ones. It is also common place to watch young Hawaiian children steal the food and eat it, while the believer in Buddha after returning believed that the dead loved one ate it.

Some Christians go to the graves of dead loved ones and hold long conversations, they think, with the dead.

Nevertheless, the Word of the Lord says, "Thou changest his countenance, and sendest him away. His sons come to honour, and **he knoweth it not**; and they are brought low, but he perceiveth it not of them." Job 14:20, 21.

"**For the living know that they shall die: but the dead know not any thing**." Ecclesiastes 9:5.

If the wicked are burning in hell or the righteous are now in Heaven as mainstream Christian priests and pastors teach their congregations, would they not **have some consciousness** of what is going on around them?

"His breath goeth forth, he returneth to his earth; in that very day **his thoughts perish**." Psalm 146:4.

Still other pastors, who have screamed to their congregations how terrible it is for them in hell and have scared the ignorant of Scripture into being good or accepting Jesus, will try to justify or reason away the above Scriptures by stating that these Scriptures talk of the death of the body. It is the **soul** that lives on after death, they say. According to them, the soul immediately goes to Heaven at death if worthy. Then, later, at the resurrection, the body and soul will be united again.

Let us see if the Scriptures agree with that doctrine.

"And the Lord God formed man of the dust of the ground, and breathed into his nostrils the breath of life; and man became a **living soul**." Genesis 2:7.

"*And man became a **living soul***," in the original Hebrew translates "*and man became a **living creature**.*" The word "*soul*" today has been **twisted** by tradition to mean a conscious being living within mankind. Nevertheless, the Scriptures plainly teach that the soul dies.

"Behold, **all souls are mine**; as the soul of the father, so also the soul of the son is mine: **THE SOUL THAT SINNETH, IT SHALL DIE**." Ezekiel 18:4.

The Real Truth About UFO's and the New World Order

The word *soul* simply means *person*; man became a living creature. The word *spirit* and *soul* are NOT the same thing. The soul dies, but "the **spirit shall return** unto God who gave it." Ecclesiastes 12:7.

Here is the **backbone** for mainstream Christianity's belief in Heaven or hell at death. It clearly states, they say, that after the body dies, "the spirit shall return unto God who gave it." Here, again, we will see pagan thought which has turned the truth of God into a lie. Originally, the word "*spirit*" in the Scriptures simply meant "*the breath of life*." It plainly teaches in Scripture that the *breath* of God is the *spirit*. It is also reveals in Scripture that God breathed into Adam's nostrils the breath of life.

"**All the while my breath is in me, and the SPIRIT OF GOD IS IN MY NOSTRILS**." Job 27:3.

"Cease ye from man, **whose breath is in his nostrils**: for wherein is he to be accounted of?" Isaiah 2:22.

The *breath of life* and the *spirit of God* are the **same**. It is the *spirit of life* (*the breath of life*) that returns to God, not man's own spirit or soul as more than most believe. When man dies, so do his thoughts perish. (See Psalm 146:4.)

"For the **living** know that they shall die: **but the dead know not any thing**, neither have they any more a reward; for the memory of them is forgotten.

"Also their love, and their hatred, and their envy, **is now perished**; neither have they any more a portion for ever in any thing that is done under the sun.

"**Whatsoever thy hand findeth to do, do it with thy might; for there is no work, nor device, nor knowledge, nor wisdom, in the grave, whither thou goest.**" Ecclesiastes 9:5, 6, 10.

This truth about the dead from Scripture, I know, is hard to believe for Christians who have been **programmed** in their minds from a child that people have ghosts which are the souls of the dead that live on in hell or Heaven after death. I do not know of any other doctrine that **turns intelligent people into atheists** more than the doctrine of hell, the burning place of torment. Has God sent multitudes to hell before the Judgment Day to burn throughout eternity while Hitler only started burning in hell in 1945? Has Cain and all the rest of the wicked since Adam been burning for almost 6,000 years while

How THEOSOPHY DECEIVED the WORLD

the wicked who die today just begin to burn? Is God a tyrant? This doctrine of scaring the wicked into submission to God is not from the pages of the Bible, but is from sun worship, which the Roman Catholics adopted from paganism and passed it down to the Protestants.

However, there is coming the resurrection of both the just and the unjust in the very near future. We will study this wonderful promise later on.

Here is something else we must first look at. If the dead are dead as the Scriptures clearly show, who are these spirit guides that psychics and astrologers say they have? If the dead are dead, what are these UFO's that many have seen? If the dead are dead, what about the Virgin Mary who has appeared to many down through history, along with sightings of the apostles of Jesus? If the dead are dead, what about the doctrine of karma and reincarnation and out-of-the-body experiences that many say they have had? If the dead are dead, who are these supposed ghosts of relatives who have died and claimed to have revisited their loved ones?

The Bible says, "**So man lieth down, and RISETH NOT: till the heavens be no more, they shall not AWAKE, nor be raised out of their sleep.**" Job 14:12.

So, who are these ancient gods, ghosts, UFO's, and spirit guides that the occult claim to receive information and knowledge from? The Bible again **unmistakably reveals** who they are. When the Israelites turned their backs on God and worshipped Baal, Ashtaroth, and Tammuz, as we saw earlier, they sacrificed their sons and daughters to these gods; but what they sacrificed their children to was not to God or to these false gods. Again, they actually sacrificed their children to **devils who were personating these pagan gods**.

"And they served their idols: which were a snare unto them. **Yea, THEY SACRIFICED THEIR SONS AND THEIR DAUGHTERS UNTO DEVILS.**" Psalm 106:36, 37.

"But I say, that the things which the Gentiles sacrifice, they sacrifice to devils, and not to God: and I would not that ye should have fellowship with devils." 1 Corinthians 10:20.

However, just as there are **demons** which are evil angels, so are there **angels of God** who will unite themselves with God's people.

"Are they not all **ministering spirits**, sent forth to minister for them who shall be heirs of salvation?" Hebrews 1:14.

The Real Truth About UFO's and the New World Oder

"The **angel** of the Lord encampeth round about them that fear him, and **delivereth them**." Psalm 34:7.

Apostate Hebrews who **blended Judaism with ancient Spiritualism** and taught it were called **Cabalists** on the other side of the cross. Apostate Christians on this side of the cross who blended occult sciences with Christianity were known as the **Gnostics**. The founder of Gnosticism was the sorcerer **Simon Magus of Samaria**[21] who is recorded in Scripture. (See Acts 8:9–26.) The Gnostics also borrowed their doctrines from Plato and the Kabbalah. The Gnostics have evolved into the Rosicrucians. It is interesting to note that the Rosicrucians say they are brothers "**of the Illuminati**."[22] It is also eye-opening to discover that the ancient Gnostics, like New Agers today, sought to communicate with spirits. A Gnostic Archon (ruler) and a divine being was El Shaddai.[23] This was the name of the ruler of evil spirits of which a popular so-called Christian song was named after. Although El Shaddai is found in the Hebrew language as a name for God, Satan has **often** used God's name to draw people to himself. Jesus warned: "For many shall come in my name, saying, I am Christ; and shall deceive many." Matthew 24:5.

Keeping in mind that God said in Daniel 11:45 that this final conflict between Him and the Devil will end in Israel, let's turn now and see how this **Illuminism** attacked the minds of Anglo-Jewish thought and **changed their thinking** about the coming Messiah to establishing **Plato's Utopian Socialist society**. This is very important to understand. Once the reader sees how Judaism has been infiltrated by Illuminism, which is Marxism today, the reader will understand what Satan's plans are today for Israel and how the Bible foretold it!

The Ashkenazi Jews who embraced the Kabbalah also embraced the gospel of the Enlightenment during the 18th century. This era of early Illuminism was known among European and Soviet Jews as the Haskalah. Like Roman Catholics in France, the European and Russian Jews received a **change of thinking**. Here from *The New Encyclopaedia Britannica* on page 639, we read the following:

---

[21]*Collier's Encyclopedia*, **Vol. 11, 1991, p. 169.**
[22]*Rosicrucian Questions and Answers with Complete History*, **Lewis, p. 25.**
[23]*A Guide to the Gods*, **Carlyon, p. 338.**

How THEOSOPHY DECEIVED the WORLD

"**The 18th century** was the time of the **Haskala**, or **Jewish Enlightenment**, in central and eastern Europe. In this period, Jews turned away from messianic beliefs and began to seek personal or national fulfillment on this Earth during their own lifetimes. Especially important was Moses Mendelssohn, whose *Jerusalem* (1783) defended the validity of Judaism and of his belief in a universal religion of reason. Together with Naphtali Herz Wessely, he produced a German Bible that served to introduce central European Jewry to German culture.

"The **Haskala** also had **influence in eastern Europe** and especially in Russia, where it was characterized by an anti-clericalism and a call for practical social and economic reforms. Hebrew–and Russian–language literature flourished among writers who declared themselves to be Russians by nationality and Jews by religion.... Jewish philosophers attacked the problem of continuity in a time when the Oral Law was **no longer** considered by most Jews to be **divinely ordained**. Among various answers, they posited Judaism as the bearer of the historical or of the moral process, as a very intense form of personal encounter with God, or as religious nationalism.

"Zionism (q.v.), in its secular aspects, can also be viewed as a result of the reform movement. Drawing upon 19th century European nationalism, and reacting to a virulent form of anti-Semitism, Zionists put forth a program of national regeneration and resettlement that culminated in the establishment of the state of Israel in 1948."

Anti-Semitic groups like the KKK and other White Supremacist groups, of which this writer is not a member, are quick to point out how Adam Weishaupt and Mayer Amschel Rothschild (who helped finance the Illuminati conspiracy to cause the French Revolution) were both Ashkenazi Jews. They point out that the population of Israel today is made up of mainly name-only Jews, many of whom are atheists; but I would like to point out that not all the Jews have embraced the Haskalah of the 18th century. Many reject it. It will be shown that this **New World Order is not a Jewish conspiracy, but a Luciferian** order that has infiltrated all nations and all religions. "The dragon deceiveth the whole world." Revelation 12:9.

However, the New World Order conspiracy is looked upon by those who have studied some history about the Illuminati and Communism

The Real Truth About UFO's and the New World Order

as a Jewish conspiracy to enslave the world into a one-world **Socialist** government. Here lies the root of the anti-Semitism in our country today.

Although it is true that the Jews have apostatized from the Word of God, so have Christians (both Roman Catholics and Protestants), Buddhists, Muslims, Hindus, and the whole world! When the Israelites turned their backs on the Lord and adopted the pagan gods around them, the Lord called them **harlots**. The act of **adopting** pagan thought and practices is symbolically spoken of by the Lord as **fornication**.

"But thou didst trust in thine own beauty, and playedst the **harlot** because of thy renown, and pouredst out thy fornications on every one that passed by; his it was." Ezekiel 16:15.

"Thou hast also **committed fornication** with the Egyptians thy neighbours, great of flesh; and hast increased thy whoredoms, to provoke me to anger. Behold, therefore I have stretched out my hand over thee, and have diminished thine ordinary food, and delivered thee unto the will of them that hate thee, the daughters of the Philistines, which are ashamed of thy lewd way.

"Thou hast played the **whore** also with the Assyrians, because thou wast unsatiable; yea, thou hast played the harlot with them, and yet couldest not be satisfied. Thou hast moreover multiplied thy fornication in the land of Canaan unto Chaldea; and yet thou wast not satisfied herewith.

"But as a wife that **committeth adultery**, which taketh strangers instead of her husband!" Ezekiel 16:26–29, 32.

In Revelation, Chapters 17 and 18, there is found a vivid picture of the whole world deceived by Babylon the Great. Babylon here is not the ancient city in Iraq, but a **symbol of the whole world** deceived into following the religious and the political philosophies that first began at Babel (Babylon), which was astrology.

"With whom the kings of the earth have **committed fornication**, and the inhabitants of the earth have been **made drunk** with the wine of her fornication. So he carried me away in the spirit into the wilderness: and I saw a woman sit upon a scarlet coloured beast, full of names of blasphemy, having seven heads and ten horns.

"And the woman was arrayed in purple and scarlet colour, and decked with gold and precious stones and pearls, having a golden

How THEOSOPHY DECEIVED the WORLD

cup in her hand full of abominations and filthiness of her fornication: And upon her forehead was a name written, **MYSTERY, BABYLON THE GREAT, THE MOTHER OF HARLOTS AND ABOMINATIONS OF THE EARTH.**

"And I saw the woman drunken with the blood of the saints, and with the blood of the martyrs of Jesus: and when I saw her, I wondered with great admiration." Revelation 17:2–6.

Notice Revelation 17:5: "And upon her forehead was a name written, **MYSTERY, BABYLON THE GREAT, THE MOTHER OF HARLOTS AND ABOMINATIONS OF THE EARTH.**"

The word *Babylon* means *confusion*. In prophetic language, the Lord is pointing out that Babylon is spiritual confusion, which is worldwide. This spiritual confusion or false worship began at the first city after the Flood for she is **THE MOTHER OF HARLOTS**.

Babylon the Great represents all the ethnic people of the world. The Jews are not the only ones who have been **deceived by her fornication** which is her **false doctrines**. The Lord plainly shows that He has His people in **spiritual Babylon**.

"And he cried mightily with a strong voice, saying, Babylon the great is fallen, is fallen, and is become the habitation of devils, and the hold of every foul spirit, and a cage of every unclean and hateful bird.

"For all nations have drunk of the wine of the wrath of her fornication, and the kings of the earth have committed fornication with her, and the merchants of the earth are waxed rich through the abundance of her delicacies.

"And I heard another voice from heaven, saying, **Come out of her, my people,** that ye be not partakers of her sins, and that ye receive not of her plagues." Revelation 18:2–4.

In Revelation 14:6–12, the most solemn message ever given to man by the Lord is found. In the following verse, the Lord is prophesying against the world (Babylon): **"For her sins have reached unto heaven**, and God hath remembered her iniquities." Revelation 18:5. Before the Lord destroys Babylon, he is calling for His people in Babylon to separate themselves from these false religions of paganism and Christianity and join hands with those "that keep the commandments of God, and the faith of Jesus." Revelation 14:12.

The Real Truth About UFO's and the New World Order

"All that the Father giveth me shall come to me; and him that cometh to me I will in no wise cast out." "For mine house shall be called an house of prayer for all people. No man can come to me, except the Father which hath sent me draw him: and I will raise him up at the last day. I am he that liveth, and was dead; and, behold, I am alive for evermore, Amen; and have the keys of hell and of death. I am Alpha and Omega, the beginning and the end, the first and the last. I Jesus have sent mine angel to testify unto you these things in the churches. I am the root and the offspring of David, and the bright and morning star. And the Spirit and the bride say, Come. And let him that heareth say, Come. And let him that is athirst come. And whosoever will, let him take the water of life freely." John 6:37; Isaiah 56:7; John 6:44; Revelation 1:18; Revelation 22:13, 16, 17.

How THEOSOPHY DECEIVED the WORLD

The Lord will **shift the people** of the world like wheat in these last days. He will **separate** the wheat from the chaff, the sheep from the goats, the real believers from the pretenders.

"**The Lord knoweth them that are his.** And, Let every one that nameth the name of Christ **depart from iniquity**." 2 Timothy 2:19.

Jesus will do something in these last days that very few anticipate. Jesus is calling the New Ager, the Buddhist, the Muslim, and the Jew, who can hear His voice and will obey it, to turn from Spiritualism and Socialism and "**worship him that made heaven, and earth, and the sea, and the fountains of waters**." Revelation 14:7.

Jesus is calling the Hindu and Chinese people to accept His invitation:

"All that the Father giveth me shall come to me; and him that cometh to me I will in no wise cast out." John 6:37.

"Come unto me, all ye that labour and are heavy laden, and I will give you rest." Matthew 11:28.

"Thus saith the Lord the King of Israel, and his redeemer the Lord of hosts; I am the first, and I am the last; and **beside me there is no God**." Isaiah 44:6.

Jesus will bring the Black man who hears His voice and obeys it into His fold. Jesus will bring the White man who hears His voice and obeys it into the same fold. Jesus in these last days will bring the Jew, Hispanic, Arab, American Indian, and Oriental peoples, who have ears to hear and obey His voice, **into one movement** before the great and terrible day of the Lord. Jesus will bring the Roman Catholic and the Protestant, who have ears to hear what the Spirit is saying unto the churches, into the same fold.

"And other sheep I have, which are not of this fold: them also I must bring, and they **SHALL HEAR MY VOICE; AND THERE SHALL BE ONE FOLD, AND ONE SHEPHERD**." John 10:16.

Our Lord is not prejudiced, but neither is Satan. Satan is also calling the Black, the White, the Oriental, the Buddhist, the Muslim, the Hindu, and the Chinese peoples to choose his side. Satan is calling the Roman Catholics and Protestants, who do not want to obey the Gospel of Jesus Christ, to join **ONE FOLD**. All who do not obey the Good Shepherd will place themselves on the side of the Evil One. Satan is using the **intoxicating philosophies of Socialism** to unite the world against its real Creator.

The Real Truth About UFO's and the New World Order

"And all that dwell upon the earth shall worship him, whose names are not written in the book of life of the Lamb slain from the foundation of the world." Revelation 13:8.

The illusions from the Kabbalah, the Jewish book of magic, and later the ideology of Illuminism (the Haskalah) did, indeed, infiltrate and change the thinking of most of these modern Jews. These two fountains which flowed through the minds of the modern Jewish community did not come from the living water from which all blessings flow, but came from the Euphrates of **spiritual Babylonia** which the God of Abraham, Isaac, and Jacob will dry up shortly! The mixture of Spiritualism and atheism from the Kabbalah and from the Jewish philosophers of the 18th and 19th centuries **intoxicated the minds** of Jewish thought and spirituality. As we have read, many have turned from the ancient Hebrew Scriptures of the Old Testament and have become atheists. The era of the Haskalah or the Enlightenment Movement of the 18th century caused many European Jews to **embrace** the precepts of **Communism**. No? To the average Christian mind, **this is shocking** and **unbelievable**, especially among Pentecostal and Baptist pastors who are twisting the Bible prophecies from Jeremiah and Ezekiel to show that the **literal return of Israel to Palestine was foretold**.

Reader, this literal return to Palestine of the people from Europe and America who are calling themselves Zionists or Ashkenazi Jews **cannot be sustained by the Holy Scriptures**. Absolutely not! Literal Israel was **divorced from God in A.D. 34** after the Jews of the flesh of that day rejected Christ Jesus as their Messiah and after they rejected the Gospel and stoned Stephen. (See Acts 7:1–60.) From here, the God of Abraham, Isaac, and Jacob **turned to the Gentiles**. Furthermore, it was foretold by the ancient Jewish prophets that the wall which **divided** the Jew from the Gentile was to be **broken down by the Messiah**. Speaking about that Christ who was to come, Isaiah said in Chapter 42, verse 1: "He shall bring forth judgment to the **Gentiles**." Again, in Isaiah 60:3 we read: "And the **Gentiles** shall come to thy light." Jesus, who was this Messiah, **came to make the Jew and Gentile one, not to establish a temporal kingdom of which** the Jewish nation would **rule** all the other nations. "There is neither

How THEOSOPHY DECEIVED the WORLD

Jew nor Greek, there is neither bond nor free, there is neither male nor female: **for ye are all one in Christ Jesus**. And if ye be Christ's, then are ye Abraham's seed, and **heirs** according to the promise." Galatians 3:28, 29.

Christian authors, who are using the Old Testament prophets' predictions about the literal city of Jerusalem to sustain and support their own predictions of what they think will happen to Israel in these last days, **have lost sight** of the predictions about *New Jerusalem* of which literal Jerusalem is only a **shadow**.

The reader must understand that the literal city of Jerusalem was first destroyed by the ancient Babylonians. The ancient Hebrew Jews living at this time were taken by force to Babylon for 70 years. This was foretold in Jeremiah 25:8–11. In Jeremiah 27:22, we read: "They shall be carried to Babylon, and there shall they be until the day that I visit them, saith the Lord; then will I bring them up, and restore them to this place." The remnant of the Hebrew Jews of this time were punished for their idolatry. For 70 years, they were to be captives in Babylon, but after the termination of these years the prophets also foretold the restoration of the first temple and of the Holy City.

However, the prophets who prophesied of the restoration of Jerusalem lived before Nehemiah led the captive Hebrews back to Jerusalem after their 70-year captivity in Babylon reached its fulfillment. All of these prophecies concerning the restoration of Israel were pointing to the Hebrews during the Babylonian captivity, not to the 20th-century exodus of the American and European Jews who established modern Israel in 1948.

Then, who is really behind the successful accomplishment by Zionists to secure Palestine as a separate Jewish State? Again, Daniel the ancient Hebrew prophet reveals the answer to this puzzling question in Daniel 11:45: "**And he shall plant the tabernacles of his palace between the seas in the glorious holy mountain; yet he shall come to his end, and none shall help him**."

Reader, the true God of Abraham, Isaac, and Jacob reveals in Daniel 11:45 that **Satan** will **use** modern Israel to bring the ignorant of Scripture **under** his banner. The Evil One will soon move his tabernacles (headquarters) to Israel! It will not be set up in the city of David, but *between* the seas in the glorious holy mountain. Again, the seas are

The Real Truth About UFO's and the New World Order

the Mediterranean Sea, the Sea of Galilee, and the Dead Sea. The glorious holy mountain is, of course, Jerusalem.

As discussed, the evolution of the Atlantean Plan to establish a Utopian **world federation** can be traced to Plato, then accelerated during the European Renaissance, and still later can be traced in the 18th century to Deism a.k.a. the **Enlightenment a.k.a. Illuminism**. It evolved among the Ashkenazi Jewish societies as the **Haskalah**. The Haskalah was nothing less than a Jewish version of the same Deism of the 18th century that Voltaire and Paine promoted by pen and voice. It was during the period of the **Enlightenment Movement** that many Ashkenazi Jews **dropped** their Judaism and **switched to atheism** and **nationalism** out of which **political** Zionism and **Socialist** Zionism emerged. **Instead** of looking for the **arrival** of the promised Messiah which was foretold by Old Testament Jewish prophets which the Hebrews in the first century in A.D. 31 crucified, these European Jews **turned their minds towards establishing a Jewish homeland and nationalism**.

It should be noted that the Ashkenazi Jews have suffered terrible persecutions from the sixth century to our present day. Amazingly, just as the Hebrew Jews were **thrown out of their homeland** in Palestine during the destruction of Jerusalem by the pagan Romans in A.D. 70, so were these Armenian Jews **thrown out of their original homeland** by Armenians who became Muslims.[24] The pagan Roman Empire forbid the Hebrews to ever return to Jerusalem. The Roman Empire continued their expulsion of Jews from living in Jerusalem until its fall in A.D. 476. In A.D. 70, the remnant of the Hebrews who escaped the Roman massacre of the Hebrew Jews in Jerusalem scattered in different directions. Some settled in Galilee or Europe and Russia while some **fled to Spain**. The Hebrew word **for Spain is** "*Sepharad*,"[25] and this small remnant of Hebrew Jews in Spain, as we saw earlier, became known as **Sephardi Jews**.

Meanwhile, as the Ashkenazi Jews emerged in the sixth century and were thrown out of Armenia and scattered, the Semitic Jews found that they had both religious and cultural differences between them. The Sephardic and Ashkenazi Jews **became rivals** and went on to

---

[24]*Encyclopaedia Judaica*, **Vol. 3, pp. 721, 722.**
[25]***The Jews: Their History, Culture, and Religion***, **Finkelstein, p. 221.**

How THEOSOPHY DECEIVED the WORLD

even war on each other. Sephardic Jews have kept themselves in separate congregations to this day.[26] Ashkenazism, however, has grown to where it has completely **eclipsed** the Sephardic division of Jewry. There are very few original Hebrews among Jewry today.

It was from the Ashkenazi Jews that both Jewish mysticism (Theosophy) and political Zionism emerged which led to the establishment of the State of Israel.[27] As pointed out, Jewish Theosophy was **adopted** by the Ashkenazi in Armenia. They adopted the Kabbalah which **blended** Hebrew Judaism with Babylonian pantheism and magic around the time of the rebuilding of the first temple in Jerusalem by apostate Hebrew priests living in Babylon. It should be noted that the **Kabbalah** was greatly influenced by the national religion of Persia,[28] which was **Zoroastrianism**. Its prophet and founder was **Zoroaster**, and his religion (commonly called fire worship) was embodied in the Zend-Avesta. It was written by his disciples in Zend, which was an ancient Iranian language. It was Zoroaster who made popular the belief in hell, the burning place for wicked souls. Zoroastrianism was centered around a deity named Ormazd and the constant struggle between the forces of light and the forces of darkness, which was nothing less than a distorted recollection of the real conflict between Christ and Lucifer. This pagan concept was vividly portrayed in the movies of *Star Trek* and *Star Wars*.

Not only have the Ashkenazi and the Sephardic Jews been rivals, but the Ashkenazi Jews themselves have always been split into different religious and political circles. When Shabbethai Zebi, the self-proclaimed messiah and also a Cabalist,[29] proved himself to be a false christ in 1666, not only was this a great embarrassment but was an overwhelming disappointment to these Jews. Many abandoned their faith because of it. Then, in the third quarter of the 18th century, another billowy wave of deception came pouring upon the religious community of the Ashkenazis. The ***red* fog** of the Enlightenment Movement began to cover these people. Deism began to push out Ashkenazi Judaism from being taught among the young

---

[26]*Encyclopaedia Judaica*, Vol. 3, p. 722.
[27]*Encyclopedia Americana*, Vol. 2, 1978, p. 436.
[28]*Encyclopaedia Judaica*, Vol. 10, p. 495.
[29]*The Jewish Encyclopedia*, 1925, p. 252.

The Real Truth About UFO's and the New World Order

student population.[30] As a result, **a new generation** of Jews sprang up. The **Haskalah**, which had its roots in the general Enlightenment Movement in Europe which had its roots in Plato's myth about **Atlantis**, as we have seen, drove out Judaism as the European Enlightenment Movement had done to papal Christianity in France and Protestant Christianity in the schools found in America! Once the European Jews were **de-Judaized**, then the **ideologies of Zionism** and **nationalism emerged**. Moses Mendelssohn was considered to be the father of the Enlightenment Movement among the Jews. Political Zionism's **father** was Theodor Herzl (1860–1904), and Herzl was also the founder of the World Zionist Organization. Herzl believed that the problem with anti-Semitism would be resolved with **Socialism's promise of a world federation with racial equality**. At first, Herzl set his sights on having a mass conversion of Jewish youth to Socialism and also a mass exodus from anti-Semitic countries to Israel for they were strangers in the countries where they lived and considered themselves homeless. At this time, the Turks still occupied Palestine, and Herzl did not consider only Palestine in becoming a Jewish settlement. Before the founding of the World Zionist Organization, the Zionists were scattered in rivaling groups. It was, however, Theodor Herzl who was able to unite the rivaling Zionists into the World Zionist Organization that helped Ashkenazi Jewry to establish the Land of Israel as their homeland.[31]

Reader, keep in mind that the Hebrew prophet Daniel warned that Satan shall establish his headquarters in Israel in these last days as Daniel 11:45 clearly predicts. Keep in mind that there are many branches of the Jewish faith today, and some Zionists did **abandon** their belief that the Holy Scriptures were given by divine revelation. Keep in mind that the apostle John was shown that it would be **businessmen** (merchants) of this world that would bring this last drama between Christ and Satan to its **climax** (Revelation 18:23). Keep in mind that Jesus said, "**MY KINGDOM IS NOT OF THIS WORLD.**" John 18:36. Keep in mind that the Kingdom of God will be established when the earth is made anew (Revelation, Chapter 21), **not in this present world** of which Zionism, New Agers, the pope, and

---

[30]*Encyclopaedia Judaica*, Vol. 8, pp. 1435, 1436.
[31]*Ibid.*, Vol. 8, pp. 407–420.

How THEOSOPHY DECEIVED the WORLD

well-known Protestant television evangelists are all promoting. **This is a strong delusion from the Arch Deceiver himself.** Keep in mind that **not all Jews are Utopian rebel conspirators**. Not one in a hundred thousand understands these things, much less is a convinced disciple. Most Jews today are like most Christians. They are caught up in worldly pursuits of moneymaking and pleasure-seeking. Like Christians, the glamour of Hollywood and sports has occupied most of their free time and has replaced their interest in religious things as secondary. Both Christians and Jews have been **blinded** by the attractions of this world whereas the prophecies about these pending events **go on unnoticed**. However, both Christians and Jews will see more and more how the Devil has **hoodwinked us all** as these prophecies from Daniel and Revelation unroll.

In these last days, there will be Jews, Muslims, Hindus, Buddhists, Confucians, and Christians from both Catholic and Protestant faiths who will make the Holy Scriptures the only standard in which to base their faith. They will turn to seek salvation from the Lamb of God. They will see that their religions are based in falsehood and will separate themselves from all Theosophy. All the people of the world will be separated into just **two movements** – either with Lucifer or with Christ Jesus.

The prophet Hosea, writing under the inspiration of the Holy Spirit, prophesied that a **remnant** of those who are the descendants of the Ten Lost Tribes **will unite themselves again** with the true God of Israel in the last days! They will realize that Jesus was and is the Messiah! They will also play a part in proclaiming the Loud Cry of the Third Angel of Revelation, Chapters 14 and 18. In the book, *The Story of Prophets and Kings*, the author points out how both Amos and Hosea foretold how **latter-day Jews** will accept Jesus as their King of kings and Lord of lords. It reads:

"The prophecies of judgment delivered by Amos and Hosea were accompanied by predictions of future glory. To the **ten tribes**, long **rebellious** and **impenitent**, was given no promise of complete restoration to their former power in Palestine. Until the end of time, they were to be 'wanderers among the nations.' But through Hosea was given a prophecy that set before them the privilege of having a part in the final restoration that is to be made to the people of God at the close of earth's history, when Christ shall appear as King of kings and Lord of lords. 'Many days,' the prophet declared, the ten tribes were to abide 'without a king, and without a prince, and without a sacrifice, and without an image, and without an ephod, and without teraphim.' 'Afterward,' the prophet continued, '**SHALL THE CHILDREN OF ISRAEL RETURN**, and seek the Lord their God, and David their king; and shall fear the Lord and His goodness **IN THE LATTER DAYS.**' Hosea 3:4, 5."[32]

This is already happening! Some Jews from both the Ashkenazi and Sephardic congregations have realized that the Hebrew who was born in Bethlehem and was crucified by erring Jews in A.D. 31 was the Messiah of whom the prophets foretold.

However, all races have been **deceived by Theosophy** which began on the pages written in the Kabbalah. As God used Hebrew fingers to write the Scriptures, so did Satan use Hebrew fingers to write the Kabbalah, the Jewish book of magic. During the Persian Era, it was apostate Jews who communicated Jewish Theosophy during the rebuilding of the first temple. However, it did not become written as the Kabbalah until the destruction of the second temple in A.D. 70. History does record that it has been the Anglo-Jews, the Ashkenazi, who have preserved and promoted the Kabbalah since the sixth century on this side of the cross. **This Jewish Theosophy is Spiritualism's Bible**. As we saw, **all forms** of occultism are rooted and grounded in it. All learned occultists refer to the Kabbalah as their authority. Both the Illuminati and Freemasonry are based in this Jewish Theosophy.

Satan is trying to unite all faiths under one roof. If the reader will simply go to the public library and search the encyclopedias on modern Judaism and Freemasonry, immediately the most hardened skeptic will see that Freemasonry is Jewish Theosophy[33] and has been a world revolutionary tool of Satan's which he is using to bring his final conflict to Israel as Daniel 11:45 predicted. Ashkenazi Jewry is pseudo-Judaism. It is a **hybrid** occult religious movement that is truly against the real Messiah of both the Old and New Testaments and so is Freemasonry, contrary to what you may have heard.

---

[32]*The Story of Prophets and Kings*, White, p. 298.
[33]*A New Encyclopaedia of Freemasonry*, Vol. 1, Waite, p. 417.

How THEOSOPHY DECEIVED the WORLD

Adam Weishaupt, the founder of the Illuminati, was also a Freemason. As established, he was initiated into Freemasonry at the Munich, Germany, lodge in 1777[34] just after he founded the dangerous secret society of the Illuminati of Bavaria.[35] Benjamin Franklin, Thomas Paine, and Thomas Jefferson, as we saw, were all revolutionaries of Freemasonry. **They were experts in the Kabbalah.**[36]

The Masons even had another order in Europe called the ***Illuminated Theosophists*** that were instituted in Paris by fellow Mason Benedict Chastanier, who subsequently succeeded in introducing it in London, England.[37] This doesn't mean that all Masons are Ashkenazis, but Freemasonry is nothing less than a **basket** to gather all religions. As pointed out, most politicians and wealthy merchants in the United States have been Freemasons.

When Hitler's hideous Nazis began their genocidal pursuits to remove the Ashkenazi off the face of the earth, multitudes of Ashkenazi Jews fled to the United States. The bulk of their population worldwide was located in the United States at this time.[38] Let's look now at who was really working behind the scenes to give the Ashkenazis the Land of Israel so they could not only establish a Jewish State, but, reader, the capital of this New World Order scheme. This Luciferian scheme has been **veiled** under the order of Freemasonry, the Theosophical Society, and Zionism.

While H.P. Blavatsky was busy promoting Jewish Theosophy through her Theosophical Society and Nicholai Lenin was beginning to make his debut and Zionists were becoming Marxists, Baron **Edmond Rothschild** was busy setting the stage for the Ashkenazi's exodus to the Land of Israel in the late 1800s.

Keep in mind that Jesus, who was, is, and is to come the **real** founder and finisher of Judaism and Christianity, foretold through His prophets and apostles that the merchants of Babylon the Great (the world) would deceive all nations by using the **deceptions of sorcery** (Revelation 18:23). It would attempt to establish this occult society in the

---

[34]*Mackey's Revised Encyclopedia of Freemasonry*, Vol. 1, p. 474.
[35]*Ibid.*, pp. 474, 475.
[36]*The Occult Illustrated Dictionary*, Day, Kay & Ward, p. 56.
[37]*A New Encyclopaedia of Freemasonry*, Waite, p. 64.
[38]*Encyclopaedia Judaica*, Vol. 3, p. 722.

The Real Truth About UFO's and the New World Order

Land of Israel (Daniel 11:45), "**YET HE SHALL COME TO HIS END, AND NONE SHALL HELP HIM.**"

There are no other families on earth that history does record that have had more financial, religious, and political power which controlled the people of the known world besides the Rothschild families in the Old World and their business partners, the Rockefeller families, in the New World. We will see shortly what John D. Rockefeller, Jr. and David his son accomplished in helping establish the Ashkenazi Jews in the Land of Israel.

It is also important to remember that those who persist to reject the Saviour of this world are called in 1 John 2:22 "*antichrist*."

"And this is the record, that God hath given to us eternal life, and this life is in his Son. **He that hath the Son hath life; and he that hath not the Son of God hath not life.**" 1 John 5:11, 12.

It was astonishing to me when I read from the Jewish encyclopedia entitled *Encyclopaedia Judaica*, Vol. 3, page 475, that a geographical compilation seen in the 14th century *Travels of Sir John Mandeville* states that the Caspian Jews (Armenian) are the "**FUTURE GOG AND MAGOG.**" There are two books of the Bible which warn of Gog and Magog. They are the books of Ezekiel in Chapters 38 and 39 and Revelation, Chapter 20:7–10.

Jesus, shortly before he was crucified and resurrected, warned of **false prophets** and **false teachers**. There have always been false systems of both Judaism and Christianity. Both Jews and Christians have been deceived by the Dragon as have New Agers. Jesus foretold that Satan's deceptions, which will lead up to the **final climax** of the war between good and evil, shall deceive the very elect of God if possible. Ezekiel, Daniel, and John foretold that Satan would use the Land of Israel to connect the people of this planet with him. They prophesied that this would take place in the **LATTER DAYS**.

For over a quarter of a century now, I have been puzzled about the confusion there is in Christendom about who Gog and Magog are, and if there will be a **literal** battle of Armageddon or if it is just a **spiritual** battle. Some theologians try to reason away the prophecies about Gog and Magog found in Ezekiel, Chapters 38 and 39, which prophesy about a **world federation** against God as conditional and only applying to the ancient Hebrew Jews. However, I would like to

How THEOSOPHY DECEIVED the WORLD

point out that Ezekiel, Chapters 38 and 39, and that of Revelation, Chapter 20, were not pointing back to the ancient Hebrews and the nations of that day for the prophet and the apostle, writing under the inspiration of the Holy Spirit, said:

"Son of man, set thy face against **Gog, the land of Magog**, the chief prince of Meshech and Tubal, and prophesy against him, And say, Thus saith the Lord God; Behold, I am against thee, O Gog, the chief prince of Meshech and Tubal:

"**Gomer**, and all his bands; the house of Togarmah of the north quarters, and all his bands: and many people with thee…. After many days thou shalt be visited: **in the LATTER YEARS** thou shalt come into the land that is brought back from the sword, and is gathered out of many people, against the mountains of Israel, which have been always waste: but it is brought forth out of the nations, and they shall dwell safely all of them.

"And thou shalt come up against my people of Israel, as a cloud to cover the land; it shall be in the **LATTER DAYS**, and I will bring thee against my land, that the heathen may know me, when I shall be sanctified in thee, O Gog, before their eyes.

"Thus saith the Lord God; **Art thou he of whom I have spoken in old time by my servants the prophets of Israel, which prophesied in those days many years that I would bring thee against them?**" Ezekiel 38:2, 3, 6, 8, 16, 17.

"And when the **thousand years are expired**, Satan shall be loosed out of his prison, And shall go out to deceive the nations which are in the four quarters of the earth, **Gog and Magog**, to gather them together to battle: the number of whom is as the sand of the sea.

"And they went up on the breadth of the earth, and compassed the camp of the saints about, and the beloved city: and fire came down from God out of heaven, and devoured them.

"And the devil that deceived them was cast into the lake of fire and brimstone, where the beast and the false prophet are, and shall be tormented day and night for ever and ever." Revelation 20:7–10.

Ezekiel said that God shall deal with the people who unite with Magog in the "**LATTER YEARS**," "**IT SHALL BE IN THE LATTER DAYS**." John said God will deal with Magog and all his bands at the end of the **1000-year reign** with Christ Jesus in Heaven.

The Real Truth About UFO's and the New World Order

The final destruction of those who are antichrist will occur after the second resurrection. There are **two resurrections**. God's people will be resurrected at the **first** resurrection *before* the 1000-year reign with Christ, while the **wicked** will be resurrected *after* the 1000 years. As there are two resurrections, so will there be **two Armageddons**. The **first** is when Christ comes to rescue His people from Satan and his people *before* the millennium, and then again at **the final** destruction of all the wicked and Satan himself *after* the millennium.

Just who is Magog? **Magog was a real person.** He was the second son of Japheth (Genesis 10:2) who migrated from the mountains of Ararat and settled around the Black Sea of which in Jesus' day it was known as Scythia,[39] whose people were Anglo-barbarians. In these last days, this land has become known as Russia. Japheth's eldest son Gomer (Genesis 10:2) was the **father** of all Celtic peoples who populated the nations of Europe and in the North.[40] Gomer had sons named **Ashkenaz**, Riphath, and Togarmah, and it was from them that the Anglo-Saxon race **originated**. One of these Celtic descendants of Japheth, Gomer's son Ashkenaz, was not only the founder of ancient Armenia, but some of his descendants in the sixth century adopted Jewish Theosophy (Spiritualism) and became known as the **Caspian Jews or as Ashkenazi Jewry**.[41] Again, it is here that the reader can find the origin of the Ashkenazi Jews. In the Middle Ages and after, the Ashkenazi Jews spread all over Europe (except for the Mediterranean countries) and blended their German language with Hebrew.[42] Ezekiel the Hebrew prophet lived in the days when the ancient Hebrews were captives of the Babylonians. When Ezekiel prophesied against Magog, Gomer and all his bands, Togarmah, and the other nations who joined them, he was referring to their descendants for Magog and Gomer were very dead.

Keeping in mind that Magog's and Gomer's descendants are not the Hebrews but are the origin of not only the Anglo-Saxon peoples, but also of the Anglo-Jews known as Ashkenazim today, let's again look at another branch of Anglo-Jewry that began in the eighth century.

---

[39] *Young's Analytical Concordance to the Bible*, Young, pp. 47, 627.
[40] *Ibid.*, Young, p. 426.
[41] *Encyclopaedia Judaica*, Vol. 3, pp. 473–475.
[42] *Encyclopedia Americana*, Vol. 2, 1978, p. 436.

How THEOSOPHY DECEIVED the WORLD

The Khazars, sometimes credited with Armenian origin,[43] had lived in Magog in what is now south Russia and had adopted Judaism. These Celtic Jews were imitated in the course of time by many of the people.[44] God foretold through the prophet Ezekiel that the descendants of Magog (Russia) and Gomer (Anglo-Europeans) would in the "**latter days**" form an alliance with other nations in defiance to God. Daniel the prophet said that their headquarters would be established "*between*" the seas in the holy mountain. John in Revelation 16:16 called this area Armageddon. The word "*Armageddon*" means the "*hill of Megiddo*."[45] *Megiddo* means the "*place of God*."[46] The valley of Megiddo lies between the seas with Jerusalem to the south and Mount Carmel to its north.

Very soon all the inhabitants of this world **will be united into just two groups** – those who obey the Gospel and have accepted Christ Jesus as the true Messiah of the world and those who do not. While the deceptions of Jewish Theosophy are exposed, many Ashkenazi and Sephardic Jews will see how their ancestors from both races had serious erroneous beliefs and how they had misinterpreted the Scriptures of the Old Testament. Even though the God of Abraham divorced the literal Israelites as a nation, **they can and will be saved individually**. Theosophy, however, is Spiritualism. It has deceived not only the Jews, but also Muslims, Buddhists, Hindus, Christians, New Agers, and all those who belong to secret societies which draw from its precepts. However, there are those in these occult divisions who have seen the warnings about Babylon the Great and its open violation of the law of God and contradictions in their own beliefs who will hear the Messiah's voice saying to them:

"And I heard another voice from heaven, saying, Come out of her, my people, that ye be not partakers of her sins, and that ye receive not of her plagues." Revelation 18:4.

Babylon the Great (Revelation, Chapters 17 and 18) is representing in Scripture the whole world with all of its diversities of races and religions in total **spiritual confusion**. As anciently there was a

---

[43]*Encyclopaedia Judaica*, **Vol. 3, p. 472.**
[44]*The Jews: Their History, Culture, and Religion*, **Finkelstein, p. 221.**
[45]*Young's Analytical Concordance to the Bible*, **Young, p. 50.**
[46]*Ibid.*, **Young, p. 652.**

The Real Truth About UFO's and the New World Order

literal Babylon, so is there a **spiritual Babylon.** Just as ancient Babylon had a tower that represented the power of the people who erected it, so does **modern Babylon** today have a tower that serves as a shrine or seat of its power. This modern Tower of Babel will be placed in the Land of Israel by modern-day Nimrods. Gog and Magog and Gomer and all his bands are pointed out in the Old Testament Scriptures as being the **ringleaders** in this international conspiracy against the God of Abraham.

Gog and Magog and the nations that are in league with them are symbolizing all of the various ethnic groups and religions of peoples who refuse to acknowledge Christ as the Saviour of the world. Those who reject the Creator of this world are accepting the world's worst tyrant. He will lead human agents to set up their edifice as a shrine to show their **defiance** against God's great design. This is what Nimrod did. This is what New World Order advocates shall do. However, this modern capital of Babel (Babylon) will not be placed on the plains of Shinar, but **between the seas in the holy mountain**, which is Megiddo Valley in the Land of Israel.

Now coming back to the prophecies concerning the Land of Israel, the Ashkenazis had experienced a **spiritual drought** during the **Haskalah** (Enlightenment Movement). When Alexander II was assassinated in Russia, the Ashkenazis both in Eastern European countries and in Russia were vexed sorely by persecutions from the non-Jewish community. Between 1800 and 1900, over a million Jews fled from persecution and poverty they were forced to experience in the Old World to seek a better life in the United States.[47] In **1870**, a **training farm** had been established in Mikveh, Israel. During the mass exodus from Russia and Eastern Europe (Magog and Gomer), on July 7, 1882, a small group of **14 Hibbat Zionists** landed at Jaffa and made their way to the Mikveh farm. Shortly afterwards, others came totaling to 50.[48] **This began the migration of Russian and European Jews to the Land of Israel.**

In the meantime, Russian Ashkenazis and Eastern European Jews who remained in these countries and had been **de-Judaized** by the Haskalah (the Enlightenment Movement), like Marx, Lenin, and Trotsky, joined Marxism.

---

[47]*Encyclopaedia Judaica*, Vol. 9, p. 515.
[48]*Ibid.*, Vol. 9, p. 515.

How THEOSOPHY DECEIVED the WORLD

To help counteract the weapon Marxists and Socialists use when exposed, when they cry *anti-Semitism*, and to help perhaps the Jewish reader who is eyeing the pages of this book to see that this is not anti-Semitism but just recorded history, below I will quote from this Jewish encyclopedia which openly admits that Eastern and Russian Ashkenazis who remained in the Old World between the years of 1880 and World War I **did, indeed, become Marxists**.

"Of all the schools of thought that were arising within the Zionist movement in its very first few years, **Socialist Zionism** was, at least in practice, the most important. In the work of its founding father, Nachman Syrkin, and a few years later, of the younger, **MARXIST, Ber Borochov, A SOCIALIST EXPLANATION OF THE 'PLIGHT OF THE JEWS' WAS CONSTRUCTED**."[49]

Yes, reader, believe it or not there are Communist and Socialist Jews. However, reader, believe it or not there are also Catholic Marxists, Protestant Marxists, New Age Marxists, and atheistic Marxists. There are Anglo Marxists, Black Marxists, Oriental Marxists, Hispanic Marxists, etc., etc. Marxism is not just a Jewish conspiracy to enslave the world. As we continue to unveil this huge deception, the reader will see that this problem really lies with Lucifer who has used the minds and fingers of human antichrists to write and promote this *red* revolution. Ironically enough, reader, there are even New Age Jews. According to *The New Age Encyclopedia*, pages 242 and 243 under the heading *Judaism, New Age,* many Jews have attracted themselves to the themes of the New Age Movement. However, at first some Jews were uncomfortable with New Age materials that have blended many Christian references to attract Christians, but today there are groups of Jews who have begun to approach New Age ideas through its metaphysical and mystical teachings.

According to *The New Age Encyclopedia*, the roots of **New Age Judaism** can be traced to three **Hasidic Ashkenazi rabbis** named Zalman Schachter-Shalomi, Shlomo Carlebach, and Joseph H. Gelberman.[50]

Schachter-Shalomi is said to have been deeply interested in Timothy Leary and LSD back in 1959, He had taken the drug, and

---

[49]*Encyclopaedia Judaica*, **Vol. 16, p. 1047.**
[50]*The New Age Encyclopedia*, **pp. 242, 243.**

The Real Truth About UFO's and the New World Order

this experience changed his life and his outlook on his religion. LSD lessened his estimation of Judaism's uniqueness and caused him to seek greater spiritual depth in Judaism's tradition. **He went on and founded a New Age Jewish center called B´nai Or.** After moving to Philadelphia and then again to Berkeley, California, Schachter-Shalomi's **Aquarian Minyan** center has emerged. Today, he has evolved into a much sought-after leader by other New Age groups.[51]

Shlomo Carlebach who is also an **Ashkenazi Hasidic rabbi**, on the other hand, emphasizes one's ability to **alter** one's consciousness without the use of drugs. This New Age Jewish rabbi uses his guitar and stories about Hasidic rabbis to attract young Jews to Theosophy.

Joseph Gelberman migrated from Eastern Europe during World War II and became an Orthodox rabbi, but he left his calling and developed his own metaphysical Judaism and is very active in seeking interfaith contacts and inviting non-Jews to participate regularly in the activities of his Little Synagogue which he founded.

By the end of the 1960s, New Agers saw streams of Jews flowing into their ranks because of the mystical New Age doctrines which derived out of the Kabbalah. While Jews are attracted by the use of the Kabbalah, **New Agers then lead them into Hinduism.**[52]

While the Haskalah was busy de-Judaizing young Ashkenazi students beginning in the third quarter of the 18th century, another *red* scourge of **national Socialism** began to rise up against Marxism in Austria and Germany. Hitler's Nazism arose in opposition to the Platonic Atlantean Plan of Marxism. Hitler thought that the Atlantean Plan of Communism to establish a world federation was a Jewish conspiracy working through secret societies of Freemasonry to enslave the whole world. **Hitler was a shaman himself** and was much studied into occultism. Hitler knew that Freemasonry is Jewish Theosophy which originated on the pages of the Kabbalah (Cabala) of which Freemasonry freely admits. In *Mackey's Revised Encyclopedia of Freemasonry*, Vol. 1, page 166, it is stated that the secrets of the Cabala were first taught by God himself and after the Fall, angels communicated to Adam and Eve. From Adam it passed over to Noah,

---

[51]*The New Age Encyclopedia*, pp. 242, 243.
[52]*Ibid.*, p. 243, 244.

How THEOSOPHY DECEIVED the WORLD

Abraham, and then to Moses. The secrets of the Cabala were, according to this encyclopedia of Freemasonry, written down by a theosophical rabbi named Simon ben Jochai who was living at the time of the destruction of the second temple (A.D. 70). However, these Cabalists conveniently ignore what God warned Moses of what he will do to those who teach and promote Theosophy (witchcraft).

Hitler, who was a learned shaman but Scripturally retarded, was determined to establish the Nordic Thule plan in direct opposition to Communism's Atlantean Plan that had derived out of the pages of Plato's writings. Both Plato's Golden Age of Atlantis and Hitler's Golden Age of Thule were, as we saw earlier, rooted and grounded in Greek and Nordic mythology. Nevertheless, multitudes went into untimely graves defending these deceptions. Certain it is that **THE DRAGON "DECEIVETH THE WHOLE WORLD."** Revelation 12:9.

Now, going back to the prophecies regarding modern Israel and how it is today filling history pages of what was predicted centuries ago, let's again look at what both history and Jewish sources said established the State of Israel in 1948.

Before the rise of Hitler during World War I, the British captured Jerusalem from the Turks on December 9, 1917. This set the stage for Lucifer's final effort to try to take complete control over the people of this planet. Satan's ambitions and words when he was in Heaven are recorded in the book of Isaiah in Chapter 14:12–16.

"How art thou fallen from heaven, O Lucifer, son of the morning! how art thou cut down to the ground, which didst weaken the nations! For thou hast said in thine heart, I will ascend into heaven, I will exalt my throne above the stars of God: I will sit also upon the mount of the congregation, in the sides of the north:

"I will ascend above the heights of the clouds; I will be like the most High. Yet thou shalt be brought down to hell, to the sides of the pit. They that see thee shall narrowly look upon thee, and consider thee, saying, Is this the man that made the earth to tremble, that did shake kingdoms." Isaiah 14:12–16.

The drama between Christ and Lucifer has been continuing now here on earth for 6,000 years. However, this time Satan is using human

The Real Truth About UFO's and the New World Order

agents to try to overthrow Christ Jesus. As Satan tried to usurp the throne of Christ in Heaven, so does he want to place his capital in the Land of Israel. The prophecies predict that he will manage to use deceived humans in setting up his headquarters in Israel, **"YET HE SHALL COME TO HIS END, AND NONE SHALL HELP HIM."** Daniel 11:45. We have not yet reached in time the fulfillment of this prediction, but these prophecies that were sealed **"TILL THE TIME OF THE END"** (Daniel 12:9) **are today unfolding before our very eyes**.

In Revelation 18:23, there lies two key words that unlock Satan's secret plans about how he is going to control the masses of human beings so he can use them to **make war on the Lamb** by making war on His people who stay loyal to Jesus during this time when nobody will be able to "buy or sell, save he that had the Mark, or the Name of the Beast, or the Number of his name." Revelation 13:17. These two words which help us understand these prophecies are **MERCHANTS** and **SORCERIES**. What is a merchant? He is a businessman. The prophecies of Daniel and Revelation point to businessmen as Satan's agents who will use the influence of money to bring the gullible **under Satan's banner**. These human agents would be well-known businessmen who are the well-known leaders of Babylon the Great (the world); "**for thy MERCHANTS were the GREAT MEN OF THE EARTH**." Revelation 18:23.

Besides controlling world commerce, what else would these famous businessmen be doing during these days of the Time of the End? The apostle said, "For by thy **SORCERIES were ALL NATIONS DECEIVED.**" Revelation 18:23 (last part).

Keep in mind that Daniel the Hebrew prophet foretold that the headquarters (tabernacles of his palace) of these human agents, who would be against the Father and His Son, would move to the Land of Israel "**between**" the seas in the holy mountain. However, the Scriptures go on to reveal:

"**And at that time** shall **Michael** stand up, **the great prince** which standeth for the children of thy people: and there shall be a time of trouble, such as never was since there was a nation even to that same time: and at that time **thy people shall be delivered, every one that shall be found written in the book.**

How THEOSOPHY DECEIVED the WORLD

"And many of them that sleep in the dust of the earth shall awake, some to everlasting life, and some to shame and everlasting contempt. And they that be wise shall shine as the brightness of the firmament; and they that turn many to righteousness as the stars for ever and ever.

"But thou, O Daniel, shut up the words, and seal the book, **EVEN TO THE TIME OF THE END**: many shall run to and fro, and knowledge shall be increased.

"**Many shall be purified, and made white, and tried; but the wicked shall do wickedly: and none of the wicked shall understand; but the wise shall understand.**" Daniel 12:1–4, 10.

Now, it is time to investigate the **merchants** who have been behind this plot foretold from Scripture to eventually establish the capital of this partly religious and partly political alliance in the Land of Israel.

As we have seen from their own words that the Ashkenazi Jews are not from the original stock of Shem but are from Aryan descent or from Japheth (See Genesis 10:2), they have all but merged and mingled the whole Hebrew culture and history into their own society.

Ashkenazis have merged their language of German with Hebrew which became known as Yiddish. They have also mingled sorcery and magic into the worship of the God of Israel. If the reader is an Ashkenazi Jew and has been insulted by this statement, then I suggest you turn to your Jewish encyclopedias and read for yourself. The God of Abraham of whom Ashkenazis say they identify with strictly forbade any manner of sorcery or magic in the Torah. In all of the various divisions of Ashkenazi Jewry, it has been, however, according to the *Encyclopaedia Judaica*, Vol. 11, page 710, the "Hasidei Ashkenaz" who have been deeply involved in Spiritualism. Ashkenazi Hasidic magic has its roots in the Kabbalah of which its medieval founders Ba'al Shem-Tob[53] and Samuel he-Hasid[54] borrowed. Remember, all secret societies of the occult are based in the Kabbalah, the Jewish book of magic. Magic is sorcery, and Bible prophecy warns that the businessmen in the Time of the End will use **sorcery** to deceive all nations into joining a **world federation** against the Author and Finisher of both Judaism and Christianity!

---

[53]*The Jewish Encyclopedia*, p. 252.
[54]*Encyclopaedia Judaica*, Vol. 11, p. 713.

The Real Truth About UFO's and the New World Order

It should be understood that not all Jews from Ashkenazim and Sephardim are involved in Spiritualism, but many of them are. It is also eye-opening to realize that the House of Rothschild are Ashkenazi Jews. From the start of the Rothschild banking dynasty, this Celtic Jewish banking family has been the number-one promoter of not only Ashkenazism, but also of the Ashkenazi taking Palestine to be their homeland.

Mayer Amschel Rothschild (1743–1812) was the son of a merchant who had five sons that established several banks in European countries.[55] In his youth, Mayer Amschel Rothschild was training to be a rabbi (master) in Ashkenazi Jewry until his father died. Then, Mayer Amschel went home to help his two brothers in their family's second-hand clothing business which was located in Frankfurt, Germany's ghetto where they lived.[56] Rothschild began to acquire his enormous wealth by first becoming an old coin collector as a sideline and buying and selling them. One of his customers was Prince William of Germany who placed Rothschild through his financial adviser, Karl Buderus, in his employment. Mayer Amschel was placed to handle the collection of drafts and mortgages owed the prince.[57] It should be noted that Adam Weishaupt's Illuminati was emerging in Bavaria, Germany, when Mayer Amschel Rothschild of Frankfurt was also emerging as a German banker. Both Adam Weishaupt and Mayer Amschel Rothschild were born in Ashkenazi families. However, Adam Weishaupt was orphaned, but later was trained to be a Jesuit and a professor of Canon Law. As we saw earlier, it was political businessmen that caused the French Revolution, and they were of Freemasonry.

As it is now, so was it in the third quarter of the 18th century. Freemasonry is nothing less than Jewish Theosophy out of which the Rosicrucians, H.P. Blavatsky's Theosophical Society, and other societies of occultism derived. They all are rooted and grounded in the Kabbalah. The international Order of Freemasonry openly admits to have been based in Jewish Theosophy. "It is an expectation for Jewish theosophy," says Waite in *A New Encyclopaedia of Freemasonry*, Vol. 1, page 417.

---

[55]*The World Book Encyclopedia*, Vol. 16, 1995, p. 488.
[56]*Who's Who in Jewish History*, Comay, p. 341.
[57]*Ibid.*, Comay, p. 341, 344.

How THEOSOPHY DECEIVED the WORLD

The Rothschild family have had members of their family who were high-ranking Freemasons. In Europe, the rulers of many nations were Masons. The founding fathers of the United States were members of Freemasonry.

The House of Rothschild are Ashkenazi Jewry's first family since the third quarter of the 18th century. The Rothschild family started their banking dynasty in Gomer (Germany). Their first patriarch was Mayer (Meyer) Amschel Rothschild. Just as Hebrew Jews kept their race pure in the days of ancient Israel, so did the Rothschild family marry within their own family members. Mayer Amschel's five sons were Amschel Mayer (1773–1855); Salomon Mayer (1774–1855) who migrated to Vienna, Austria, in 1816 and established a bank; Nathan Mayer (1777–1836) migrated to England in 1797 and established a bank; Karl Mayer (1788–1855) migrated to Naples in 1821 and established a bank; and then James (1792–1868) the younger son moved to Paris in 1812 where he established a bank. The five banks became known as the House of Rothschild.[58] Mayer Amschel died in 1812, however, his son Amschel Mayer took control of his father's bank in Frankfurt, Germany, while his other sons expanded in their banking businesses.[59]

Now James, the younger son of Mayer Amschel who settled in Paris and established a bank, married his seventeen-year-old niece from Vienna named Betty and through her had four sons of whom the youngest was Edmond (1845–1934).[60] **It was Edmond James Rothschild who was to play the most significant part in establishing the Ashkenazi Jews in the Land of Israel.**

Before the rise of Theodor Herzl who united the rivaling factions of Zionism, Rabbi Samuel Mohilewer, a leader of one of these rivaling factions known as the Lovers of Zion movement, and Joseph Feinberg, who had already established a little Ashkenazi settlement in Israel, approached Edmond Rothschild for they were desperately in need of financial help.[61] The atheistic Socialists and Marxist Zionists

---

[58] *Who's Who in Jewish History*, Comay, pp. 341–344.
[59] *The World Book Encyclopedia*, Vol. 16, 1995, p. 488.
[60] *Who's Who in Jewish History*, Comay, pp. 346, 347.
[61] *Ibid.*, Comay, p. 348.

The Real Truth About UFO's and the New World Order

and Jewish Theosophists were clashing in those days. Edmond Rothschild gave these two Zionists thirty thousand francs to help establish one of the first Zionist settlements which was started *"between"* the Mediterranean Sea, the Sea of Galilee, and the Dead Sea. In 1896, Rothschild turned down the Socialist/Zionist Theodor Herzl's request[62] when he approached him. At this time, Herzl did not realize that Edmond Rothschild had already begun to help the theosophical side of Ashkenazism and had involved himself for the rest of his life with the struggle to revive the soil of the Holy Land which had laid destitute under the Ottoman Empire, which was still controlling Jerusalem. All this was transpiring in the early 1800s.

Protestant Christians have a **natural instinct to side** with the Jews upon hearing anything that may have a ring of anti-Semitism attached to it. To most Protestant Christians, the emancipation of Jews and their return to the Land of Israel gained much support. Bible-believing Christians, generally, sympathize with the Hebrew Jews for our Saviour and all who wrote the Scriptures were Hebrews save Luke, who was a Greek physician. However, these Jewish Theosophists and Zionists, as a whole, **are not Hebrews**, and there is **no promise** in the Scriptures for the Nation of Israel to be restored. **This truth has been veiled for centuries.** When these things begin to come to light, Ashkenazis shout *anti-Semitism*. Even this is a misnomer for this originally applied to the Hebrew Jews who were descendants of Shem. Ashkenazis are descendants of Japheth. The Ashkenazis have cleverly wrapped themselves up in the Hebrew culture whereas Jewish Theosophy of Ashkenazim **is looked upon as the original religion** of Abraham and Moses. The miracles performed by God during the days of Moses, the prophets, and even those of Jesus are believed by some to have been performed by magic rather than by the miraculous power of our Creator. Nonetheless, there were a few Hebrew Zionists involved, but Zionism was mainly an Ashkenazim movement.

Amazingly, as the God of Abraham told a Hebrew to go and look for a Promised Land and Abraham became the father of the Israelites and Ishmaelites, so did Baron Edmond Rothschild think that he was chosen to help bring Ashkenazi Jewry to the Promised Land.

---

[62]*Encyclopaedia Judaica*, Vol. 8, p. 412.

How THEOSOPHY DECEIVED the WORLD

Edmond Rothschild even had a Hebrew name. He used it when it was convenient. It was Avraham Binyamin.[63]

The Hovevei Zion were among the **first settlers** in the 1880s.[64] **They came from the land of Magog (Russia)**.[65] Rothschild gave **huge sums of money** to assure that there would be a colonization of Israel. He brought grape vines which in the past also helped his family fortune to grow. Rothschild even built wine cellars at two settlements at Rishon le-Zion and Zichron Ya'acov to help with the wine industry he also founded in Israel.

Baron Edmond Rothschild from Paris had become the "**father of the colonies**" and was known by the Hebrew phrase "*ha-nadiv ha-yadu'ah*" (the well-known benefactor).[66] Strangely enough, the prophecy from Revelation 18:23 foretold that merchants who would be promoting doctrines from sorcery would be "**THE GREAT MEN OF THE EARTH.**" Rothschild by 1901 gave a grant of **14,000,000 francs which bought 62,500 acres of Israel**.[67]

However, this well-known merchant began to receive resentment from Zionists because of his seemingly philanthropical acts towards the establishment of the State of Israel.

Rothschild had set barons over his investments in Israel. Baron Edmond Rothschild was a **humanist intellectual**, and a **liberal in Ashkenazism**, so there was constantly friction between the Russian farmers and the baron's barons who were not Jewish. Unexpected religious problems began to surface. Russian rabbis demanded that all farm work should cease for a sabbatical year. Rothschild got around this demand by **fictitiously transferring** the landholding he had to non-Jewish owners for that year. These methods were some of the reasons the more religious Russian Zionists wanted him out. One of the leaders of the Lovers of Zion movement, Ahad Ha-am (a Hebrew), complained that Rothschild's aid as charity robbed the settlers of self-reliance and failed to serve the national awakening of Zionism. This Russian delegation of Zionists hoped to recapture the religious fervor

---

[63]*Encyclopaedia Judaica*, Vol. 14, p. 345.
[64]*Ibid.*, Vol. 14, p. 343.
[65]*Ibid.*, Vol. 14, p. 343.
[66]*Who's Who in Jewish History*, Comay, p. 348.
[67]*Encyclopaedia Judaica*, Vol. 14, p. 343.

The Real Truth About UFO's and the New World Order

they once had. When the delegates demanded reforms in the administration of the Palestine colonies, Baron Edmond told them, "**These are my colonies, and I shall do what I like with them.**"[68]

The first eight years of Edmond Rothschild's involvement with the establishment of settlements in the Land of Israel were not connected with any Zionist movement. He had his own self-interest. However, by the end of the century, Edmond Rothschild yielded to the Zionist's demands and handed over his administrative powers to the Jewish Colonization Association. Naturally, Theodor Herzl was at the start a critic of Edmond Rothschild's colonies in Palestine and eclipsed Rothschild in popularity and power. About three years before Rothschild was pressured to hand over Palestine's colonies to the Zionists on August 29–31, 1897, **Herzl managed to bring the rivaling Zionists together for the first time**. Almost a year earlier, Edmond Rothschild had rejected Herzl's ideas about Zionism. However, **Herzl's First Zionist Congress held in Basle** established the powerful **World Zionist Organization** which struggled because of opposing Zionist factions. Nevertheless, it continued and went on to lead Zionism to eventually take over the Land of Israel and establish it as a homeland for all Jews. **Like the Europeans before him**, Herzl was trying to **promote a renaissance** among the Jews.

At this time, Herzl was not only striving with rivaling factions of Zionists, but also with the power of the Turkish government for the Ottoman Empire still had control of the Land of Israel. Herzl went to the sultan and tried through several meetings to allow the Zionists to establish an independent Jewish State, but the sultan demanded money for the improvement of Turkey's financial situation and offered other areas in the Ottoman Empire besides the Land of Israel. Herzl rejected the offer.[69] From there, Herzl turned to Britain to seek help. Here he met Lord Rothschild who suggested that the Zionists establish a homeland at the Sinai Peninsula which was under the protection of the British Empire.[70] However, with the help and influence of Lord Rothschild of England, Herzl began to gain sympathy for the World Zionist Organization. However, he died of heart problems

---

[68]*Who's Who in Jewish History*, Comay, p. 348.
[69]*Encyclopaedia Judaica*, Vol. 8, p. 414.
[70]*Ibid.*, Vol. 8, pp. 414, 415.

How THEOSOPHY DECEIVED the WORLD

and pneumonia in 1904. Herzl never saw the fulfillment of his hopes and goals of Zionism.

As the first Jewish colonies were being set up in the Land of Israel, the **Fabian Society**, as we saw earlier, was busy promoting Socialism and was determined to establish the Atlantean scheme of a Utopian world federation. England was where the headquarters of the Fabian Society was located. The Fabians had their own ideas in forcing upon the world international Socialism. However, these same Platonic ideas, which led to the Enlightenment Movement, Herzl also shared.[71] Around the same time, Annie Besant and Mahatma Gandhi were busy promoting Socialism in India. The same beliefs were also being promoted in the land of Magog by Nicholai Lenin who also originally came from Ashkenazism, but like Karl Marx, was de-Judaized by the Haskalah (Enlightenment Movement).

During this turmoil, these European Jews were in **total confusion**. The **religious side** of the Zionists were **clashing** with the **atheistic Zionists**. Herzl was in the middle of all this, and having heart problems this continued strife of these rivaling Zionists put him into an early grave. Herzl was a "**political Zionist**" which had successors after his death promoting his ideologies. However, an opposing faction known as the "practical Zionists" whose leader, Chaim Weizmann from the religious side of Zionism (Lovers of Zion), succeeded in winning control of the World Zionist Organization. Weizmann was a disciple of Ahad Ha-am, the Hebrew rabbi who had demanded Edmond Rothschild to **reform** his administrative policies of which Rothschild later was forced to do. Ahad Ha-am was a religious reformer and wanted to restore religious order in Israel.[72]

While the Theosophical Society was busy promoting Hindu Marxism in India, George Bernard Shaw, George Orwell, and H.G. Wells were at the same time promoting humanistic Socialism from England as World War I was raising its ugly head. By World War I, Zionism was transformed, however, into a mass movement and a major political force whose headquarters at the outbreak of World War I were in the land of Gomer (Berlin) which quickly re-established in Copenhagen,[73] when Hitler began to gain power in Germany.

---

[71]*Encyclopaedia Judaica*, **Vol. 8, pp. 407, 420.**
[72]*Who's Who in Jewish History*, **Comay, p. 348.**
[73]*Encyclopaedia Judaica*, **Vol. 16, p. 1049.**

The Real Truth About UFO's and the New World Order

While the Marxist Zionists in Magog were helping Lenin's revolution against Tzar Nicholas II and his government and the world was engaged in a terrible war, Socialist Britons announced to the world that the Jews were going to have Palestine as their homeland. This was set up by **Arthur Balfour**, who was the first lord of the British Admiralty and who later became Britain's foreign secretary, and Chaim Weizmann, who earlier was a leader of the opposition group of younger Russian Zionists, the Democratic Fraction.[74] In 1916, Arthur Balfour became Britain's foreign secretary and discussed with fellow Cabinet members in 1917 about the possibility of allowing Palestine to become the National Home for Jewish people. At this time, the Communists had overthrown the Tzar and on November 2, 1917, the War Cabinet of England approved this proposal as the "**Balfour Declaration**,"[75] which was named after its foreign secretary. The Balfour Declaration was addressed to **Lord Rothschild**.[76]

In the meantime, Woodrow Wilson and a Socialist Briton by the name of **Edward Mandel House**, who was at this time the president's aide, were busy going to different parts of the world trying to promote a **world federation** movement called the **League of Nations**. Many countries joined except for one very important one, the United States. Back then, we had some loyal American politicians who wanted to keep America free and independent and had the foresight to tell that joining the League of Nations would mean giving up the sovereignty of the United States for the League of Nations was a Socialist trap to get all nations to hand over their weapons to them. If controversy should arise, then the nation would not have the ability to defend itself. After many years of constant pressure by merchants and politicians to join the League of Nations scheme, **it met defeat in the United States**.

Keeping in mind that generally it is the powerful "**merchants**" who become members of Parliament or congressmen, senators, and presidents, let us again go on and see how they are, indeed, filling the pages of recorded history which was foretold by the God of Abraham centuries ago through Hebrew prophets and apostles of Jesus

---

[74]*Who's Who is Jewish History*, Comay, p. 419.

[75]*Ibid.*, Comay, p. 420.

[76]*The Universal Jewish Encyclopedia*, 1943, p. 238.

How THEOSOPHY DECEIVED the WORLD

Christ as they wrote while they were moved by the Holy Spirit.

While Edmond Rothschild was buying up the land *"between"* the Mediterranean Sea, the Sea of Galilee, and the Dead Sea that will become, as prophecy says, the site where the god of this world in the near future will establish his headquarters, the Rockefeller family were doing what they could to promote this New World Order scheme on this side of the Atlantic.

Like Mayer Amschel Rothschild, John D. Rockefeller, Sr. became the **patriarch of a family of merchants and politicians**. John D. Rockefeller, Sr. made a fortune in oil. He had five children, and the youngest was John D. Rockefeller, Jr. of whom we will focus on. John D. Rockefeller, Jr. had six children, five of whom were sons by the names of John D. Rockefeller, III, Nelson, Laurance, Winthrop, and David.

In this volume, we have **focused mainly** on the rise and evolution of the Atlantean Plan of Plato and how it was promoted down through the centuries through merchants, politicians, and with violence by Marxist revolutionaries. To close this last chapter in this controversy between Christ and Lucifer (Satan), we need to learn how John D. Rockefeller, Jr. **put in motion** agencies before his death in 1960 that are still uniting religions and nations today to move towards that day foretold in Scripture – Armageddon.

There is not enough space to write everything that John D. Rockefeller, Jr. did to promote this same Atlantean Plan of the New World Order, but here are a few facts.

Like the famous merchant Edmond Rothschild, John D. Rockefeller, Jr. was a humanist intellectual, but unlike Edmond Rothschild, John D. Rockefeller, Jr. **in his earlier years professed** the Protestant faith. He was raised in a Baptist Church. However, he later founded in 1930 an **Interfaith church** in Riverside, New York. Earlier, he started an **Interfaith college** called **Union Theological Seminary**. At his Riverside church, John D. Rockefeller, Jr. desired to unite secular humanism with religion. The arches of his gothic edifice contained figures of the heros of the Enlightenment Movement such as Dante, whose writings helped inspire the European Renaissance, and Hegel, one of the heros of the 18th-century European Enlightenment Movement whose writings helped Karl Marx write his 40-page booklet,

The Real Truth About UFO's and the New World Order

The Communist Manifesto. Also seen on one of the arches of Rockefeller's church is another one of his heros, Charles Darwin, whose theory of evolution even the pope of Rome, John Paul II, has publicly embraced. The figures of Moses, Muhammad, and Confucius are also there.[77]

In 1908, John D. Rockefeller, Jr. was already busy helping the New World Order scheme to unite the world into a one-world Socialist government and a one-world religion when he founded the **Federal Council of Churches** which evolved into the **World Council of Churches** whose American headquarters I visited in the fall of 1996. The World Council of Churches' headquarters in America are in John D. Rockefeller, Jr.'s 19-story building at **475 Riverside Drive, Riverside, New York**. The World Council of Churches is nothing less than a basket like Freemasonry to collect all pagans, Christians, and Socialists together under one roof.

To collect the major businesses into one basket, another British Socialist secret society of businessmen was set up in Paris in 1919. Its name is the Royal Institute of International Affairs. President Wilson's aide, Edward Mandel House, and former President Herbert Hoover were members. In 1921, the Council on Foreign Relations, Inc. emerged out of this secret society of businessmen.[78] The CFR was set up by Edward Mandel House and the Rockefeller family. It is America's number-one elite secret society. The majority of our most well-known politicians and businessmen have been or are, since 1921, members of this powerful society. Alan Greenspan, the chairman of the Federal Reserve, has been an active member for years. Its number-one chairman has been John D. Rockefeller, Jr.'s son, David Rockefeller. All major decisions on American policies abroad or domestic must first receive an approval from these merchants and politicians. They are actually a state within a state. They control our political system because most congressmen and senators are members. Every president from Wilson to Clinton were or are members, save Reagan. Clinton and Albright have been, unfortunately, members for years.[79]

Twenty years later, another agency was set up with the help of

---

[77]*The Rockefellers: An American Dynasty*, **Collier/Horowitz, p. 153.**
[78]*Council on Foreign Relations Annual Report 1979–1980*, **p. 5.**
[79]*Council on Foreign Relations Annual Report 1995*, **pp. 142–144.**

How THEOSOPHY DECEIVED the WORLD

Above, my wife is holding the 1990 Fall/Winter Wainwright House Coming Events Guide *we received when visiting there. This is the same* Wainwright House Guide *out of which I quoted some of their faculty members and their involvement with Theosophy. It was from this school of Theosophy that the United Nations emerged.*

The Real Truth About UFO's and the New World Order

John D. Rockefeller, Jr. in Rye, New York. It has been one of the biggest New Age centers in which to learn Theosophy in the country. The center is called the Wainwright House. They claim to be a Judeo-Christian organization, as we saw earlier. However, just one glance from a Christian who is rooted and grounded in the Bible into the publications of the Wainwright House will show that it is a **house of Spiritualism**. It, too, was set up to use the power and influence of money to lure unsuspecting and gullible Christians into Jewish Theosophy, which has its roots grounded in the Kabbalah.

The New Age Hassidic Rabbi Joseph Gelberman, according to the *1990 Fall/Winter Wainwright House Guide*, on pages 31–33 was listed as a member of its faculty. Another name listed in the Wainwright House's faculty is Kenneth Cohen who is on the faculty of Boulder Graduate School in Colorado. Cohen is an internationally-known New Age scholar and master of Chinese healing arts. Gail Greenstein leads workshops for the Wainwright House. Greenstein teaches yoga, psychology, and New Age spirituality. Nancy Moshé is the associate editor of the *Wainwright House Guide* and has had a long standing interest in Eastern approaches to spirituality. Another faculty member of Anglo-Jewish descent is Dr. Peter Laurence, the Interfaith director of the Wainwright House. Dr. Lawrence along with two Catholic priests, Daniel Martin and Luis Dolan, work together in heralding all faiths to unite together. Others on the faculty of the Wainwright House are members of the Baha´i faith. Its founder, Baha´u´llah, claimed to be the Messenger of God for this age. He taught that universal peace and unity are inevitable, as well as the unity of science and religion. This is the main theme that flows through the halls of this **house of Spiritualism**. Another faculty member listed is Diana Lee Beach who claims to be a minister of the Gospel. She is an Episcopalian priest and serves, according to the *1990 Wainwright House Guide*, on the faculty of the New York Theological Seminary. Beach is a disciple of the late Carl Jung (1875–1961), an occult psychiatrist and philosopher and New Age prophet. Jung was one of the most influential New Age psychiatrists of the 20th century. He was from Switzerland and was fascinated by paranormal topics all of his life, among them alchemy, mediumship, and witchcraft.[80] There are New

---

[80]*The Mystical Year*, Time-Life Books, Alexander, VA, p. 64.

How THEOSOPHY DECEIVED the WORLD

   Above, there is a photograph of the Wainwright House I took in Rye, New York. This interfaith organization was established to not only teach Theosophy, but is also the very organization that founded the United Nations. John D. Rockefeller, Jr. was one of its most well-known founders. It was John D. Rockefeller, Jr. who gave $8.5 million towards the building of the United Nations. It was Nelson Rockefeller, John D. Rockefeller, Jr.'s son, according to the nationwide best seller, The Rockefellers, pp. 232–241, who convinced American politicians to establish it.

The Real Truth About UFO's and the New World Order

Age universities of Jung's witchcraft. Barbara Bliss, who is another faculty member at the Wainwright House, is a graduate of the C.G. Jung Institute of Zurich and is a Jungian analyst who teaches Jung's contribution of the spread of Spiritualism. Winifred Clark, a Wainwright House trustee and staff member, studied Jungian psychology and attended lectures at the Jung Institute in Zurich. There is a Carl G. Jung Institute of New York and another Wainwright House faculty member, Robin van Löben Sels, is another Jungian analyst in private practice in New York City and Ridgefield, Connecticut. She is a supervisor at the C.G. Jung Institute of New York.[81] Another faculty member of the Wainwright House, Andrew Flaxman, conducted four seminars January 15 through February 5, 1990. One of his seminars was entitled "***Benjamin Franklin, American Initiate***." Flaxman examined the historical account of Franklin's connection with Freemasonry and Rosicrucianism.[82]

The Wainwright House, since its founding in 1941, has drawn many famous names to its mansion in Rye, New York. Again, the warning in Revelation 18:23 points to merchants (businessmen) of the world who would be foremost in **drawing** the people of **all** nations into the **ranks** of **Spiritualism**. I first became aware of the Wainwright House by reading a booklet written by Robert Keith Spenser entitled *The Cult of the All-Seeing Eye* which was published in 1964 by The Christian Book Club of America, P. O. Box 638, Hawthorne, CA 90250.

Spenser points out with good documentation how high officials of the United States government and the United Nations were working through the Wainwright House to continue the goals of Theosophy and its symbols and its Novus Ordo Seclorum. Spenser also points out if the naive supporters of both the Wainwright House and its child, the United Nations, were exposed to their secret doctrines they would recoil in horror from its evil teachings and sever any connection with them.

Theosophy's most cherished symbol has been the **All-Seeing Eye** within the delta (triangle). The Egyptians called it the Eye of Ra or Osiris. This pagan emblem **can be traced back** to the Chaldeans as the Solar Eye. The All-Seeing Eye or the Solar Eye was the **left eye**

---

[81]*The Wainwright House 1990 Fall/Winter Guide*, pp. 31–34.
[82]*Ibid.*, p. 30.

How THEOSOPHY DECEIVED the WORLD

and was adopted throughout the Old World as the Eye of Jove or Jupiter, the Eye of Phoebus or Apollo, the Eye of Baal, and as the Eye of Providence. The Eye of Jove appeared in front of Jove's temple at Peloponnessus.[83]

While on the island of Cebu in the Philippines, my wife and I saw a Roman Catholic Church with a huge **All-Seeing Eye** displaying itself on its front wall. In Arabia, all ancient temples were decorated with the All-Seeing Eye, and it was a Muslim emblem of *"Allah"* which means *"I am that I am."*[84] Now, it has managed to be adopted as an emblem of the United States which is proudly displayed on the back of the dollar bill. If the reader will examine his dollar bill, he will see that the 13-level pyramid is not capped. This idea was inspired by occultist politicians who were Freemasons. The All-Seeing Eye is proudly displayed on the apron of the Worshipful Master of their lodges. This All-Seeing Eye found on the back of the dollar bill was also adopted by Aleister Crowley, the infamous pope of Satanism and hero of the heavy metal music culture. The All-Seeing Eye has always been, since the ancient days of Babylon, the most significant symbol of heathenism and can, indeed, be seen on some Roman Catholic Churches as well.

As established, New Age Spiritualists believe that all people and their gods originated from Atlantis. According to New Age philosophy, the gods are the UFO's who gave the Atlanteans the secrets of how to develop a **huge crystal** in which Atlanteans powered ancient flying machines and their ships. However, the Atlanteans misused this crystal and caused explosions and the island paradise sunk into the Atlantic Ocean. According to New Age philosophy, some Toltecs and Aryans survived and made their way to Egypt and the north and founded colonies there. The Toltecs (Atlanteans) built the pyramids in which the capstone of the pyramid of Gizeh, which is missing today, was said to have been **capped of pure crystal** in honor of their chief deity. This floating triangle with the **Solar Eye** above the pyramid on the dollar bill is symbolizing this chief **Solar Deity** who gave its builders the metaphysical knowledge of **levitation** to build these pyramids.

---

[83]*The Cult of the All-Seeing Eye*, Spenser, p. 32.
[84]*Ibid.*, Spenser, p. 32.

The Real Truth About UFO's and the New World Order

The Wainwright House is nothing less than a modern school of metaphysics which has camouflaged itself as a Judeo-Christian center. These modern Chaldeans and Atlanteans are seeking from the Solar Deity and his spirit guides this forbidden knowledge that the ancient Toltecs, Egyptians, Druids, and Chaldeans received from the seducing spirits. Jesus warned His people who stay loyal to Him in these last days that Lucifer's Magi would be able to perform miracles through the power of sorcery, and that there would come from Theosophy "false Christs, and false prophets, and shall shew great signs and wonders; insomuch that, if it were possible, they shall deceive the very elect." Matthew 24:24. The Wainwright House has a flyer they send out to Christian pastors throughout the U.S. It is called *The Interfaith Community*. I have a copy of the flyer dated May 1990 that states:

"**On the eve of the 21st century, the spiritual traditions – Hindu, Buddhist, Chinese, Jewish, Christian, Islamic – are no longer separated but involved in a global spiritual process.**"

New Agers are determined to unite naive Christians into their movement. They are determined to replace the Christian Bible with the Bible of Spiritualism. Just as Bible-believing Christians are told by the Author and Finisher of Christianity to "go ye therefore, and **TEACH ALL NATIONS**, baptizing them in the name of the Father, and of the Son, and of the Holy Ghost" (Matthew 28:19), so do trained New Age intellectuals go forth teaching Theosophy from its Bible, the Kabbalah (the Jewish book of magic). One of the biggest training seminaries to merge naive Christians into the ranks of Spiritualism is John D. Rockefeller, Jr.'s Union Theological Seminary in Riverside, New York. From here, these New Age professors are sent forth to other seminaries which are Christian. Slowly but surely, a subtle gospel of **New Theology a.k.a. Liberation Theology** is introduced to unsuspecting Christian churches by these trained **Interfaith professors**. The prophecies and doctrines from the Holy Scriptures which warn about Baal worship and its deceptions, which Eastern religions, Islamics, Catholics, and Protestants have all mingled, is set aside. Then, Pluralism and religious tolerance takes their place. The Third Angel's message of Revelation, Chapter 14, which is warning about the hour of God's judgment, Babylon's fall, and the Mark of the Beast is replaced with a gospel of peace and safety and ecumenism. This New Theology not only leads professors of theology to teach their students

How THEOSOPHY DECEIVED the WORLD

that all religions are good, but subtly throws out creation, the Deity of Christ, Jesus as Saviour, His virgin birth, and His coming kingdom on earth.

Malachi Martin, the most studied theologian in the Roman Catholic hierarchy, wrote in his book how New Theology had infiltrated Roman Catholic seminaries and eventually New Agers and Socialist priests took over the Vatican. Martin admitted that the most powerful religious orders of the Roman Catholic Church – Jesuits, Dominicans, and Franciscans – were swept into New Age Spiritualism and Marxism through the promotion of New Theology.[85] We shall study the rise and evolution of Pluralism and the fusion of Spiritualism, the Papacy, and the Protestants as predicted by Scripture in Volume Five entitled *Ancient Prophecies About The Dragon, The Beast, and The False Prophet*.

John Paul II, however, is very aware of what has happened to his church. While humanist intellectuals from the CFR, New Agers from the Wainwright House, and occult, Socialist politicians are busy trying to unite the world into an international Global Village, the leader of the Roman Catholic Church **has his own ideas** about uniting the world into a New World Order. John Paul II is also a revolutionary and **is racing to become the head** of this Babylon the Great, and the prophecies of the Bible predict that the Papacy and its leader at that time **will sit at the head of this world federation**. This we will study more in both Volume Four entitled *Ancient Prophecies About Mysticism and Hollywood and The Music Industry* and also in Volume Five entitled *Ancient Prophecies About The Dragon, The Beast, and The False Prophet*.

John Paul II, who is in the autumn of his years, predicted the following about the Land of Israel. This was seen Sunday, April 3, 1994, on the front cover of *Parade* magazine:

"We trust that, with the approach of the year 2000, Jerusalem will become the city of peace for the entire world and that all the people will be able to meet there, in particular the believers in the religions that find their birthright in the faith of Abraham."

However, the worst of all the agencies John D. Rockefeller, Jr. set in motion through other fellow businessmen and interfaith New Age adherents was, believe it or not, the United Nations! The United

---

[85]*The Keys of This Blood*, Martin, pp. 259– 273.

The Real Truth About UFO's and the New World Order

Nations was actually set up by these occult-seeking and promoting disciples of the Wainwright House in 1941.[86] John D. Rockefeller, Jr., like Edmond Rothschild, had the tenets of Spiritualism and humanism mixed up in his beliefs about God. "For thy **MERCHANTS** were the **GREAT MEN** of the earth; for by thy **SORCERIES** were all nations deceived." Revelation 18:23 (last part).

There are many cross connections that link the Rothschilds and the Rockefellers who are families of merchants and politicians. One is the Federal Reserve. Both families of the Rothschilds and Rockefellers assisted in the establishment of it in 1913, and both families presently own the controlling interest in this nongovernmental private central bank. In Volume Two, *The New Age Movement and The Illuminati 666,* the history of the Rothschild family's connection is revealed. Volume Four, *Ancient Prophecies About Mysticism and Hollywood and The Music Industry*, has a documented study of how international businessmen are working to implement a **cashless society and a Socialist government** and how Hollywood and the Music Industry have for years been the number-one heralds of this New World Order scheme. It also shows how our Lord foretold it and what we should do when no man can buy or sell unless he receives the Mark, the Name of the Beast, or the Number of his Name.

We are still living in the time of unfulfilled Bible prophecy. Daniel's prophecy that foretold of Satan moving his tabernacles (headquarters) to the Land of Israel between the seas in the holy mountain has yet to take place. However, the edifice for it has risen up, and it is the United Nations. The United Nations is the modern Tower of Babel.

Alice Ann Bailey, a pythonist and one of the most sought-after occult authors, wrote to her disciples in her book, *Externalization of the Hierarchy*, that this New World Order scheme of occultists would reach its goal of uniting the world under their banner under the auspices of Freemasonry and the United Nations.[87] Alice Bailey was connected with the Wainwright House, which founded the United Nations. She also told her *red* revolutionaries that the United Nations would eventually gain control of the weapons of all the nations through

---

[86]*The Wainwright House 1990 Fall/Winter Guide*, **Introduction page.**
[87]*Externalization of the Hierarchy*, **Bailey, pp. 510, 512.**

How THEOSOPHY DECEIVED the WORLD

The above photograph was taken in the summer of 1996 when my wife and I again visited the United Nations Meditation Room. This photograph shows both the mural and the pagan altar to the Unknown God inside the Meditation Room of the U.N. The U.N. Meditation Room is 30 feet long and 18 feet wide at the entrance which faces north north-east. It is nine feet wide at the other end. It is wedge-shaped. The U.N. Meditation Room was designed in the form of a pyramid laying on its side. As pointed out earlier, the pagan god Hermes is the god of merchants, bankers, thieves, fortunetellers, and heralds. In pagan mythology, Hermes' throne was said to be of a single piece of solid gray rock. It is not by chance that the U.N. Meditation Room altar is of a solid gray lodestone, and this god of merchants, bankers, and fortuneteller's sign is proudly displayed in the mural painting for it was, indeed, merchants, bankers, and fortunetellers from the Wainwright House who actually founded the United Nations!

The Real Truth About UFO's and the New World Order

disarmament treaties.[88] After gaining control of all weapons from the various nations, then they will use them on those who oppose them and who cling to God's Word.[89]

Right from the start, the United Nations' founding fathers also included members of the Council on Foreign Relations. A founding committee for the United Nations met in San Francisco. Council on Foreign Relations member Nelson Rockefeller, the son of John D. Rockefeller, Jr., was among the voices urgently promoting the United Nations scheme. Also among them were the Assistant Secretary of War and CFR member, John J. McCloy, and the notorious Alger Hiss, the Communist sympathizer and alleged Russian spy. Alger Hiss wrote the charter of the United Nations which was adopted June 26, 1945.

It was pointed out earlier that the god Hermes is, among ancient and modern Spiritualism, the author of all occult sciences. He was Bel in one Babylonian tradition and Nebo to the Canaanites and Mercury to the Romans. His symbols were the **swastika** and the **caduceus**. Hermes was also the **god of merchants, bankers, and thieves**. It is very apparent that the merchants and politicians who founded the United Nations actually knew what they were doing when they designed the **United Nations Meditation Room** inside this modern Tower of Babel. This writer has been there several times. To get into the Meditation Room, you must be accompanied by an armed guard. What is even more chilling is when I first went into the Meditation Room back in 1985. The Meditation Room is painted in what to me looked like electric blue and the room is wedge-shaped. **It is shaped like the pyramid of Gizeh with its cap stone missing, only laying on its side.** In the middle of the room is a **dark, gray block of crystalline iron ore** which weighs six and one-half tons. It is rectangular in shape, and it is a lodestone from Sweden and is strongly magnetic and possesses polarity. This chunk of dark, gray crystalline iron ore is used as a **pagan altar** dedicated to the **Unknown God**, the god whom man worshipped under many names and in many forms.[90]

The U.N. Meditation Room, its mural with its occult signs of Hermes, the sun-god, and the moon goddess, and its altar were promoted by

---

[88]*The New Age Movement and The Illuminati 666*, Sutton, p. 207.
[89]*Externalization of the Hierarchy*, Bailey, pp. 276–279.
[90]*The Cult of the All-Seeing Eye*, Spenser, pp. 8, 9.

How THEOSOPHY DECEIVED the WORLD

The United Nations was founded by occult businessmen from the Wainwright House. The photograph above I took while visiting the Wainwright House in Rye, New York. This is the original pagan altar which was in the United Nations Meditation Room. This is seen on the second floor of the above mansion. The above pagan altar has the following inscription on it: "300 lb. Agba tree altar from French Equatorial Africa formerly in the United Nations Meditation Room was presented to the Laymen's Movement and Wainwright House by Dag Hammarskjöld on May 3, 1957."

The Real Truth About UFO's and the New World Order

Alice Bailey's Lucis Trust, the World Council of Churches, and a group known as the **Friends of the Meditation Room**.[91] They were a group set up specifically to promote the construction of this pagan sanctuary. Friends of the Meditation Room was a branch of the **Laymen's Movement for a Christian World, Inc.** whose international headquarters are at the Wainwright House. The two most important members of the Laymen's Movement for a Christian World, Inc. were John D. Rockefeller, Jr. and former President Dwight D. Eisenhower who was, like the Rothschild family, an Ashkenazi Jew. This pseudo-Christian organization has a magazine they send out called *The Laymen's Movement Review*. In their May/June and July/August 1959 and July/August 1962 issues, there were listed speakers for the Laymen's Movement for a Christian World, Inc. who have been Norman Cousins, Ralph Bunche, Frank P. Graham, William Ernest Hocking, and Kirtley F. Mather; all of whom have Communist-front records.[92] This should not be so shocking to the reader if he or she remembers that New Age occultism adopted Socialism. Mahatma Gandhi, remember, was indeed a Marxist Hindu. It was Eisenhower who handed over, in the presence of the astonished and puzzled eyes of General Patton, East Berlin and the Balkans to the Soviet Union at the close of World War II. Eisenhower **was a very active member** of the Rockefeller-run Council on Foreign Relations.

The **original altar**, which was in the Meditation Room at the U.N. before Sweden gave the U.N. its present altar, is at the **Wainwright House**. This original altar came from French Equatorial Africa and is made from the Agba tree and weighs 300 pounds. There is a plaque on the altar stating that this altar was presented to the Laymen's Movement and the Wainwright House by **Dag Hammarskjöld** on May 3, 1957.

It should be noted that it was also Dr. Frank Laubach, Union Theological Seminary graduate and author of *Letters of a Modern Mystic*, who had lobbied in 1946 at the Paris Peace Conference for the establishment of the Meditation Room. It was another modern mystic who studied at the Union Theological Seminary who founded the Temple of Understanding movement in 1960. The Temple of Understanding

---

[91]*The Cult of the All-Seeing Eye*, Spenser, p. 10, 11.
[92]*Ibid.*, Spenser, p. 12.

How THEOSOPHY DECEIVED the WORLD

    I took this photograph in the fall of 1996 while visiting the United Nations Meditation Room which is located in the United Nations building. Jesus through His apostle John warned in Revelation 18:23 that the Dragon would use businessmen (merchants) to promote the deceptions of Spiritualism (sorcery). As pointed out, Hermes is worshipped among occultists as the god of merchants, bankers, fortunetellers, healing, and medicine. One of his signs that occultists used to invoke him among his ancient pagan worshippers was known as the wand of Aesculapius or the caduceus of which the American Medical Association adopted as the symbol of their organization. Who founded the A.M.A.? Who helped finance its founding? It was none other than the occult businessman and banker, John D. Rockefeller, Jr. and his partner in promoting interfaith and internationalism, Andrew Carnegie.
    Who gave $8.5 million to buy the land and help finance the United Nations? It was John D. Rockefeller, Jr. It is not by chance that the sign of the god of banking and merchants is symbolically painted in abstract art in the mural painting above. In the center, you can see the wand of Hermes. The symbols of the sun-god and the moon goddess are displayed on the left and right of the wand.

The Real Truth About UFO's and the New World Order

Movement's focus is to build a pagan temple to house all the six major religions of the world. Its founder is Judith (Juliet) Hollister. A complete history of the Temple of Understanding Movement and my interview with its founder and the Wainwright House connection is written in Volume Five of this series of Time of the End prophecies. The Temple of Understanding Movement has now evolved into a **spiritual United Nations**.

I wonder with amazement how Protestant pastors cannot see that the United Nations is trying to swallow up the whole planet into its unholy belly. When the U.N. makes a statement about the good things this or that church is doing in the world, this is looked upon with great admiration. This organization was founded by the people of Spiritualism and those who are uniting with it have, like the ancient Hebrew leaders, turned their backs upon the temple of the Lord and his Law which forbids any manner of Spiritualism and have faced the east and have bowed their knees to Baal!

It was planned by these merchants of modern Babylon that the Land of Israel would be used as the site which is to be the Seat of their world federation. Slowly but surely, the last scenes of this drama between Christ and Satan are unfolding. It was Edmond Rothschild who gave the money to buy the land to place the capital of the New World Order in the Land of Israel. It was John D. Rockefeller, Jr. who gave the $8.5 million to build the United Nations. Before this, the first Jews to step foot on the Land of Israel came from the land of Magog (Russia) and Gomer (Germany). As pointed out so many times in this book, there has been a **Socialist revolution** going on since the founding of the Illuminati of Bavaria, Germany. On November 2, 1917, the War Cabinet of Britain approved Arthur Balfour's Declaration in allowing Palestine to be given as a national homeland for the Jews. This declaration was signed and placed in a letter to be presented to Lord Lionel Walter Rothschild. He was a Zionist and the most powerful Ashkenazi in England. Edmond Rothschild had been from the French branch of the Rothschild family.

About 31 years later, an Ashkenazi Jew who had been a Marxist Zionist read another victory declaration for the Socialist revolution on May 14, 1948, in Tel Aviv, Israel. He declared the establishment of the State of Israel. He became a member of the Marxist Zionists

How THEOSOPHY DECEIVED the WORLD

   Jesus foretold through his apostle John in Revelation 18:3, 15, 23 that it would be the merchants (businessmen) of Babylon the Great (the whole world) whom Satan would use to not only stop God's remnant people from being able to buy or sell (See Revelation 13:16, 17), but to also deceive all nations into joining an alliance against Jesus. The inspired Scripture warned, "For by thy sorceries (Theosophy) were all nations deceived." Revelation 18:23.

   The Wainwright House was founded by the Laymen's Movement for a Christian World, Inc. One of its very active members was none other than former President and Council on Foreign Relations member Dwight Eisenhower. After the Rothschild family colonized the Land of Israel, the Rockefeller family working through the Wainwright House and the Council on Foreign Relations used Dwight Eisenhower's influence as president (1953–1961) to give the newly-established State of Israel hundreds of millions of U.S. tax payer's money to buy military equipment, ammunition, spare parts, training aircrafts,[93] etc. It was the United Nations that actually played the biggest role in establishing the State of Israel. It was businessmen from the Wainwright House who founded the United Nations. David Ben-Gurion said that the United Nations would eventually be set up in Israel. Daniel the prophet foretold Satan's last headquarters would be established between the seas (the Mediterranean Sea, the Sea of Galilee, and the Dead Sea). See Daniel 11:45.

[93]**Encyclopaedia Judaica,** *Vol. 6, pp. 543, 544.*

The Real Truth About UFO's and the New World Order

in 1905.[94] He went on to become modern Israel's first Prime Minister. His name was David Ben-Gurion. Very few, indeed, are there today who realize that this great hero and leader of the exodus of American and European Jews to the Land of Israel was a Zionist guerrilla fighter in his youth. Throughout his life, he professed Socialist Zionist ideas until his death.[95] Now the reader may understand why there have been so many White, blue-eyed German and Russian-sounding Jews running Israel, for most of them originated from these areas.

Amazingly, on January 16, 1962, David Ben-Gurion unwittingly announced what the real God of Israel foretold through Daniel the Hebrew prophet. What the former prime minister so proudly proclaimed to the world was, ironically enough, also foretold in Bible prophecy to be one of the last acts that Satan would be allowed to lead human agents to do before the end of this present world. This late Socialist Zionist said:

"With the exception of the U.S.S.R. as a federated state, all other countries will be **UNITED IN A WORLD ALLIANCE** at whose disposal will be an **INTERNATIONAL POLICE FORCE**. All armies will be abolished and there will be no more wars. In Jerusalem the United Nations (a truly United Nations) **WILL BUILD A SHRINE** to the prophets to serve the federated union of all continents. This will be **THE SEAT OF THE SUPREME COURT** of mankind to settle all controversies among the federated continents, as prophesied by Isaiah." *Look* magazine, January 16, 1962.

The United Nations is going to move to the Land of Israel! This is the ultimate goal of the businessmen and politicians of the New World Order and of the New Age Movement. This is also the plan of the hidden **Prime Minister** of this world. However, the sure Word of prophecy says:

"And he shall plant the tabernacles of his palace between the seas in the glorious holy mountain; YET HE SHALL COME TO HIS END, AND NONE SHALL HELP HIM." Daniel 11:45.

"Many shall be purified, and made white, and tried; but the wicked shall do wickedly: and **none** of the **wicked** shall **understand**; but the **wise** shall understand." Daniel 12:10.

---

[94]*Ben-Gurion: The Burning Ground 1886–1948*, Teveth, p. xvii.
[95]*Chronicle of the 20th Century*, Dec. 1973, Chronicle Publications, p. 1073.

INDEX

A

Abiff, Hiram,   89, 90
Acupuncture,   140
Adam and Eve,   242
Adams, John,   82, 84
Adonis,   204
All-Seeing Eye,   36, 258, 259
Allah (I am that I am),   259
American Revolution,   63, 75, 82
Anarchy,   46, 80, 149
Animal Farm,   160
Ankh,   112
Anti-Semitic,   210, 223, 248
Antichrist,   30, 31, 50, 60, 74, 75, 118, 137
Applewhite, Marshall,   27, 28, 178
Aquino, Michael,   125
Arcane School,   185
Arch Deceiver,   233
Argüelles, José,   65, 66, 68, 69, 71
Armageddon,   238, 239, 253
Artemis,   110, 111
Aryan race,   37, 38, 208
Ashkenazi Jews,   63, 159, 210, 212, 214, 222, 231
   Adopted Hebrew culture, language & history,   210, 211
   Adopted the Kabbalah (6th Century),   213, 218, 230, 231
   Balfour Declaration,   252, 268
   Daniel foretold Satan's last headquarters,   229-231, 239
   David Ben-Gurion's connection,   268, 270
   Divided into many factions,   251
   During Hitler's time,   235, 236
   East European,   228, 251
   God divorced Israel as a nation in A.D. 34,   208
   Ha-ad, Ahad,   249
   Hasidei Ashkenazi,   213, 214, 222, 234, 245
   Hasidic are deep into Spiritualism,   212, 213, 242, 245
   Haskalah Era (Enlightenment),   63, 222, 223, 228, 232, 240, 241
   He-Hasid, Samuel,   245
   Herzl, Theodor,   232, 247, 248, 250, 251

Ashkenazi Jews (CONT.),
    Hibbat Zionists,   240
    Hovevei Zion,   249
    Marx, Lenin, and Trotsky were,   240, 241
    Mendelssohn, Moses,   223, 232
    Not Hebrew but Aryan,   212, 245, 246
    Origin of,   211, 212, 230, 234, 238, 248
    Over one million migrated to U.S. from 1800-1900,   235, 240
    Preservers and promoters of the Kabbalah,   214, 234, 245, 256
    Protestant pastors are in a strong delusion about,   209, 210, 228-230, 248
    Rothschild connection,   247-250, 252, 268
    Rothschild family were first family of,   246, 252
    Russian,   239, 249-252
    Shem-Tob, Ba'al,   245
    State of Israel founded mainly by,   210, 211, 213, 215, 216
    Switched from Messianic to Nationalism,   223
    United Nations, modern Tower of Babel, is to move,   240
    Zionism founded mainly by,   210, 231
Ashtaroth (Ashtoreth),   114, 116, 123, 204
Assyrian Empire,   203
Astrology,   20, 68, 107, 122, 168, 201, 204-206, 213
Atlantis myth,   19, 21, 22, 25, 26, 34, 36, 41, 43
    Atlanteans believed to be the origin of the Aryans,   36, 37
    Both Socialism and Communism are based in the,   153, 160-163, 193, 232, 253, 259, 260
    Divided into ten kingdoms,   25, 26, 31
    European Renaissance connection,   22, 31, 75, 148, 211, 230
    Gods of believed by New Agers to be the UFO's,   21, 24, 25, 36, 37, 41, 97, 184, 259, 260
    Golden Age of,   22, 36, 70, 148, 153, 243
    Illuminati connection,   19, 63, 184
    New Age Movement is promoting this Atlantean Plan,   34, 36, 40-43, 46, 65, 70, 161, 184, 197, 211, 242, 243, 251, 259, 260
    New World Order advocates are centered around,   19, 24, 31, 63, 184, 243
    Plans to divide this world into ten divisions,   46, 97
    Plato's connection,   26, 31, 148, 153, 160-163, 230, 243, 251, 253
Atlas,   25
Author and Finisher of Christianity,   23, 245, 260
Aztecs,   21, 23, 57, 65-68, 71, 207, 218

B

Baal worship,   119
Babel,   202, 204, 206
Babylon the Great,   67, 107, 114, 224, 225, 235, 239, 240

Babylon the Great (CONT.),
  Symbolizes the whole world,   235, 239, 240, 244
Babylonian mythology,   15, 201, 203, 204
Back to Eden,   143, 146
Baha´i faith,   256
Baha´u´llah,   256
Bailey, Alice,   157, 183-185, 262
Balancing of the energies,   141
Balfour Declaration,   252, 268
Ballard, Guy and Edna,   186
Beatles, The,   192
Ben-Gurion, David,   270
Besant, Annie,   157, 161-164, 182, 183, 251
Bible prophecy,   17, 24, 26, 29, 46, 50, 56, 57, 60, 61
  Foretold Jews will accept Jesus as Messiah,   235
  Foretold that Satan will personate Christ,   50
  Foretold Satan's last headquarters,   211, 229, 235, 236, 239, 244, 270
  Foretold the 1000-year reign of Christ,   238
  Foretold UFO's,   23, 42
  Foretold world federation against God at the Time of the End,   46
Blavatsky, Helena,   32, 36, 37, 157, 165, 180, 184, 246
  Apostle of the New Age,   180
  Atlantean Plan connection,   163
  Co-founder of the Theosophical Society,   181, 182
Blood
  Forbidden to eat,   143-145
Bolívar, Simón,   94, 95
Bolsheviks,   163
Bowie, Jim,   88
Bradlaugh, Charles,   162
British invasion,   160, 163
Buddha,   105, 177, 218

C

Cabot, Laurie,   102
Caduceus,   49, 52, 264, 267
Cakes,   110-113, 116
Carter, Jimmy,   42
Caspian Jews,   212, 236
Castaneda, Carlos,   190, 191
Castro, Fidel,   157
Cattle get cancer,   131
Cayce, Edgar,   40, 41, 165
  Sleeping prophet,   41

Celtic peoples, 212, 238, 239
Chakras, 138
Channels for Satan's electric currents, 141
Chariots of the Gods?
   Von Däniken, Erich, 34
Charmer, 121, 130
Ch'i, 139, 140
Chinese therapeutic touch, 140
Chocolate has caffeine, 145
Christianity, 17, 20, 22-24, 52, 60-62, 73, 75, 78, 80, 85, 94, 98, 103, 131, 141, 161, 227
   Not to use violence, 96
   Protestant, 20, 22, 104, 113, 120, 135, 163
   Roman Catholic, 20, 26, 28, 37, 71, 74, 78, 86, 106-114, 120, 135, 213
Christians
   Apostasy of, 28, 54, 59, 86, 101-104, 117, 118, 135-138, 150, 164, 167, 168, 192, 217, 218, 224, 233
   Mainstream will unite with New Agers, 241, 254, 256, 260, 266
Church Universal and Triumph Threat, 188
Clinton, Bill, 65
Clovis, 78
Columbus, Christopher, 213
Common Sense, 23, 75
Communism, 29, 110, 155-165, 242
   Is Socialism, 162
   Leninism/Stalinism, 153
   The papal connection, 62
Communist Manifesto, The, 156, 254
Consulter with familiar spirits, 121, 130
Conway, Moncure
   Unitarian preacher, 162
Council on Foreign Relations, The, 254, 261, 264
Coven Lothlorien, 101
Crockett, Davey, 88
Crowley, Aleister, 32, 37, 38, 40, 45, 190, 192, 259
Cumbey, Constance, 62
Cush, 43, 45, 94, 202

D

Dante, 253
Darwin, Charles, 155, 254
De-Christianize, 155
Deism, 74, 75, 231

Deists
   Jefferson, Franklin & Paine were,   156
   Swapped kingdom of Christ for Plato's Atlantis,   31
Deity of Christ,   74, 261
De-Judaized,   232, 240, 242
Delphi,   128
   Priest of,   53, 127
Demons,   23, 43, 55, 100, 128, 129, 142, 178
Denver, John,   65
Devas,   100, 105
Diana,   113, 116, 218
Divination,   121, 126, 131, 138, 141, 142
Dolan, Luis,   256
Donnelly, Ignatius,   36, 37, 163
Dragon,   30, 48, 57, 116, 120, 138, 153, 155, 157, 196, 203-207
Druids,   101, 212

E

E. Coli 0157H7,   132-134, 145
E.T.,   28
Easter,   113
Eber,   207, 208, 211
ECKANKAR,   188, 189
Eckart, Dietrich,   37, 38
Ecumenical movements, two,   46, 196
Edison, Thomas,   165
Egyptian mythology,   15, 21, 28, 48
Eisenhower, Dwight D.,   266
Elam,   213
Electromagnetic energy,   140
Enchanter,   121, 130
Enchantment,   130
Engels, Friedrich,   155, 163
Enlightenment Movement,   65, 94, 98, 228, 230-232, 240, 251, 253
Epopt of the Illuminati,   32
European Enlightenment,   253
European Jews,   211, 240, 270
European Renaissance,   63, 75, 86, 148, 211, 253
Eve,   127
Extraterrestrial beings,   21, 42, 66, 69, 97, 197
   Believed to be the ancient gods of mythology,   21, 38, 42, 48
   Bible exposes as demons,   42
   From the Dog Star Sirius,   15, 17, 28, 32
   Satan will come as Christ,   17, 43

Extraterrestrial beings (CONT.),
   Supposedly visited Atlantis, 41, 42
   Will publicly appear today, 42, 43

F

Fabian Socialism, 163
Fabian Society, 159-163, 182, 251
Father of Lies, 208, 218
Fatima, 109
Fearful sights of supernatural character will soon appear, 42
Federal Beef Processors, 134
Flood, The, 196, 197, 199, 201
Force, The, 138, 139, 140
Ford, Gerald, 88
Ford, Henry, 88
Fox sisters, 156, 180
Franklin, Benjamin, 64, 75, 82, 84, 156, 258
Frazer, Sir James, 108
Freemasonry, 81-94, 234
   A basket to gather all nations & religions, 235, 262
   American Revolution connection, 63, 64, 82, 84, 85
   Caused world revolution, 95
   French Revolution connection, 79, 81, 85, 86, 156
   Jewish Theosophy, 216, 217, 234, 235, 242, 246
French Revolution, 63, 79, 82, 86, 95, 148, 149

G

Galactic Age, 34, 68
Galactic Federation, 46
Gandhi, Mahatma (Mohandas), 98, 163, 164, 251
Gardner, Gerald, 40
Garland, Judy, 54
Geller, Larry, 54
God of Abraham, 48, 115, 197, 210, 229, 239, 245, 252
Goddess of Liberty, 86
Goddess of Reason, 79, 80
Godhead, 150
Golden Age, 22, 31, 243
Gomer, 238-240, 251, 268
Good Shepherd, 142
Gout, 145, 146
Gramsci, Antonio, 165
Great battle against God Almighty, 196

Great White Brotherhood, 37, 38, 69, 107, 129, 181, 183, 186
Greeley, Andrew, 71, 72
Greeley, Horace, 163, 166
Greenspan, Alan, 254
Gullible Americans, 98, 159, 163, 167
Gullible Christians, 98, 167, 180, 256

H

Ha-am, Ahad, 249
Hades, 25
Hale-Bopp comet, 27, 28
Halloween, 102
Hallucinogenic drugs, 190
Ham
   Son of Noah, 207
Hammarskjöld, Dag, 266
Harmonic Convergence, 65, 69, 70
Hasidei Ashkenazi, 212, 245
Hasidism, 212, 214, 241, 242
"He shall come to his end", 208, 270
He-Hasid, Samuel, 245
Heathen deities will manifest themselves, 42
Heaven's Gate, 27, 28
Hebrew Jews, 208, 210-214
Hegel, 253
Hermes, 45, 52, 94, 264
Herzl, Theodor, 232, 247, 248, 250, 251
Hexagram, 216
Hibbat Zionists, 240
"Him ye will receive", 50
Hindu pantheism, 164
Hislop, Alexander, 203
Hiss, Alger, 264
Hitler, Adolf, 37, 40, 63, 153, 197, 235, 242, 243
   Connection with the New Age Movement, 37
   Thule, 40, 243
   Thule Society, 37, 63
   Wanted to establish his Thule Society instead of, 40
Holistic medicine, 137, 140
Holy God of Israel, 151
Holy Scriptures, 23, 29-31, 119, 121, 168, 219, 228, 239, 240, 260
Holy Spirit, 31, 74, 233, 237, 253, 260
Homer, 26, 203, 218
Hoover, Herbert, 254

Hopi Indians, 66, 105
Horus, 107, 204, 218
Hot Cross Buns, 112, 113
House, Edward Mandel, 252
House of prayer for all people, 209
Hovevei Zion, 249
Humanist Renaissance, 22
Huxley, Aldous, 190

I

I Am movement, 186
Illuminati, 19, 32, 63, 79, 81, 84, 85, 87, 150, 216
   Adam Weishaupt, 19, 79, 81, 86, 95, 246
   Communism connection, 63, 155, 222, 223
   New Age connection, 32, 182
   New World Order connection, 31, 95, 182, 223, 234, 235, 268
Immortality of the soul, 17, 53, 131, 138, 218, 219
Inanna, 107
Incas, 21, 23
Ingram, Eunice, 140
Interfaith organizations, 103
   Christianity's connection, 260
   Interfaith Forum, 103
   John D. Rockefeller, Jr.'s connection, 253, 260, 261
   Wainwright House's connection, 256, 260
Iridology, 137, 138, 141
Ishtar, 15, 48, 107
Isis, 106, 111, 204
Isis Unveiled, 165, 181, 182
Israel, Land of, 98, 229, 244, 261, 262

J

Jacobinism, 78, 79, 81, 85
Japheth
   Son of Noah, 207, 208
Jefferson, Thomas, 25, 64, 75, 82, 94, 156
Jesus, 17, 24, 50, 59-61, 75, 93, 131, 152, 153, 157, 169, 171, 210
   As Saviour, 129, 169, 196, 225-229, 239, 261
   Foretold false christs, 50, 61, 74, 260
   Foretold fearful sights in the skies, 42, 97
   Foretold majority of earthlings will reject Him, 59, 98, 118, 119, 148, 149, 208, 214, 233, 237
   Foretold merchants uniting against Him, 24, 52, 56, 235, 236, 244

Jesus (CONT.),
   His coming kingdom,   31, 96, 150, 151
   His people will reign 1000 years in Heaven,   237, 238
   Second Coming,   17, 23, 96, 131, 150-152, 196
Jewish Colonization Association,   250
Jewish mysticism,   231
Jewish Theosophy,   217, 218, 231, 234, 235, 239, 246-248, 256
Jews,   209, 223
   Ashkenazi,   234, 235, 238, 239, 245
   Descendants of the Ten Lost Tribes,   233
   Divided into two mainstreams,   210
   Hebrew (Sephardim),   213, 230, 231, 239
   Not solely behind Marxism as believed by Right Wingers,   241
   Not solely behind the New World Order conspiracy,   211, 223
John Paul II, Pope,   110, 254, 261
Judge, W.Q.,   165, 166, 180, 182
Jung, Carl,   256, 258
Jungian psychotherapists,   139, 258

K

Kabbalah (Cabala),   64, 214-218, 222, 231, 235, 242, 246
   Jewish book of magic,   213, 228, 234, 245, 260
Kachinas,   105
Kant, Immanuel,   75
Karma and reincarnation,   52, 180, 181
Khazars,   239
King David,   216
King Hezekiah,   136
King Louis XVI,   78
King Nebuchadnezzar,   116, 120, 212
King of kings,   59, 233
King Saul,   105, 169-178
King Solomon,   216
KKK,   197, 208, 223
Kloss, Jethro,   143, 146
Krishna,   105
Kulkulcán,   18, 68, 204, 218
   Name means bird serpent,   19, 20, 68

L

Land of Nimrod,   203
Latter days,   115, 234, 236, 237, 239
LaVey, Anton,   100, 124

Layard, Austen Henry,   203
Laymen's Movement for a Christian World, Inc.,   266
League of Nations,   252
Leary, Timothy,   65, 192, 241
Lemuria,   37, 41
Leninism/Stalinism,   36, 161
Liberation Theology,   260
Lincoln, Abraham,   167
Lincoln, Mary Todd,   168
Little Hitlers,   211
Lovers of Zion Movement,   247, 249, 251
LSD,   65, 190-192, 241
Lucifer a.k.a. Satan,   50
Lucis Trust,   266

M

Mackey, Albert G.,   94, 242
MacLaine, Shirley,   41, 65, 73, 74, 79, 81
Magog,   236-240, 249, 252, 268
Mahatmas,   66, 69, 105, 165, 180, 181
Maitreya,   69, 105, 185
Manson, Charles,   32, 124
Mao, Chairman,   159
Mark, Name, and Number,   244
Martin, Daniel,   256
Martin, Malachi,   62, 261
Marx, Karl,   36, 153, 155, 157, 162, 163, 216, 240, 251, 253
Marxism,   36, 148, 240, 252
   Catholic Marxists,   192, 241
   Hindu Marxists,   192, 251, 266
   Jewish Marxists,   192
   New Age Marxists,   241
   Protestant Marxists,   192, 241
Mason, Diane,   103, 106
Mayan Indians,   17-19, 21, 57, 67, 68, 218
Mayan Initiation Center,   17, 18
McCloy, John J.,   264
Meat eating
   Dangers of,   132, 133, 135
Meditation Room of the U.N.,   264, 266
Megiddo
   Meaning of,   239
Melton, J. Gordon,   27
Mendelssohn, Moses,   223

Merchants of modern Babylon,   56, 78, 244, 252, 258, 262, 268
Mercury,   52, 264
Mesopotamian peoples,   48, 107, 203
Metaphysics,   45, 56, 94, 98, 99, 121, 126, 129, 168, 179, 184, 242
Michael shall stand up,   244
Microcosm,   180
Miracle of Philadelphia,   82
Mishnah,   212
Mojo bag,   125
Montgomery, Ruth,   41
Monvel,   79
More, Thomas,   148
Mother Earth and Father Sky,   97, 106
Mother of Harlots,   107, 156, 225
Muhammad,   217, 218
Murray, Jacqueline,   24

N

Nazca Valley,   24, 36
Nazism,   38, 40, 197, 235, 242
Nebo,   264
Necromancer,   97, 121, 130
Nehemiah,   212
New Age vegetarianism,   97
New Agers,   15, 17, 21, 34, 37, 40, 45, 53, 67, 69, 74, 106, 113, 135, 137, 259-261, 270
New heaven and a new earth,   151, 152
New Jerusalem,   151
New Theology,   260, 261
New World Order,   19, 23-26, 31, 95, 96, 136, 142, 153, 184, 211, 223, 235, 240, 253, 261, 268, 270
"*Night Prowler*",   124
Nimrod,   19, 43, 45, 67, 94, 96, 107, 148, 201-204
Nineveh,   202, 203
Ninus,   204
Novus Ordo Seclorum,   64, 65, 78, 258

O

Obi-Wan Kenobi,   28
Observer of times,   121, 129
Ochshorn, Judith,   117
Olcott, H.S.,   165, 166, 180
Old Jerusalem,   151

Olympians, 52, 53
OM..., 69
Order of the Solar Temple, 27, 28
Ordo Templi Orientis, 38
Orwell, George, 157, 160, 251
Osiris, 21, 106, 204
Ottoman Empire, 248, 250
Ouija board, 126

P

Paine, Thomas, 75, 76, 79, 82, 157
Pan, 100, 104
   Is Satan, 104
   Worshipped among New Agers, 104
Pantheism, 138, 139, 190, 213
   Hindu, 164
Parapsychology, 45, 97, 130
Paris Peace Conference (1946), 266
Passing through the fire, 121, 122
Pauley, Jane, 132
Pharmakeia, 191
Phoenix, 28
Pike, Albert, 32, 87, 216, 217
Plato, 22, 25-27, 63, 75, 86, 153, 155, 160, 161, 164, 203, 218, 232, 242, 253
   Father of the Atlantean Plan, 22, 148, 161
   New Age apostle, 148
   Timaeus and the *Critias* and the Atlantis myth, 22
Pluralism, 260, 261
Plutarch, 22
Poseidon, 25, 26
Presley, Elvis, 54
Propagandists, 160, 163
Prophet, Elizabeth Clare, 186, 188
Prove all things, 61
Psychedelic drugs, 191, 192
Psychic healers, 139, 140
Pyramids, 259
   Pyramid of Gizeh, 259
Pythians, 53, 127
Pytho, 53, 127
Pythonist, 34, 97, 128, 141, 163, 262

Q

Queen Isabella,   213, 214
Queen of Heaven,   107, 110, 113, 116
Quetzalcoatl,   17, 19, 66-69, 204, 218

R

Ramirez, Richard,   124
Rather, Dan,   132, 133
Reagan, Nancy,   105
Red revolutionary,   156, 160, 161, 262
Reflexology,   137-141
Reign of Terror,   80, 98, 148, 149
   To be repeated worldwide,   149
Renaissance,   63, 75, 86, 148
Rivera, Geraldo,   122
Robespierre,   78
Robison, John,   62
Rockefeller, David,   254
Rockefeller family,   236, 253, 262, 268
Rockefeller, Jr., John D.,   253, 254, 256, 261, 266, 268
Rockefeller, Nelson,   253
Roman Catholics,   106, 107, 109, 112-114
Roosevelt, Eleanor,   180
Roosevelt, Teddy,   168
Rosicrucians,   64, 213, 222, 246, 258
Rothschild, Baron Edmond,   247-250, 253, 268
Rothschild family,   196, 223, 236, 246, 247, 253, 262
Rothschild, Mayer Amschel,   223, 246, 247
Russian Jews,   222, 223, 230, 239-241, 249

S

Salmonella poisoning,   134
Satan a.k.a. Lucifer,   31, 43, 48, 50, 68, 75, 100-105
   Has deceived all religious movements,   116, 121, 122
   Invisible Prime Minister of the world,   26
   Satanism,   100-103, 124, 125
   Symbolized as a Seven-headed Dragon,   20, 48
   Uniting the whole world today against Bible-believers,   57, 59, 61, 150, 155-157, 193, 203, 227, 243
   Uses famous businessmen,   78, 244, 253, 262, 268, 270
   Uses human agents to war against Christ and His,   20, 26, 31, 155-157
   Will personate and manifest himself as the ancient gods,   19, 50

Satan a.k.a. Lucifer (CONT.),
   Worshipped as the gods of astrology, 19, 20, 48, 50, 53, 56
Satanism, 102, 103, 124, 125
Schlesinger, Richard, 134
Scythia (Magog), 238
Seat of the New World Order, 268, 270
Secret Doctrine, The, 165, 181
Semiramis, 107, 116, 201-204
Semitic, 207, 212, 213
Sephardim, 210, 213, 230, 231, 239
Sephardim Jews, 210, 213, 230, 231, 234
   Hebrew remnant, 210, 213, 230, 231
   Semitic, 210, 230
Shamanism, 190-192, 242
Shamash (sun-god), 107, 108
Shaw, George Bernard, 36, 157-159, 164, 251
Shaw, James, 89, 90
Shem, 207, 208, 211, 213
Sirius
   Star of the Sea, 108
   Stellar Maris, 108, 114
   Virgin Mary symbol, 107
Sirius, the double star (Dog Star), 15, 21, 24, 28, 32, 42-43, 48, 106-108
   Isis, 107, 108
Siva, 110
Six hundred sixty-six (666), 30, 141, 206
Sleeping Christian pastors, 167
Sleeping Christians, 167
Socialism, 147, 148, 153-165
   Atheistic Socialists, 164
   British Socialists, 159, 160
   Ethical Socialists, 164
   New Age Socialists, 152, 163, 167
   Zionist Socialists, 247, 248
Solar Deity, 181, 259
Space goddess, 113
Spanish Inquisitions, 214
Spirit guides, 34, 37, 41, 45, 54, 69, 130, 142, 185-189
Spirit of Antichrist, 23, 30, 59, 74, 120, 137, 139
Spirit of Christ, 137
Spirit of divination, 127, 128
Spiritual D-days, 157
Spiritual feminists, 117, 122
Spiritualism, 34, 50, 57, 119, 122, 125, 137, 138, 157, 167-170, 179, 181-184, 188, 245, 246, 256, 258

Stalin, Joe,   40, 159
Star of David (Magen David),   216
Star Trek,   28, 231
Star Wars,   28, 231
State of Israel,   223, 231, 243, 249, 268
Steiger, Brad,   53, 54
Steiger, Sherry,   54, 55
Stein, Diane,   101
Steiner, Rudolf,   165
Stellar Maris
   Virgin Mary,   108, 114
Stewart, Richard,   104
Sufis (Muslim sect),   217

T

Tammuz,   18, 107, 112-114, 123, 203
Temple of Set,   125
Theosophical Society,   37, 156, 161, 164-167, 182-184, 235, 246, 251
   Made war on Christianity,   166, 167, 179, 186, 235
   Marxist connection,   156, 164, 165, 183
Theosophy,   165, 231, 239, 243, 256, 258
Thompson, Michael,   104
Thule Society,   37, 38, 40, 63
Time of the End,   29, 113, 244, 245, 268
Titans (Teitans),   25, 197
Toltecs,   18, 19, 21, 68, 218, 259
   Believed to be the Atlanteans,   21, 259
Tower of Babel
   Modern,   52, 240, 262, 264
Trotsky, Leon,   157
True Shepherd,   31
Twitchell, John Paul,   188, 189
Two ecumenical movements,   46, 196
Two key words,   244
Typhon,   89, 92
Tzar Nicholas II,   162, 252

U

UFO's,   15, 17, 23, 34, 42, 43, 53, 66, 97, 107, 131, 139, 160, 181, 221
Unarius Academy of Science,   51
Union Theological Seminary,   253, 260, 266
Unitarians,   104, 105
United Nations,   29, 34, 97, 152

United Nations (CONT.),
   Founded by Spiritualists,   193
   John D. Rockefeller, Jr.,   261, 264
   Meditation Room,   264
   Modern Tower of Babel,   262, 264
   Pagan altar to the Unknown God,   264, 265
   Plans to move to Israel,   262, 268, 270
   Uniting the world against God,   262, 264
Unknown God,   264
Uric acid,   145, 146
Urim and Thummim,   170, 172
Utopian Age,   63, 197
Utopian World Federation,   148
Utopians,   98, 211

V

Valentino, Rudolph,   54
Vegetable and fruit juice fast,   145
Vegetarianism,   97, 131, 132, 135-137
   My experience with,   132, 143, 145, 146
Ventriloquism,   128
Venus,   108, 123, 204, 205
Vernal equinox,   18, 68, 113
   Adopted by Christians,   113
   At Yucatán peninsula,   18
   Called Easter,   113
   Pagan festival celebrated worldwide,   18
Voltaire,   75, 79, 94, 156, 157
Von Däniken, Erich,   34, 35

W

Wainwright House,   113, 255-262, 266, 268, 269
   Dwight D. Eisenhower connection,   266
   John D. Rockefeller, Jr. connection,   261, 262
Washington, George,   82, 95
Webb, Sidney,   159
Wedge, Thomas,   125
Weishaupt, Adam,   23, 40, 63, 78, 79, 94, 95, 157, 161, 223, 235, 246
Weizmann, Chaim,   251, 252
Wells, H.G.,   36, 157, 160, 251
White, Ellen,   42
White Supremacists,   38, 208, 223
Wicca,   101-104, 114, 116, 117, 122

Wilson, Woodrow, 252, 254
Witch of Endor, 105, 172, 176, 179
Wizard, 121, 130
Woodstock, 70
Words, two key, 244
World Council of Churches, 254, 266
World revolution, 63, 148, 155
World Zionist Organization, 232, 250, 251

X

X-Files, 28

Y

Ye are the temple of God, 135
Yin yang, 138-140

Z

Zend-Avesta, 231
Zeus, 25, 110, 111, 204
   Father of Hercules, 25
Zevi, Sabbatai, 214, 215
Zionism, 98, 223, 228, 230, 231, 235, 241, 247-251
Zionist Congress, First, 250
Zodiac band, 141, 142, 206
Zoroaster, 218, 231

Thirty-four years in the making! Perhaps the most up-to-date and fully-documented study within seven volumes about the three-fold union of the secret societies of the Illuminati, the Papacy, and the apostate Protestants that you have ever read in your entire life! Take a historical and prophetical journey through the ages from 2200 B.C. up to the year A.D. 2005 and view, with your own astonished eyes, the real and true-to-life battle between the forces of good and the forces of evil. Truly see for yourself how this terrible struggle is about to reach its climax!

BEWARE IT'S COMING—
THE ANTICHRIST 666
$11.00

The New Age Movement and The Illuminati 666
$11.00

THE REAL TRUTH ABOUT UFO's AND THE NEW WORLD ORDER CONNECTION
$11.00

ANCIENT PROPHECIES ABOUT MYSTICISM HOLLYWOOD AND THE MUSIC INDUSTRY
$12.00

ANCIENT PROPHECIES ABOUT THE DRAGON THE BEAST AND THE FALSE PROPHET
$12.00

IN GOG THEY TRUST?
$10.00

IN GOG THEY TRUST? (still under construction)
$12.00

TO ORDER, PLEASE CALL OUR TOLL-FREE NUMBER
1-866-899-1877
SUNDAY-THURSDAY 9-9
PLUS POSTAGE & HANDLING

Please allow 3 to 6 weeks delivery

Also visit our website
www.18441888.com

Sim & Sons' Publishing House
10624 S. Eastern Avenue
Suite A, #177
Henderson, NV 89052